W0080411

Uncertainty and Communication

Also by the author

LITERARY COMMUNICATION FROM CONSENSUS TO RUPTURE: Practice and Theory in Honecker's GDR

FUNCTIONS AND FICTIONS OF COMMUNICATION

LANGUAGE – MEANING – SOCIAL CONSTRUCTION: Interdisciplinary Studies (*editor with D. McLaughlin*)

RETHINKING COMMUNICATIVE INTERACTION: New Interdisciplinary Horizons (*editor*)

Uncertainty and Communication

New Theoretical Investigations

Colin B. Grant
University of Surrey

© Colin B. Grant 2007

All rights reserved. No reproduction, copy or transmission of this
publication may be made without written permission.

No paragraph of this publication may be reproduced, copied or transmitted
save with written permission or in accordance with the provisions of the
Copyright, Designs and Patents Act 1988, or under the terms of any licence
permitting limited copying issued by the Copyright Licensing Agency, 90
Tottenham Court Road, London W1T 4LP.

Any person who does any unauthorised act in relation to this publication
may be liable to criminal prosecution and civil claims for damages.

The author has asserted his right to be identified as
the author of this work in accordance with the Copyright, Designs and
Patents Act 1988.

First published 2007 by
PALGRAVE MACMILLAN
Houndmills, Basingstoke, Hampshire RG21 6XS and
175 Fifth Avenue, New York, N.Y. 10010
Companies and representatives throughout the world

PALGRAVE MACMILLAN is the global academic imprint of the Palgrave
Macmillan division of St. Martin's Press, LLC and of Palgrave Macmillan Ltd.
Macmillan® is a registered trademark in the United States, United Kingdom
and other countries. Palgrave is a registered trademark in the European
Union and other countries.

ISBN-13: 978–0–230–51762–2   hardback

This book is printed on paper suitable for recycling and made from fully
managed and sustained forest sources. Logging, pulping and manufacturing
processes are expected to conform to the environmental regulations of the
country of origin.

A catalogue record for this book is available from the British Library.

Library of Congress Cataloging-in-Publication Data

Grant, Colin B.
  Uncertainty and communication : new theoretical investigations /
Colin B. Grant.
     p. cm.
  Includes bibliographical references and index.
  ISBN 978–0–230–51762–2 (alk. paper)
  1. Communication. 2. Uncertainty (Information theory) I. Title.

P91.G693 2007
302.2–dc22
                                                                    2007017070

10   9   8   7   6   5   4   3   2   1
16   15   14   13   12   11   10   09   08   07

For Beatriz, Anna and Eva

Table of Contents

List of Figures

Acknowledgements

Part of Chapter 4 was published in *Soziale Systeme* in 2004. The remaining chapters in this book are published here for the first time. They derive from papers and seminars I have presented between 2000 and 2006 at Heriot-Watt University, Edinburgh, and the universities of Sheffield, Oxford, Rio de Janeiro, Paraná, Viçosa, Ghent, Amsterdam, Shanghai and Warsaw.

I am grateful to John Benjamins for permission to reproduce the diagram of Karl Bühler's organon model of language functions, to Christopher Gauker for permission to quote from his manuscript 'Zero Tolerance for Pragmatics' and to Lucius and Lucius for permission to quote from my 2004 article 'Uncertain Communication: Uncertain Systems'.

1
Why Communication Is Not as Certain as We Might Think

1. Rethinking 'information'

One might wonder why mathematics could offer a starting point for a series of 'theoretical investigations' on human communication. After all, the two fields appear rarely to come into contact with each other. And yet it was Claude E. Shannon's *Mathematical Theory of Communication* (1948) that offered a breakthrough in the theory of information which has fascinated philosophers and social scientists ever since. In our everyday contexts and dealings we tend to associate information with concrete data, possibly evidence or news. By contrast, in his studies of telegraphy, Shannon rethought information as a *measure of uncertainty*. This theoretical news is a paradox: are information and uncertainty part of each other? Information in this sense is the selection of a message from a range of possibilities. This range forms a kind of background or penumbra to the message selected. And, as Dirk Baecker has pointed out, the fact that information always relates to a range of options which are not selected means that information is a relation of form (e.g. speech) and nonform (e.g. silence) or message and redundancy (the range of unselected messages). I develop this relational aspect further in these investigations as the *porous form* of communication. This theory of communication as a porous form of selected message and redundancy suggests the need to explore the unmarked spaces of communication, the interstices or gaps, the unspoken languages 'no-one has ever spoken or will ever speak'.[1] Baecker argues that communication is the 'determination of the indeterminate but determinable with the

1

aim of understanding the determinate' (Baecker, 2005: 23). I would suggest that the indeterminacy of the range of communication options we have at our disposal in different cultures, different languages, different media and different social roles is not actually determinable at all. The porous form of communication actually means that even when we think we choose a clear, stable form, the penumbra of unselected information remains. The relationship between the form of our communications and their non-forms is irreducibly dynamic. We communicate in order to accompany the dynamic of our interactions with the world. To be communicable as a social agent is not to be determinable.

Now this might seem rather remote from much of the literature in communication studies where there is a strong tendency to deal with discrete forms of text or discourse and where strong philosophical assumptions are made about how we interact, understand and exchange information with each other. This book sets out to explore such issues and to understand communication as an uncertain dynamic more directly in a series of philosophical investigations.

2. So, has uncertainty crept up on us from behind?

The sociologist Zygmunt Bauman argues in *Liquid Life* that the pace of cultural, economic, technological and social change in our lives today is such that relationships, habits, norms and conventions, organizational forms, and institutions (from political parties to the church and the universities) have become precarious: '[i]n short: liquid life is a precarious life, lived under conditions of constant uncertainty' (Bauman, 2005: 2). And since one core facet of globalization means connectedness through mediated communication, that sense of precariousness affects communication. Bauman is not alone in reflecting on the liquidity of life today: there is a growing body of research in vague logic,[2] social theorists discuss the 'risk society' and the 'community of contingency' which unites citizens in an increasingly trans- or postnational world; psychologists discuss the multiple voices of the self. Uncertainty, it seems, is the mark of our *hypercritical modernity*.

From government eavesdropping to Internet crime, reality TV to computer-mediated communication and mobile telephone texting, the forms of human communication continue to undergo significant change. The heightened awareness of the diversity (and risk) of communication can be witnessed in old and new media, in changing patterns of face-to-face interactions, the flux of identity, the blurring of the distinction between real and virtual and the global interconnectedness of our media worlds. These manifestations are not in themselves the chief concern in this study. Rather, the objective is to examine these changes as manifestations of uncertain communication. To date, theories of interaction have been slow to conceptualize communication in terms of its instabilities: social communication models have tended to remain heavily indebted to a normative, Enlightenment-inspired 'semantic of interaction' (to borrow Niklas Luhmann's term):

> The semantic of interaction laid down in the 18th century is concerned with a person-to-person relation. At the same time, it *interprets* itself as a model of society.
>
> > (Luhmann, 1993: 153 – my translations and emphasis)

> an understanding of interpersonally enriched reciprocity is no longer compatible with functional needs and forces the retreat of interaction theory into communality.
>
> > (Luhmann, 1993: 122 – my translations)

So the semantic of interaction was a social code, an epistemic order in which the face-to-face model is abstracted to form a model of social relations. This is especially visible in the concept of 'publicness' or the public sphere and the pressure for rational debate which emerged at the time of the Enlightenment (one will recall that Edmund Burke was quick to speak of the 'monstrous fiction' of that publicness). And yet the transition from mercantilism to capitalism required new forms of economic and social organization, which created a gap between the assumed reciprocity of face-to-face encounters and the new asymmetries of social functioning. To see 'dialogue' as a model for society became an act of nostalgia. Was there, one might even ask, *ever* a dialogue?

The semantic of interaction, which informs Jürgen Habermas's vastly influential work, has forfeited its claim to (universal) normative validity. A communication theory of society needs to explore the new spaces of what could be termed *post-nostalgic* communication, covering a complex field which requires the broadest possible range of approaches beyond current disciplinary confines, in which even normative accounts can at best be seen as competing with other social codes or semantics. This study seeks to examine some of the implications for our understanding of the communicating subject and society when communication is examined as a complex uncertainty.

A problem remains, however, and Shannon's mathematical model cannot be crudely imported. That problem is the fuzzy factor par excellence: the human factor. Information theorists such as Shannon have tended to exclude the self and other sources of human vagueness such as semantics or pragmatics and focus instead on a concept of uncertainty embedded in information generation in a discrete channel. According to Shannon, entropy in an information-theoretical sense means uncertainty or the 'rate of generating information' (Shannon, 1964: 58) – there is uncertainty, since what is said could easily be different: 'information is a measure of one's freedom of choice when one selects a message' (Shannon and Weaver, 1964: 9). The field of application may well have been engineering, but the modelling of uncertainty and the uncoupling of information and meaning have made a productive contribution to a theory of uncertain communication in the human sciences.

This is the age of the network society, the information society, the communication society, the global information culture. In heightening our sense of *connectedness* in a global village, the complex communicative networks of a globalized world also heighten our awareness of the different ways in which connections are actually made. Connections are in an almost literal sense *contingent*, capable of multiple configurations. And so, the more we communicate about communication, the more acute our consciousness of its uncertainties or connectability becomes. We might be aware of unsolicited prizes to refurbish kitchens from far-off call centres, the terrorist dependency on the mass media system (relayed by Al Jazeera, now a household name), spam from apocryphal royalty, hacking, viruses and worms and so on.

As communications systems have gained in complexity, the need for 'protection' of those communications has grown as well. The *Oxford English Dictionary* reveals that the term 'tapping' (as used in the 'tapping of communications') can be traced back to the mid-nineteenth century at the time of the Franco-Prussian War; the description of telephone lines as being 'secure' is recorded in the

1960s, while the term 'hacker' appears in the mid-1970s; new communications media require new forms of encryption (a term also first
recorded in the 1960s). The networks of globalization mean more
connections, and more connections mean more contingencies or
people selecting from a range of connections at a given point in time
and place, connecting with others selecting from a range of connections at a given point in time and place. It is thus no coincidence that
this is also the age of *risk society* in which citizens are connected by a
sense of contingency in which modernity has become 'liquid' or
hypercritical. This is the paradox of the world communication society
to which Klaus Japp (2003) refers.

Although media communications and their contingencies are
important facets of communication complexity, they do not mark
some kind of linear transition from a previously stable or certain communication world to a somehow unstable one. The gap between the
semantic of interaction and forms of social and economic organization was not merely a misalignment between the 'truth' of dialogue
and new, concrete experience. Rather, the assumption of universality
of the semantic of interaction was inherently a theoretical claim with
a powerful discourse supporting it. The complexities of communication today merely impel us to revisit the truth claims of that semantic as one historically rooted discourse among others.

Communication is fundamentally uncertain in many different
forms, of which the medium (from cave paintings to the Internet) is
but one. Light and smoke were used as communication media in
ancient North American, Egyptian and Chinese civilizations; military
survival manuals to this day warn of the risks of using light as a communication signal. Flashing a mirror too rapidly could be 'misread' by
a pilot as enemy fire, while prolonged targeting of the cockpit of a
rescue aircraft might blind the pilot. There are also uncertainties of
context (institutional, temporal, cognitive, cultural), uncertainties of
the self (autonomy, identity, physicality), uncertainties of language
(reference, meaning, the problematic concept of 'truth') and uncertainties of interaction: what is understanding? How is 'meaning'
shared? What is, as Manfred Frank (1995) has asked, the 'reality guarantee' of intersubjectivity?

Miraculously, none of these uncertainties have irrupted onto the
world with the advent of mass media systems. In this way, communication media complexity can be conceptualized as increasing our

consciousness of the paradox of connection and uncertainty and can be *fed back* into a new theory of social communication without levelling the deeper uncertainties just described. The task is urgent since theories of social communication have long operated with normative, universalist frameworks which are now quite seriously out of joint with their time. Social communication theory lags behind the experience of communication risks. At its most foundational level, the uncertainty of communication arises from its form: communications are incommensurable. As Donald Davidson has put it, since languages are actually 'people and their written and acoustical products' it is more appropriate to speak of an 'infinity of "languages" no one ever has spoken or will ever speak' (Davidson, 2001: 108). In extreme terms, silence – the necessary correlate of phonetic noise – is the ever-present non-form of communication. As Locke put it in *An Essay Concerning Human Understanding*:

> *Words* by long and familiar use, as has been said, come to excite in men certain ideas, so constantly and readily, that they are apt to suppose a natural connexion between them. But that they *signify* only men's peculiar ideas, and that by a perfectly arbitrary imposition, is evident, in that they often fail to excite in others (even that use the same language) the same ideas, we take them to be signs of: and every man has so inviolable a liberty, to make words stand for what idea he pleases [...].
>
> (Locke, 1997 [orig. 1689]: 366)

If we agree with Bauman that our modernity has become liquid, that the fast-frozen relations of past structures have been cast into the melting pot, resulting in a growing cleavage between an increasingly rigidified order and the various subsystems or agencies in societies, then we can observe that this 'disengagement' has not been brought about by some kind of colonization of the sphere of private subjects by the dominant, somehow ideologically saturated social system (capitalism, globalization, industrial-military complex as the embodiments of a voracious ideology), but by the 'radical melting of the fetters and manacles rightly or wrongly suspected of limiting the individual freedom to choose or to act'. The techniques of flexibilization, deregulation and liquefaction in economic and cultural processes are the 'techniques which allow the system and free agents to remain radically disengaged, to by-pass each other instead of meeting' (Bauman 2003: 5). Bauman's sociological account helps to describe the new complexities of systems and institutions and thus also provides a useful descriptive account of the complexities of the contexts in which subjects interact. If contexts are liquid and the relations of yesteryear molten, then they inform the uncertainties of the macro- and microcontexts in which our communications take place. Sociological accounts of uncertainty not only articulate meaningfully with theories of communicative understanding, but also account for the *contingencies* of plural cultural forms in which questions of communication become increasingly evident. Globalization describes the increased intensity of cultural contact (with varying accounts of cultural incommensurability, universal values, multiculturalism and putative clashes among civilizations). As Butler, Laclau and Žižek note:

> Cultures are not bounded entities; the mode of their exchange is, in fact, constitutive of their identity. If we are to begin to rethink universality in terms of this constitutive act of cultural translation [...] then neither a presumption of linguistic or cognitive commonness nor a teleological postulate of an ultimate fusion of all horizons will be a possible route for the universal claim.
>
> (Butler, Laclau, Žižek, 2000: 20–1)

Cultural contact and the increasing amounts of 'translations' across cultures thus make it appropriate to question the nostalgia for universal accounts of shared civilizational or communicational values based on a 'pre-established universality of the speech act' (Butler, Laclau, Žižek, 2000: 3) as a normative communication framework. In the field of communication theory, these complex contextual shifts in and among cultures and systems, however these might be defined, mean that new theoretical investigations of uncertain communication are opportune.

What follows then is not a sociological theory grounded in communication but a series of interdisciplinary theoretical investigations of communication based on the integration of a necessarily complex range of disciplinary approaches. The primary concern of this book is a critique of universalist accounts of communication theory which resolve uncertainty or at best consider it to be soluble on the basis of a universal semantic of rationality. The methodological framework rests firstly on an interpretative reconstruction of significant theoretical antecedents in the opening chapters: Edmund Husserl's phenomenology of intersubjectivity, Mikhail Bakhtin's socio-cultural epistemology of dialogism, Jürgen Habermas's critical theory of communication and finally, Niklas Luhmann's systems theory. In many ways, the book sets a course between Habermas's *Theory of Communicative Action* and Luhmann's *Die Gesellschaft der Gesellschaft*. However, whereas Habermas's work displays a sociological bias by drawing upon the works of Piaget, Austin, Popper, Weber, Adorno, Durkheim, Mead and Parsons, the current work focuses less on sociology and more on the philosophical dimensions of communication theory.

This difference in focus manifests itself clearly in Chapters 5 and 6 of the current study. *Uncertain Communication* drops the sociological methods and normative claims of *Communicative Action*. Here, the reconstructive method of the first chapters makes way for detailed theoretical explorations of uncertainties in human interaction and agency. Thus, the sociologically salient categories of lifeworld, modernity and rationalization and the normatively charged accounts of rationality and reason to be found in Habermas's *Theory of Communicative Action* also yield to conceptually focused theoretical inquiries into interaction and the communicating subject. Chapters 7 and 8 develop case studies of the theoretical antecedents and conceptual investigations in order to evaluate the implications of a theory of uncertain communication for the study of communications in intercultural communication and the uncertainties of globalized communication in the age of interconnected media.

3. Contingency

The social theorist Talcott Parsons introduced the concept of 'double contingency of interaction' in *The Social System*, first published in 1951. In his thoughts on interaction processes Parsons argued that reactions to a communicative sign may cover a range of possibilities, 'selection within which is contingent on ego's actions'. This contingency is effectively doubled since interaction also depends on the actions of *alter*. The selection of a meaning is therefore a selection from a range 'which covers the contingent alternatives not only of ego's action, but of alter's and the possible permutations and combinations of the relation between them' (Parsons, 1967: 11). In this way, the potential for noise is multiplied.

Double contingency is inextricably linked to uncertainty, since ego's communications are communications selected from a range and interact with alter's communications, which select from a range. As a result of this complex relationship between contingency and selection in interaction, an 'extra hazard of conflict' is introduced (Parsons, 1967: 48). In a situation of double contingency alter's reaction does not depend on what ego is. A more apt description of the contingencies of interaction would be: 'Depending on *which of several alternatives open to me I take*, I will set *alter* a problem to which he will react in terms of the alternative system of his own which is oriented to my action' (Parsons, 1967: 94). In his radical and extremely influential reworking of systems theory published as *Social Systems* in 1986, Niklas Luhmann, Parsons's doctoral student in the 1960s, took contingency to a new level of theoretical abstraction as follows:

> Complexity [...] means selection pressure, selection pressure means contingency and contingency means risk. Every complex state of affairs is based on a selection of relations among its elements [...]. The selection positions and qualifies the elements, although other relations would have been possible. We borrow the tradition-laden term 'contingency' to designate this 'also being possible otherwise'.
> (Luhmann, 1995: 25)

Here, then, Luhmann defined contingency as a factor of uncertainty in the process of selecting from a range in a complex context. His radical concept of contingency is taken further in this study. Arguably, we are faced with multiple contingencies: selections of ego from a communication range, selections of alter from ego's range and other communications and forms of communication themselves. In concrete terms, a form of what may provisionally and inadequately be described as *overload* is a real risk in the globalized worlds of surveillance, appeals for vigilance on municipal transport systems, false alarms, colour-coded states of alert, new warnings of environmental damage or terrorism and electronic 'jamming' by banks, insurers and kitchen designers. In these 'liquid' contexts, the self is required to manage acute contingencies in communication by coping with the plurality of knowledge systems and their discourses and the risks of 'too much' information. Debates on multiculturalism and secularism are a poignant illustration of this multiple context of competing worlds and their knowledge systems. This uncertainty poses a major challenge to human agents in world communication society.

As noted above, all too often communication theories in a range of disciplines resolve uncertainties by invoking the paradigms of inter-subjectivity and dialogue or consensus with universalist claims or rational motivation and understanding, for example. A theory of uncertain communication adopts as its object of analysis more than simply the mutability of linguistic structures; instead, it must take account of a dynamic and vague theory of communicative signs used by actors in social contexts. Communication does not merely take place as a stable factor in a complex environment; rather, communication is itself a factor of uncertainty which drives interaction. This happens as a 'matter of course' and yet, even so, we might be aware of the lack of saturation of our communications (Derrida, 2001). There is always a remainder – what is not said in the multiple languages no one will ever speak. From this point it should be possible to elaborate a formal model of *communication* which challenges existing normative or universalist accounts and where an outcome of understanding is not imposed either before the communicative event – or after it.

4. Limits of normativity

As discussed above, the uncertainty of communication is not coterminous with processes of globalization in the late twentieth century. It has been neglected by virtue of the dominance of the semantic of interaction and the assumption that speaker intentions and references can be stabilized as such in another mind. And yet the discourse of this semantic leaves a number of stones unturned. It is possible to return to these stones and work out alternative semantics where uncertainty of intention, reference, meaning and, therefore, also understanding are crucial theoretical components.

If Wittgenstein introduced the linguistic turn in the early twentieth century, now we are faced with the communicative turn (Loet Leydesdorff). The linguistic turn is best described as the shift from the philosophy of consciousness to a philosophy of natural language as exemplified in the *Philosophical Investigations* (1968) in particular, where the term 'language game' emphasizes the fact that the speaking of a language is an activity or 'form of life'. Here, Wittgenstein no longer conceptualized language as an invariable essence pointing to eternal truth or God. 'Meaning' is generated in games amounting to complexes of elements of discourse and other action forms, while grammar consists of a package of interactional norms. By virtue of the force of such pragmatic agreements, meaning is constituted not in terms of the 'impact' of an utterance, but in terms of the pragmatic-interactional possibilities of its 'connections'. As Wittgenstein said: 'The rules of grammar may be called "arbitrary", if that is to mean that the *aim* of the grammar is nothing but that of the language' (Wittgenstein 1968: 138e). The language game is not constructed and conceptualized on the basis of an objective essence, but instead as the result of relations among speakers. In other words it can be said that meaning is not a given being, an ontological fact, but socially constructed.

Wittgenstein also sees the sign in its quality as a sign *for* someone; the living being is always defined by the fact that it possesses the faculty to use a language of signs (1991: 192). Language is a complex of non-arbitrary or contextually contingent rules, but this does not mean abandoning understanding. Thus, language games are about relations and connections. Uncertainty is theoretically and empirically central to communication. It is increasingly acknowledged that language games, which include guessing riddles, jokes and translating, raise *local* truth claims in situations, settings and contexts, whose norms are therefore contingent and depend on their use by actors in those very information-rich circumstances. The *Philosophical Investigations* are an important point of departure for the current study, for Wittgenstein bids farewell to the notion that the meanings of words are their correspondences with the thing named: 'Something red can be destroyed, but red cannot be destroyed, and that is why the meaning of the word 'red' is independent of the existence of a red thing' (Wittgenstein, 1968: 20). Language dynamics mean that names do not have 'fixed or unequivocal use' (1968: 37). Thus a gap emerges with force between idealized logics and everyday language, which is no approximation to a putative truth or reality outside it. Moreover, the *Investigations* inquire into the ambiguity and vagueness of language – the relationship between interpretations and the objects of interpretation, the contention that 'meaning it' is 'also something private' (1968: 113), that words are 'arbitrary signs' and the impossible distinction of the 'undertone' from the experience of speaking (1968: 155). These questions take the study of language and communication beyond its discrete forms, logics, truth claims and correspondence theories. In other words, to borrow a concept from George Spencer Brown, we can begin to understand communication as a dialectic of marked and unmarked space, of interpretation and object, undertone and speaking, private language and grammatical fictions, arbitrary signs and agreed rules. This means the study of communication is the study of the non-form within the form and the form within the non-form (where the form is porous). In Wittgenstein's words: 'The common behaviour of mankind is the system of reference by means of which we interpret an unknown language' (1968: 82). But what are these neglected or unmarked forms?

Austin's speech act theory further developed philosophical pragmatics by viewing the utterance as an act of either felicity or infelicity, stressing the importance of appropriate circumstances for a given act. Felicity conditions include such conditions as a conventional procedure having a conventional effect, the appropriateness of the status of interlocutors, correct execution of a procedure and intentions and sincerity; for successful performance 'the circumstances in which the words are uttered should be [...] appropriate'. More significantly, a connection is made between such pragmatic conditions of appropriateness, status, sincerity and truth: 'for many purposes the outward utterance is a description, *true or false*, of the occurrence of the inward performance' (Austin, 1971: 9). Austin's theory of utterances as (social) action operated within a strong normative framework, distinguishing normal from parasitic language use, equating felicity conditions with truth conditions: 'If the performative utterance "I apologize" is happy, then the statement that I am apologizing is true' (Austin, 1971: 53). Even if, when an act goes wrong, it is an *infelicity*, and not a falsehood, felicities are tied up with truth claims.

Austin's influence on linguistic philosophy marginalized non-normal or deviant use as a direct result of a theory of knowledge based on the mapping of language onto truth conditions. Here, it is striking that only primitive languages are said to contain 'ambiguity, equivocation or vagueness':

> Language as such and in its primitive stages is not precise, and it is also not, in our sense, explicit: precision in language makes clearer the force of the utterance, or 'how [...] it is to be taken.'
>
> (Austin, 1971: 72–3)

When Austin described non-serious language use as the 'etiolations of language' (1971: 22) or language used 'in ways parasitic upon its normal use', he closed down the space Wittgenstein had opened between form and non-form, undertone and speaking. While the study of contextual felicity conditions as an inquiry into language acts as a dynamic process, Austin imposed a more restrictive normative framework on categories of the language game or speech act, consigning uncertainty to the realm of infelicity and primitive language. This normative framework heavily informs Habermas's theory of universal pragmatics and sustains the semantic of interaction.

By contrast, the contention put forward in these investigations is that 'appropriate circumstances' are fluid, vagueness and lack of precision unavoidable and the multiple contingency of communication means that there are many sidings and they are constitutive of communication. In other words, 'how an utterance is to be taken' depends precisely on how it is taken. The silencing of uncertainty (the explicit exclusion of 'parasitic forms of communication') continues in the speech act theory of J.R. Searle in near-identical form:

> This principle [what can be meant can be said] has the consequence that cases where the speaker does not say exactly what he means – the principal cases of which are nonliteralness, vagueness, ambiguity, and incompleteness – are not theoretically essential to linguistic communication.
>
> (Searle, 1970: 20)

And yet they are. Searle's position might be consistent with truth-theoretical pragmatics, but in terms of the communication, risks of everyday life remain problematic. Nonliteralness, vagueness and ambiguity are indeed theoretically essential, and a philosophy of language shorn of such vagueness actually serves to *undermine* communication; it is incommensurability which makes communication possible. We communicate for there is more to life than meeting alter's expectations and stating the obvious. Robert Brandom refers in this context to the 'relativity of inferential significance'; it is axiomatic that inferential significance is not 'preserved in communication' (Brandom, 1998: 478; 480). If communication derives from finite words and syntactical forms and truth statements it must become sterile – a predictable exercise in redundancy.

As noted above, important theoretical stones have remained unturned in the theory of communication. Some of the precursors of a theory of uncertain communication can be found in the philosophy of pragmatism at the turn of the nineteenth and twentieth centuries and are represented by William James, Charles Horton Cooley, John Dewey and George Herbert Mead and the *pragmaticism* of Charles Sanders Peirce. They require especial mention since the interactional connections between self and society are also foundational here. In Peirce's 'Logic as Semiotic: The Theory of Signs' (1897–1910) the sign is described as a ground or *representamen* or 'something which stands to somebody for something'; this sign, which stands for an *object*, creates a sign 'in the mind of someone' and so has a 'mental *Interpretant*' (Peirce, 1955: 100). What is interesting in the current undertaking to develop a theory of uncertain communication is that there is a tension in Peirce's semiotics between, on the one hand, a cultural universalism based on the law of 'general ideas' in which the conventional sign is shared by all (Peirce, 1955: 102) and, on the other, the relative autonomy (although Peirce does not use this term) of the receiver of a sign. Thus, the representative character of a symbol lies in its capacity to *determine* (Peirce's words) the Interpretant. By contrast, in his slightly later essay 'Issues in Pragmaticism' (1905), Peirce explicitly addressed the question of vagueness which seems, at first sight, to raise certain questions about that very universalist premise (of a shared cultural world): 'A sign is objectively *general*, in so far as, leaving its effective interpretation indeterminate, it surrenders to the interpreter the right of completing the determination for himself' (Peirce, 1955: 295). Since '[...] no man's interpretation of words is based on exactly the same experience as any other man's', a 'vague residuum' always persists. This stone will remain turned throughout the following chapters.

This tension brought about by the vague residuum of communication is clearly relevant to a theory of semiotic uncertainty. In his seminal study on Peirce (originally 1967), Karl-Otto Apel referred to this vague indetermination of the interpreter as the commonsensical 'open factor' or 'choice of goals' within a system of universalist imperatives. Peirce had sought to resolve the tension by identifying the rationalizing core in both the recognition of universal laws and the choice of goals as a 'fatefully predetermined, eschatological *summum bonum*' (Apel, 1995: 179–81). An important element in Peirce's semiotic is thus the relevance of the vagueness and contradictoriness of commonsense judgements. Apel's synthesis of pragmatism aptly demonstrates the relevance of uncertainty:

> The reality of laws must be assumed to be unchanging and actual, but this is not enough to explain that possibility which Pragmatism had always counted upon when it explicated all concepts in terms of possible, that is, predictable experience. If the real is all that which can be the object of a true proposition, then there must be such a thing as 'real vagueness'.
>
> (Apel, 1995: 184)

It is the theoretical connection between vagueness as an expression of uncertainty and its theoretical pragmatic counterpart in autonomy or 'freedom' which is amenable to renewed theoretical investigation. This is the space in which we explore the relations between the realm of real and universal possibility and that vagueness which is 'analogous to the indecision of a person' (cited in Apel, 1995: 188). The openness of cultural conventions and the uncertainties of actors are core components of a theory of uncertain communication.

Philosophical accounts of intersubjectivity are no less significant in a theoretical account of uncertainty in communication. One core influence here is Edmund Husserl's theory of intersubjectivity, which, despite its limitations, is crucial for its philosophical account of a certain paradigm of understanding and interaction which is not modelled in either cognitive or informational terms but in transcendental terms:

> Only by starting from the ego and the system of its transcendental functions and accomplishments can we methodically exhibit transcendental intersubjectivity and its transcendental communalization, through which, in the functioning system of ego-poles, the 'world for all,' and for each subject *as* world for all, is constituted.
>
> (Husserl, 1997 [orig. 1936]: 185–6 – emphasis in original)

In general terms, Husserl attempted to escape the confines of the Cartesian ego by positing a dynamic relation between the phenomenon (as it appears to the subject) and consciousness. It is in this overarching, transcendental relationship that the ego is conceptualized as a subject embedded in the world of others and phenomena. To the extent that the subject constitutes the importance of the phenomena around him, it relates itself to a perception of the phenomenon in its character as the other. The orientation to the other enables the subject to overcome its isolated, monadic status. Husserl argued that only a transcendentalism firmly committed to the fundamental ego as producer of meaning and inhabitant of a pre-objective, pre-scientific world could make the reconciliation of subjectivism and objectivism possible. The theory of intersubjectivity has been a dominant paradigm in interaction theories across a range of social and human sciences and will be challenged below.

Peircean semiotics, the *Philosophical Investigations*, information theory and the theory of intersubjectivity form distinct but interrelated facets of communication theory. Their distinctiveness makes them all the more productive from a plurality of perspectives. In addition to these historical antecedents, distinct approaches to communication have emerged since the 1960s, in particular across the human and social sciences, often without entering into any form of cross-disciplinary exchange. The shift to natural language philosophy introduced by Wittgenstein and refined by Austin and Searle naturally informed two communications-theoretical sociologies in the 1960s: Erving Goffman's ethnography (heavily influenced by Husserl and Alfred Schütz) and Harold Garfinkel's ethnomethodological approach. Building on some important aspects of social interactionism and influenced by George Herbert Mead and H. Blumer, Erving Goffman's studies of the dramaturgical aspects of social interaction in *Life as Theatre* (1959), *Interaction Ritual* (1967) and *Strategic Interaction* (1970) continue to exert a significant influence on contemporary studies of communication. One of Goffman's most important insights lay in identifying the performative norms of social interaction. Focusing on the role played by 'impression management', Goffman departed from the notion that interactions are unproblematic givens by emphasizing the background norms which induce certain theatrical performances – the way in which the individual '[...] presents himself and his activity to others, the ways in which he guides and controls the impressions they form of him [...]' (Goffman, 1959: xi). Goffman's studies in strategic interaction also challenged the assumptions of the transmission model of communication by introducing a significant noise factor into the communication moves we make:

> Whenever students of the human scene have considered the dealings individuals have with one another, the issue of calculation has arisen: When a respectable motive is given for action, are we to suspect an ulterior one?
>
> (Goffman, 1970: 85)

In this view, communications lose innocence or transparency, and the assumptions we might be tempted to make about how we infer meaning or gain access to speaker intention and indeed hearer reception or response are questioned. And yet, notwithstanding the 'calculative, gamelike aspects of mutual dealings' (Goffman, 1970: x) or the individual's capacity to 'acquire, reveal and conceal information' (Goffman, 1970: 4) through a complex repertoire of concealment, revealment and misrepresentation strategies, Goffman's account does not really resolve or adequately address the implications of this noisy communication for our intuitive and traditional understandings of dialogue, shared meaning or even understanding. He argues both that the 'intentional transmission of information' is 'a human process arising when the signs mean to the sender what they mean to the recipient [...]' (Goffman, 1970: 5) and endows the observer with the near-miraculous capacity to peel away the layers of concealment and communication gamesmanship to 'get behind the apparent facts in order to uncover the real ones' (Goffman, 1970: 17). Clearly, at least one question remains: how do we know when we have found them? In other words, the problem of intentionality and inference remains unresolved, and uncertainty seems surmountable.

Although Goffman's work came to be criticized for a focus on deceit, insincerity and the 'manipulation' of others' opinions, today it is uncontroversial to argue that communicative interaction involves a range of strategies, self-presentations and codes (performed in particularly dense form in the reality TV genre). There is no neat distinction between the sincere and insincere in communication (as political communications in the USA, Iran and North Korea demonstrate), and even if there were, we would have to infer or impute sincerity or insincerity to the speaker in interaction. Recognition of these risks of communication itself involves recognition of the flux of discourses, selves, receptions and contexts. And so it is right to argue for the need to reconstruct the relations between self and society where the dialectic between autonomy and organization takes centre stage.

Garfinkel's *Studies in Ethnomethodology* (1967) also sought to expose the background assumptions of everyday communicative interactions. Shifting the phenomenological emphasis on intersubjective meaning construction to a study of how meanings come to be assumed locally, Garfinkel saw ethnomethodology as 'the investigation of the rational properties of indexical expressions and other practical actions as *contingent* ongoing accomplishments or organized practices of everyday life' (Garfinkel, 1989: 11 – my emphasis). Here, too, connections with uncertainty will be made.

The need to conceptualize communication in terms of uncertainty was also central in another core work in social psychology in the 1960s. Inspired by information theory and cybernetics, Watzlawick, Beavin Bavelas and Jackson's classic account, *Pragmatics of Human Communication* (1967), sought to develop a theory which would offer new insights into human interactions as 'complex interacting systems'. In considering the communication patterns, pathologies and paradoxes neglected by the speech act philosophy of Austin and Searle, *Pragmatics of Human Communication* criticized the concentration of psychoanalysis on 'intrapsychic processes' and instead integrated concepts in systems theory, such as stability, feedback and openness, for their capacity to capture complexity.

Accounts of communication practices, theories and contexts experienced differentiation in the 1970s and 1980s, ranging from the work of Harvey Sacks and Emanuel Schegloff in conversation analysis through to philosophical pragmatics, with noteworthy contributions from Robert Brandom and François Recanati. However, if a theory of communication is to avoid silencing uncertainty it will need to remain wary of the potential aporias of universalism and new universalist claims which even certain recent linguistic accounts make. In literary theory, too, much important work was carried out in the late 1960s and 1970s in which a variously defined reader became recognized as a key facet in literary communication where the reader was considered to respond to guided reception or complete points of indeterminacy. Derrida's concept of infinite iterability as 'the break with the horizon of communication as communication of consciousness or of presences and as linguistical or semantic transport of the desire to mean what one says [*vouloir-dire*]' and also as a rupture with the 'semantic or hermeneutic horizons' (Derrida, 2000: 8) is equally significant in this context, for it has the potential to question radically our understanding of understanding. These interrelated questions will be explored in greater detail in Chapters 5 and 6.

Partly influenced by the work of Husserl and his fellow phenomenologist, Alexius Meinong, Mikhail Bakhtin's concept of *heteroglossia*, or multivoicedness, is similarly significant as a challenge to hermetic views of communication and thus, potentially, a contribution to a better theoretical understanding of complexity:

> Alongside the centripetal forces, the centrifugal forces of language carry on their uninterrupted work; alongside verbal-ideological centralization and unification, the uninterrupted processes of decentralization and disunification go forward.
>
> (Bakhtin, 1998: 272)

It will be argued that Bakhtin and his collaborators made a highly significant contribution to communication philosophy although his reception is perhaps more developed in social psychology and literary/ cultural studies. In her *Dialogicality and Social Representations* (2004), Ivana Marková offers a social psychological account of a dialogical human condition beyond I-Thou relations. Following Bakhtin and Rosenzweig, Marková refers to the asymmetry and tensions of dialogue as a heterogeneous nexus of meanings and multivoicedness. Here, 'every individual lives in a world of others' words'. Related theories of a multiply voiced self (cf. Hermans, 1993) can also make a substantial contribution to this debate on multivoicedness in complex communication and will be pursued below.

As will be seen, epistemological questions cannot be subtracted from a study of communications, and thus the theoretical undertaking must be enriched by key philosophical debates which are often consigned to the margins, at least in mainstream communication studies with their pronounced empirical media analyses. These discussions include the revived debate around vagueness theory (from Waismann's early work to Williamson's *Vagueness* and the recent debates between Wright and Rosenkranz) and referential semantics (Putnam's *Mind, Language and Reality* and Recanati's *Direct Reference* and *Literal Meaning*). To place my cards firmly on the table, *Uncertainty and Communication* will tend to deny, *contra* Putnam, 'that there exists a unique *natural* mapping of sentences onto sets of possible worlds' (Putnam, 1997: 74).

Vagueness theories prove invaluable in underpinning a philosophical approach to the inescapable uncertainties of communication. Waismann's *Mathematical Thinking* and its reflections on arbitrary orders and the 'loose texture' of language are foundational here. Unlike conventional accounts of vagueness, however, which stress that there is always a distinction between truth and falsehood, the semiotically enriched vagueness concept proposed transfers this distinction to the level of social function. By contrast, Wright and Rosenkranz have more recently moved the debate towards uncertain logics, or multivalent/many-valued logics. Vagueness is best seen not so much as an epistemic problem, i.e. relating to the ignorance of man about the world, but as the result of contingencies of communication and cognition. In social terms, society determines *ex post facto* whether or not something is true or false. By extending the concept of vagueness to communicative interaction, it is possible to heighten awareness of the uncertainties in communication and the elaborate fictional codes constructed to simulate or impute 'shared knowledge'.

5. Social communication theory

By far the most significant milestone in the history of communication science was the publication of Habermas's *Theory of Communicative Action* (1981) and Luhmann's *Social Systems* (1986). The two great interdisciplinary works were amongst the first wide-ranging interdisciplinary accounts of social communication, drawing on cognition theories, social psychology, philosophy and social theory. The rich debate between Habermas and Luhmann defines, in major part, the theoretical horizon against which this study should be viewed. In *Knowledge and Human Interests* Habermas had considered the concepts of 'I'-identity and linguistic communication, affirming that the process of communicative understanding rests on the basis of an intersubjective relation. Language is the basis of intersubjectivity or Dilthey's concept of *Gemeinsamkeit* of shared linguistic symbols (Habermas, 1999a [orig. 1968]: 198) which offers an early indication of the core ideas of *Theory of Communicative Action*. The dialogical relation incorporates at the same time a dialectical relation between the general and the individual:

> Self-awareness constitutes itself at the intersection of the horizontal level of intersubjective understanding with others *and* the vertical level of intrasubjective understanding with oneself.
>
> (Habermas, 1999a: 199 – my translation)

This grounding of communication – as understanding and social cohesion – acquires especial importance, since Habermas attaches to it nothing less than the status of a paradigm change from the aporias of the philosophy of the subject to the intersubjectively constituted social actor. Habermas avoids clinging blindly to the philosophy of the subject and pursues the reconstruction of a rational project which in turn does not confine itself to the rationalization tendencies of technical-administrative systems and releases potential for democratic contestation. It is a form of *intersubjectivity* free of constraints on the basis of reciprocal recognition of rational subjects. In this model, actors make (criticisable) claims about their statements which can either assert or withdraw legitimation. In terms of social theory, the integration of social actors by means of communicative relations based on such accountable claims presupposes a common network of references between language and the world. This network facilitates the meeting of social actors in situations of intersubjective reciprocity. It is here that Habermas places Husserl's concept of the shared horizon of expectation grounded in the *lifeworld* (of common experience and cultural knowledge) in the communicatively generated social sphere; he drops the phenomenological method based on an understanding of the ways in which phenomena appear to subjects. When shorn of phenomenological premises, the lifeworld as a concept acquires the character of background knowledge on which all actors may draw. Each communicative speech act accordingly raises ideal claims to validity and in so doing creates a three-fold relationship consisting of a subjective dimension (of the speaker), an objective dimension (of the listener) and an intersubjective dimension (of society):

> The interpreter who understands meaning is experiencing fundamentally as a participant in communication, on the basis of a symbolically established intersubjective relationship with other individuals, even if he is actually alone with a book, a document, or a work of art.
>
> (Habermas, 1979a: 9)

Admittedly, Habermas's ideal reconstruction of everyday hermeneutics proceeds from the principle of a rationally *communicable* horizon of expectation which governs assumptions, behaviour and so forth. By adopting Husserl's concept of the lifeworld and relocating it in the concrete experience of social existence, Habermas sets out to establish a source of rational codes of behaviour in which the tendencies of rationalization (e.g. differentiation, fragmentation, diffusion and networking of social organization) cannot be realized without control: a communication-theoretical interpretation of the lifeworld concept is distinct from Husserl's transcendental concept. In consequence, communicatively generated intersubjectivity embeds the speaker in a relationship which looks beyond the world of reference of alter and ego. The legitimacy of lifeworld communications derives from an intersubjective guarantee which functions as a factor of group integration, promotion of cultural tradition and the socialization of future generations. The social-theoretical model of intersubjectivity presupposes on the one hand the (normative) recognition of rules. On the other hand, this recognition requires a measure of reciprocity which is expressed in our ability to take the attitude of the other, in Mead's famous formulation. This means that each participant constitutes himself as the ego of the other. The difference introduced by Habermas's interaction concept lies in his criticism of George Herbert Mead's theory and its failure to emphasize self-reflexivity and normativity in the relationship with the other. In other words, Mead never took the process of the internalization of the other's position seriously. Habermas's communication-theoretical correction resides in embedding 'attitude-taking' in the binding force of rules and not in empirical repetitions of conventional practice handed down over time. This means that the identity of rules does not rest on invariable observable facts, but on the pragmatically negotiated intersubjective acknowledgement, i.e. discoursal construction, of their validity. Transcendental consciousness gives way to the intersubjective recognition of claims raised in discursive contestation, which is the rational challenging of premises:

> If we now relinquish the basic concepts of the philosophy of consciousness in which Husserl dealt with the problem of the lifeworld, we can think of the lifeworld as represented as a culturally transmitted and linguistically organized stock of interpretative patterns.
>
> (Habermas, 1992b: 2.124)

The reconstruction of the ideal conditions of communicative action shifts the perspective from shared horizons of *consciousness* to the pragmatics of contexts of reference. Only a critical-pragmatic social philosophy can grasp the context of reference as a context of meaning. These contexts possess their own grammars (in Wittgenstein's sense of the term, namely as a network of relations) and operate as forms of the organization of knowledge. This means that a lifeworld without grammar – norms, rules, ideals – is inconceivable. In seeing language games as the foundations of everyday rationality, Habermas assumes that the intersubjective character of understanding does not reflect some kind of external objectivity; instead, (speech) actors find themselves in an intersubjective horizon:

> The world as the sum total of possible facts is constituted only for an interpretation community whose members engage, before the background of an intersubjectively shared lifeworld, in processes of reaching understanding with one another about things in the world.
>
> (Habermas, 1996: 14)

Whereas any similarity with the phenomenological concept of the lifeworld is not coincidental, the phenomenological model of consciousness remains constrained by a fundamental egoism, meaning that the subject is locked into the lifeworld as a pre-given (and therefore not pragmatically constructed) environment. Since previous concepts of the lifeworld remain transcendentally rooted, they fail to address the problem of the practices which generate the shared acceptance of lifeworld practices. In this way, the philosophy of the subject once again reveals its inability to avoid solipsism and leaves no room for a concept of intersubjectivity anchored in communicative practice (Habermas, 1992b: 2.212–14). Once the lifeworld becomes blind to the enactment of dissent on a rational basis, the loss of the legitimation basis of modern societies – contestation or the plurality of dissenting voices – is the inevitable corollary. The lifeworld is thus reconceptualized on a communicative-theoretical basis of rational validity claims as *counterfactual ideals*:

> A set of unavoidable idealizations forms the counterfactual basis of an actual practice of reaching understanding, a practice that can critically turn against its own results and thus *transcend* itself. Thus the tension between idea and reality breaks into the very facticity of linguistically structured forms of life.
>
> (Habermas, 1996: 4)

A fundamentally realist epistemology which assumes an objective world to which reference can be made, thus converges with a counterfactual theory of social pragmatics and a theory of reflexive development.

6. The end of the 'semantic of interaction'?

A radical turn in communication theory took place in Germany with the systems theory of Niklas Luhmann and the debates surrounding radical constructivism initiated by Siegfried J. Schmidt in the late 1970s and 1980s in particular. Despite its highly significant resonance in the German-speaking countries, this turn has not been registered by communication studies elsewhere. Luhmann proposed an unconventional reading of the lifeworld concept with direct implications for a theory of social communication, stressing the paradigm of the semantics of interaction which marked the Enlightenment. The dialogism of Enlightenment thinkers is at the same time much more than a mere topos: it is elevated to the status of a paradigm of the way in which society *should* work. Husserl and Habermas remain very much within the horizon of Enlightenment ideals to the extent that their belief in a lifeworld somehow distinct from technical-administrative power is indelibly inscribed into the counter-discourse of a rationality which sets out to correct and perfect reality in a way which recalls Marx's celebrated appeal in the *Feuerbach Theses* to thinkers to change the world:

> In its long history the description of the social life of man [...] was guided by ideals which reality did not satisfy. This was as true of the tradition of ancient Europe with its ethos of the natural perfection of man as it was for its efforts to educate and forgive sins. But this is also true of modern Europe, for the Enlightenment with its double deity Reason and Critique. And well into this century the consciousness of imperfection is retained – consider Husserl or Habermas.
>
> (Luhmann, 1997: 1.21–2 – my translation)

Luhmann's paradigm shift poses challenges which are too often consigned to the margins in some debates. For him, to describe society in terms of dialogue or interaction in the face of the multiple fragmentations of a cognitive and social order is to perpetuate metaphysics and fail in the task of creating a sociology disabused of illusions (Luhmann, 1995). However, despite the liberating space Luhmann opened up, his proposal for sociological renewal amounts to the elaboration of a supertheory with near-universal claims. Its defining characteristics reside in its capacity not to construct identity and totality, but to locate differences by use of the 'system' as an epistemological construct. The paradigm of the difference between the whole and its parts is replaced by the paradigm of internal system differentiation. In this process the general system acquires the function of the internal environment of subsystems. At a micrological level, the basic system–environment distinction must be complemented by the distinction between element and relation. There cannot be elements without relations, and there cannot be a relation without elements. The concept of self-reference relates to the unity which an element or system constitutes for itself, meaning that self-reference presupposes closure. Self-reference also expands the scope for structural coupling and internal system communication (Luhmann, 1995: 16–41). Complexity is the pressure of selection, but this pressure for selection also induces contingency and risk. Systems theory thus makes a break with the presuppositions of theories of perfectability by means of one fundamental shift. The concept of the subject is discarded and replaced by the concept of the self-referential system, the identity of which in itself is located in its difference *vis-à-vis* its environment:

> The theory of self-referential systems affirms that the differentiation of systems can only occur through systemic reference, i.e. through the fact that systems refer to themselves in the constitution of their elements [...]. Self-referential closure is therefore only possible in an environment under ecological conditions. The environment is the necessary correlate of self-referential operations [...].
>
> (Luhmann, 1995: 9 – my translation)

It is well known that the richness and controversy of Luhmann's theory derives as much from its theory of knowledge as from its theory of society. It aims above all at maximum epistemological plausibility, which undoubtedly enhances its value at a diagnostic level. Systems theory, according to Luhmann, is an observer-dependent theory where the observer is also a cognitively self-referential system. By challenging the subject–object dualism, his proposal focuses on the difference between identity (that is system identity) and difference (that is the system in an environment). His conception of the system is of course not restricted to historically verifiable institutions, but rather possesses a fundamental methodological value: '[...] every social contact is understood as a system, up to including society as the inclusion of all possible contacts' (Luhmann, 1995: 14–15). In general terms, since logically the system cannot be defined without relation to its environment, the two can be said to entertain a relation of interdependence.

Luhmann's systems theory of communication integrates cybernetic theories of self-regulation (whereby a social or cognitive system 'seeks' to regulate itself into a steady state) and some of the counter-intuitive work of information theorists such as Shannon. Information, according to Luhmann, is generated when a selective event operates selectively in the system. This selective operation in turn presupposes the capacity for the formation of differences. In this way, information comes to be viewed as the experience of difference. Clearly, information is not synonymous with communication, let alone meaning; communication is not a regulatory source but rather simply discharges the function of continuing communication which, in turn, must be self-referential. Communication does not correlate to something in the world which can be located outside communication (e.g. truth, reality etc.), but refers to itself in the sense that it communicates about something which is only considered to be located outside communication:

> The social system [...] is no longer characterized by a defined 'essence' or even by a determined morality (dissemination of happiness, approximation of quality of life, rational-consensual integration, etc.), but only by the operation which produces and reproduces society. And that is communication.
>
> (Luhmann, 1997: 1.70 – my translation)

Since there is no possibility of ascertaining the correspondence of Putnam's mapping of communication and a putative external reality, the 'referent' as it might be called, can never be anything more than a narrative self-thematization, albeit with socially constitutive properties. Since society, as part of a putative external reality, cannot be known outside communication, it can only be known inside communication. Society therefore can be said to consist of communication about communication.

Systems theories of self-reference, however modelled, have been subjected to serious criticism principally on account of their high level of abstraction and apparent remoteness from empirical problem solving. Critics such as Habermas tend to see the definition of systems as being too hermetic and therefore impervious to the independent, reflective contributions of social actors in the lifeworld. In an attempt to counter these limitations or 'aporias' of self-reference, Habermas has more recently proposed a theory of communication based on a revised realism. Here, there is no denotative or representational correspondence between language and facts, and a new concept of reference is therefore needed in order to explain how it is that we can refer to the same object on the basis of the 'objectivity of the world' ('of possible references' – 1999b: 37).[3] For Habermas, this model of reference must remain realistic in philosophical terms, in the sense that the concept of reference to an objective world is retained. His proposal makes use of a 'detranscendentalized intersubjectivity of understanding' which eschews a monadological understanding of language universes (1999b: 29) in which the number of universes directly corresponds to the number of speakers: 'By orienting themselves to unconditional validity claims and imputing accountability to each other speakers aim beyond all contingent and purely local contexts' (1999b: 25). In other words, society is cohesive because speakers are embedded into common contexts of reference which in turn make shared knowledge and consensus as a counterfactual ideal a possibility and remove the danger of social disintegration or anomie.

The aim of Habermas's recent revised realism is to bring about a reconciliation. This involves recognizing, on the one hand, the 'epistemic primacy' of a linguistically articulated lifeworld of shared culture, norms and experience, and on the other, the ontological primacy of a reality independent of language. These two premises are in themselves problematic. The lifeworld is a meaningful construct, in the sense that it is a realm which is not reduced to a 'system' with its own internal systems logic. However, the lifeworld in itself is as *contingent on communication* as the system from which it is held to be distinct. In one reading, the lifeworld could be seen as communication 'outside' the system of power, which is simply excluded from the system for being superfluous or irrelevant, but this reading is rather one-dimensional. The dependency of the lifeworld on a communicatively mediated 'reality' means that it is more than simply articulated by language. Moreover, the ontological assumption or imputation that reality is independent of language and can be referred to as objectivity flattens the cognitive autonomy (S.J. Schmidt, 1994b) of the lifeworld subject and locks him into a transcendental world which is at variance with our freedom to make constructs, disagree, and be insincere and sincere simultaneously. Thus, a paradox emerges: our imputation of reference to other worlds beyond language is a construction.

The discourses of social and cultural realities remain embedded in lifeworlds since their function is to repair background knowledge which has been 'disturbed' or fragmented by the rationalization tendencies of the differentiation of social systems. At the same time, discourses are porous – that is to say, they are a *form in an open communication environment*. As such, they are not simply embedded in or confined to lifeworlds: there is no rigid frontier between lifeworld and system, and 'colonization' operates in both directions as a kind of interpenetration, not merely as the infiltration of the lifeworld by discourses of 'power', but as the infiltration of the 'system' by a range of other discourses, such as environmentalism, feminism, minority rights and, increasingly, religion. Indeed, Habermas's model of *discursive* democracy offers a theoretical model for the capacity of discourses to inform 'systems'. Admittedly, it could always be argued that such *counter-colonization* could constitute little more than a well-defined and systems-driven sphere of communicative tolerance in order to render visible and thus also neutralize counter-discourses. And yet, given the contingencies of communication in terms of social systems and the porosity of that communication in pragmatic, semiotic and cognitive terms, there is no guarantee of system success in maintaining the defining frontier of the area of tolerance. In semiotic terms, the communicative sign is an appeal which depends on use in order to remain operational; there is therefore a constant tension between stabilized conventions of meaning and information. But this is a trivial statement. A social communication-theoretical approach must take account of the management of uncertainty and certainty or ongoing dynamic of opening and closure of communication space (Dirk Baecker, 2005).

From the 1980s onwards, constructivism, often in dialogue with systems theory, generated a wide-ranging interdisciplinary discussion about the foundational concepts which are central to communication science. As noted above, in a social-theoretical sense, the concept of contingency is a paradox, involving contact and thus dependency, but also risk, since this contact depends on a context which cannot be determined in advance; if something appears as contingent, then it appears 'as something that could be different' (Luhmann, 1990: 147). Constructivism, with its explicit epistemological programme, has always been concerned with reality construction from a plurality of disciplinary perspectives, and constructivist theories of communication are, in certain important aspects, more sensitive to the precariousness of communicative interactions.

If, as constructivist thinkers generally suggested, objectivity is a fiction, in the sense that it is the construction of an observer and not an ontological category, then the notion of reference (to what? to whom?) becomes problematic. The observer does not make contact with the external world, but instead processes it internally. In simplified terms, it can be said that cognition is a process in which the subject processes his environment by reference to his own prior knowledge. If cognition is indeed closed, in the sense that there can be no 'contact' between one mind and another, or indeed between one mind and 'reality', then interaction should be reconceptualized to take account of such closure. Social fictions also operate as complex pragmatic fictions by means of recursively linked communications and thus build stable social orders through culture as a socially obligatory semantic instantiation of world models (Schmidt, 2001: 11). For reasons of cognitive self-reference (or 'closure'), therefore, communicative interaction can be more adequately viewed as a precarious process, an ongoing *operation in uncertainty*.

7. Conclusion

This book further develops the interdisciplinary programme envisaged in the preliminary studies *Functions and Fictions of Communication* (2000) and *Rethinking Communicative Interaction* (2003), building on a range of conference presentations and invited lectures between 2002 and 2006. To conceptualize communication as an operation in pragmatic, semiotic and semantic uncertainty involves pursuing a programme which challenges stable categories. As noted in *Rethinking Communicative Interaction*, although it could be argued in the 1960s that 'the pragmatics of human communication is a science in its infancy, barely able to read and write its name' (Watzlawick, Beavin Bavelas, Jackson, 1967: 13), a communication turn has certainly taken place since then.

This book goes to press at a time when a number of debates in different disciplines in the human and social sciences appear to be taking the relationship between understanding and uncertainty, meaning and the subject to new levels. Baecker's work is clearly a case in point in communication theory but philosophical works also need to be critically integrated in a philosophy of communication. These would include Christopher Gauker's *Words without Meaning* (2003), Bernhard Waldenfels's *Studies on the Phenomenology of the Strange* (1997–9), Josef Mitterer's *The Flight from Arbitrariness* (2001) and Siegfried Schmidt's provocatively entitled *Stories and Discourses: A Farewell to Constructivism* (2003).

Mitterer, for example, seeks to reconstruct philosophy as a technique in argumentation based on a dualism by which opinions may be eliminated or discredited. There are audible echoes of Foucault in such a starting position, but Mitterer takes his critique further to challenge the epistemological foundations of such dualisms as language and reality or object and description. In this way, he can see realism and constructivism as closely intertwined. In the constructivist view, 'We make differences and therefore they exist', whereas in the realist view, 'There are differences and therefore we make them' (Mitterer, 2001: 36 – my translation). Notwithstanding the insights reconstructed briefly above, Mitterer's critique of relativistic theories (including constructivism we might say) leads him to make rather sweeping statements about the relatively low incidence of conflict in day-to-day communication: 'Many, if not most human discourses occur without conflict. Opinions complement each other or are exchanged; communication in such discourses is like a monologue with distributed roles' (Mitterer, 2001: 86 – my translation).

If communication is uncertain by virtue of its constructed or shifting correspondence with a constructed truth or reality, then the fact that conflict is not the communication norm offers no warranty for the absence of that conflict. 'Contingency management' (Schmidt, 2003b) in communication means that there is indeed contingency of the 'I' and communications. These *multiple contingencies* cannot be captured by the metaphors of dialogue, intersubjectivity or monologue since in both uncertainty is ultimately resolved. Accounts of conflict, asymmetry and communication difficulty do not actually address the fundamental insolubility of uncertainty and can only do so by recourse to an assumed common horizon. Like Mitterer, Schmidt seems uneasy about some of the more radical implications of the conclusions reached by constructivists in discussions of autonomy, self-reference and so on. Against this background, it is revealing that Schmidt refers to the 'reconciliation' of social orientation by culture and collective knowledge, for example, with cognitive autonomy (Schmidt, 1994b). The determinateness of 'cultural programmes', their regulatory capacity, renders them unreflected – that is, they exist prior to the critical reflection of autonomous individuals who 'always come too late'. Societies cannot tolerate excessive uncertainty and thus operate with the 'invisibilization of contingency' (Schmidt, 2003b: 47; 141); uncertainty, in other words, is removed from our line of sight.

And yet uncertainties *are* communications, and communication *is* a complex uncertainty for the reasons outlined above. If this is so, then contingency/uncertainty cannot be invisibilized. At best, it can be suppressed, but even so, will remain latent, silent but speaking, to emerge again at some future point. The semiotic density of language as a porous form of the spoken and the unspoken (cf. Davidson's unspoken languages, Wittgenstein's undertone concept, Luhmann's contingency and Peirce's vague residuum) makes any stabilization attempt contingent. And this is the paradox of the 'uninterrupted service of blind spots' (Schmidt, 2003b: 144 – my translation). Society is the operative oscillation of uncertainty and organization. Communications cannot lose the latent uncertainty which makes societies sensitive and responsive to change. Where uncertainty is invisibilized, democracy ends. This political dimension of uncertain communication theory might surprise some readers who assume that all works on uncertainty or relativity are postmodern apologias. These investigations take a contrary view, namely that uncertain communication theory is indeed a critical theory for a late modern society acutely aware of its apparently impending postmodernity. These new investigations are part of the hypercritical project of modernity.

2
Intersubjectivity, Dialogue and the Limits of Sharedness

1. Intersubjectivity and the understanding of intentions

The following chapter discusses first and foremost the theoretical potential and limitations of two powerful traditions within what might be termed the paradigm of intersubjectivity. Two exemplars of these traditions, broadly defined, are taken up here: the work of Edmund Husserl (1859–1938) and the work of Mikhail Bakhtin (1895–1975) and his collaborators, V.N. Voloshinov (1895–1936) and Pavel Medvedev (1892–1938).

Husserl's relevance for a theory of communication derives from the way in which he conceived of the relation between the ego and the other. He introduced the systematic phenomenological account of the lifeworld and intersubjectivity which has proved to be influential across a range of works in social communication and philosophy. These extend from Paul Ricoeur to Schütz's *Der Aufbau der sozialen Welt* (1932), Schütz and Luckmann's *Structures of the Life-world* (1973), Luckmann's *Construction of Social Reality* (1966), Marková's *Dialogicality and Social Representation* (2003) and perhaps most significantly to the communicative action theory of Jürgen Habermas. The theory of intersubjectivity culminated in Husserl's late works which include his *Crisis of the European Sciences* (1936) and the *Cartesian Meditations* (1950).[1]

Let us return to the development of the concept of intersubjectivity in the earlier works first. In the *Logical Investigations* (1901), as part of the phenomenological commitment to a descriptive understanding of the immanent meaning of psychic experiences, Husserl appears to leave the door open to a contextualized theory of meaning, where meaning varies according to the participants involved:

> Person *A* faces person *B* while on another occasion person *M* faces person *N*. Should *A* wish *B* 'the same' as *M* wishes *N*, the meaning of the volitional utterance, including the view of the persons facing each other, is obviously different.
>
> (1992: 85 – my translation)

And yet, the theory of meaning proposed in the *Logical Investigations* actually resolves the risks vague language, monological speech and oscillating meanings can bring about (these categorizations are Husserl's); the communication of messages is possible in the first place because the listener can understand the intention of the speaker (1992: 39ff.):

> If someone says *this,* then he awakens in the listener not directly the idea of what he intends, but first and foremost the idea or conviction that he intends something in his field of vision or thought to which he wishes to draw the listener's attention.
>
> (1992: 89 – my translation)

This mapping of understanding and intentionality in reference to a field of vision marks out a strong transcendentalist commitment to the 'limitlessness of objective reason' (1992: 95). Thus, while at first sight the indirect awakening of intentions certainly appears sensitive to communication uncertainty since it acknowledges the gap between convictions and the act of 'triggering' or 'awakening', integration through dialogical relations presupposes reference to a common world that anchors speakers into a relation of reciprocal intersubjectivity. As Leydesdorff argues, '[w]e are uncertain about what things mean and this generates an intersubjectivity which transcends the [sic] individual subjectivity' (Leydesdorff, MS: 6). The resolution of vagueness is barely satisfactory for the sceptic who wishes to pursue the exploration of the ideality and supposed objectivity to which Husserl refers when we know how many misunderstandings arise on a daily basis.

The *Logical Investigations* already made a clear distinction between acts of meaning and meaning *per se* where meaning is a form of objective, 'ideal unity' compared with the plurality of meaning acts which are occasional, vague and oscillating (Husserl, 1992: 84). On the basis of this distinction, the early Husserl can proceed to a semantics which distinguishes between vague and exact expressions. The distinction is strongly intuitive since theoretical and legal expressions are considered to be exact, whereas 'most of the expressions of everyday life' such as 'tree', 'animal' or 'plant' are vague (Husserl, 1992: 93). Husserl's semantic unity remains unaffected by the oscillations of subjective meaning, and consciousness is therefore already inter-monadic.

Husserl defended the view that things seen are always something more than what is actually perceived about them. In this way, he considered the lifeworld as the 'forgotten meaning-fundament of natural science' (1997: 48) – for the loss of meaning brought about by the growing separation between everyday and scientific meanings. Husserl's lifeworld concept thus oscillates between two poles: between the world as it is perceived by the subject and a world which goes beyond subject-centred perceptions (1997: 51). It is clear that this generates much potential for a universalist account of social interaction. He was not here considering empirical interaction structures, but the reasons for which various subjects can perceive an object intersubjectively. The non-I, as an element of the phenomenal world of things as they appear to the subject, is another I for Husserl. The same insight opens up an infinite scope of others; an objective nature and an objective world, and these others are therefore a *monadological community* of different selves. In this way, the early reflections on a theory of intersubjectivity acquire transcendental status and consign uncertainty to the margins. Experience can be made intersubjective because the objective world is the necessary correlate of intersubjective experience, making a harmony of the monads possible.

The concept of intersubjectivity is developed further in the later works. Thus, the subtitle of Husserl's fifth *Cartesian Meditation*, 'Uncovering of the Sphere of Transcendental Being as Monadological Intersubjectivity', sets out his primary task as a phenomenological account of the transcendental relations among monads. Although the relations between *ego* and *alter* are conceived as proceeding from monads, they are transcendental and cannot be confused with closed subjective universes (solipsism). The foundation of this intersubjective and transcendental relation is the intentionality of the ego, that is to say, the capacity to *intend* or project experience, thought, evaluation and action; intentionality takes meaning beyond my being as a monad (in Ricoeur's formulation, a consciousness 'bursting out beyond itself' – Ricoeur, 1967: 17). 'Others', as opposed to the ego, are 'psychophysical' objects in the world, with bodies and minds; they are also subjects of the experience of that world. In this dual self/other constitution, the other is experienced not as my private synthesis, but instead as strange to me and therefore intersubjective and available to everyone (Husserl uses the concept of *'Umweltlichkeit für jedermann'* [1992: 98]). The phenomenonological method of *reduction* is central to this conceptualization of *ego–alter* relations.

Phenomenological reduction is the process by which the ego abstracts from everything which gives it a transcendental constitution as an other. Here, the ego is not a mere correlate phenomenon within a universal phenomenon called 'the world'; my ego is 'an essential structure of the universal constitution in which the transcendental ego lives as constituting an objective world' (1992: 96). It is this co-relational framework which averts the risk of solipsism. However, even when one performs the methodological step of abstracting from all that transcends the ego, a layer of the world remains; this residuum is the transcendental correlate of world experience or the first part in a chain of intersubjective significations (Ricoeur, 1967: 121). So the method of phenomenological reduction is a reduction to the transcendental ego. Intentionality as the capacity to project into the other and the residuum of the objective world which remains in the phenomenological reduction places the monad in an environment *sui generis*: namely, a community of monads (*Monadengemeinschaft*).

In this model – not without paradox – all egos emerge as 'world objects' while 'intermonadological communalization' (*Vergemeinschaftung*) gives 'transcendental intersubjectivity its own intersubjective sphere in which the objective world is intersubjectively constituted' (1992: 110). The monads thus live in an intersubjective realm in which the objective world is constructed as an ideal correlate. This objective world does not actually transcend its intersubjective specific essence but is inherent in it as a form of 'immanent transcendence' (1992: 110). The resultant harmony of the monads is not a metaphysical harmony but part of the process of intersubjective communalization constituted in the 'ideality of infinite openness'.

Despite his insistence that his account was anything but grounded in solipsism, Husserl's transcendental phenomenology was heavily criticized principally for claiming that the ego has no direct access to the other and therefore relied on ego-centred intentional capabilities by which ego and alter undergo *pairing* as an associatively constituted component of other-experience (1992: 114). This intentionality is transcendent because it presupposes more than that which it actually 'makes present'. The world of the phenomena of others is as my world of phenomena and so there is an 'identity of phenomenal systems' (1992: 128). There are, on Husserl's concession, abnormalities such as deafness or blindness and yet these must also first be constituted, thus presupposing normality. Attention will return to the circularity in this assertion below. Husserl claims that although monads are *'reell'* separate, the *'irreal* reaching of the others into my primordiality' is not the stuff of metaphysical fantasy but a transcendental community. The 'open community of the monads' is constituted from the sources of ego's intentionality but as such also constituted in others in their subjective phenomenal form.

We know that Husserl embeds monads in a transcendental intersubjectivity from which the objective world is constituted. Despite the fact that intentionality derives from the perceiving ego, it is 'nonsense' to conclude that there can be an infinity of worlds; each monad might have its own distinctive world, but only as part of a transcendental unity of intersubjectivity; intersubjectivity can thus emerge as an unsurpassable horizon:

> But these worlds are then necessarily mere 'environments' of these intersubjectivities and mere aspects of a single, objective world common to them. For these two intersubjectivties do not exist in air.
>
> (1992: 143 – my translation)

Husserl thus accepts the existence of many monads and many worlds, but this multiplicity does not exist at the same time – they are, in his words, 'incompossible'. By contrast, there is *'apriori* compossibility' in transcendental intersubjectivity since the ego can think of variations as a system of alternative possibilities of which one is sublated by another and the ego itself. For it is 'the fact *ego sum* which prescribes whether and which other monads are other monads for me' (1992: 144); they can only be found by the ego, not created. In terms of a philosophy of social communication, it is noteworthy that Husserl sees 'I-Thou acts' as the source of all 'personal communication' (1992: 135).

In the last work published in his lifetime, the *Crisis of the European Sciences* Husserl returned to intersubjectivity and defined it in the following terms:

> Only by starting from the ego and the system of its transcendental functions and accomplishments can we methodically exhibit transcendental intersubjectivity and its transcendental communalization, through which, in the functioning system of ego-poles, the 'world for all,' and for each subject *as* world for all, is constituted. Only in this way, in an essential system of forward steps, can we gain an ultimate comprehension of the fact that each transcendental 'I' within intersubjectivity (as co-constituting the world in the way indicated must necessarily be constituted in the world as a human being.
>
> (Husserl, 1997: 185–6)

2. Semiotics – intersubjectivity and the appeal of the sign

Karl Bühler's semiotic theory developed in the 1930s is firmly embedded in Husserl's intersubjective epistemology. Bühler's triadic model of language, with its consideration of the expressive and appellative functions of language, can be made useful in conceptualizing communication as fundamentally *appellative* in a radical sense.

According to Bühler's famous organon model of language functions, which also proved influential for V. N. Voloshinov, language enacts three 'semantic functions' (S): expression (*Ausdruck*), representation (*Darstellung*) and appeal (*Appell*) (see figure 2.1). The last named function (the term is derived from the Latin *appellare*) is significant here. The language sign is 'a *signal* by virtue of its appeal to the hearer, whose inner and outer behaviour it directs as do other communicative signs'. This underexplored concept of linguistic appeal is intended to be a revision of the term 'triggering' in the

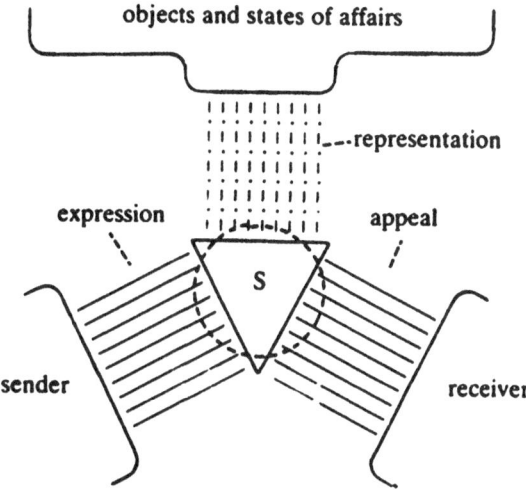

Figure 2.1 Organon model of language functions
Source: Karl Bühler, Theory of Language. John Benjamins. Amsterdam and Philadelphia 1990.

sense of a triggering of reactions and in analogy to sex appeal (Bühler, 1990: 35). The concept is conceived as being less deterministic than the rather behaviouristic term 'triggering'. It is important to establish the distinction between a predominantly producer-based triggering function and the more dynamic, receiver-focused concept of the appeal for Bühler's revision of Anton Marty's concept of 'Auslösung' was not simply a reworking of the triggering function, as Brandist (2005: 31) has recently suggested. While the speaker 'aims to trigger an act of response from the hearer [...]', that intention to trigger is an appeal. Triggering is the intention to determine; appeal is the recognition that the determination is indeterminate.

Crucially, the concept of appeal focuses on the role of the person to whom the appeal is being directed: '[...] in human and animal communication with signs it is the appeal that first and most exactly becomes evident to the analyst, namely in the behaviour of the receiver' (Bühler, 1990: 38). The concept of appeal is now proposed in a more complex sense in so much as the capacity of the sign to direct reception is modest at best. The appeal is *an open-ended communicative sign*. If the sign is an appeal, then it goes without saying that 'meaning' cannot be taken for granted: 'representation with language leaves a latitude of indeterminacy of meaning open and it can be closed by no other means than with regard to the "objective possibilities"' (Bühler, 1990: 76). The invocation of objective possibilities immediately closes down the space for autonomous reception and response; Bühler's psychology is transcendentalized because reactions to appeals are understood as 'objectively detectable reactions to *signals*' (1990: 45). Signs are not arbitrarily or contingently interpreted, but are used for practical purposes 'in *intersubjective* contact' (1990: 56 – my emphasis) where 'everything is *intersubjectively* understandable' (1990: 89 – my emphasis); the 'intersubjective communication about things' is 'necessary in human life' (1990: 120). Thus, deictics such as 'here', 'now' and 'I' are not, in Bühler's terms, incurably subjective. Bühler is quite explicit about the scope of his theoretical investigation, referring to the need for a common orientation between speaker and listener which is described as harmonious:

> As long as it is only a matter of using words like *here* and *there*, *I* and *thou* to identify something that is present in the field of perception common to both and which can hence be found with the external eye and ear, there is no need to bother with the finer details of a finer analysis of the partners' orientation within this field. We think *common sense* is enough for us to be able to understand the given conditions adequately, we believe we grasp how and why the receiver finds what the sender intends.
>
> (Bühler, 1990: 141)

The orientation is a *transcendental* rejection of the view that symbolization is based on 'arbitrary coordination' (1990: 210). The appeal of the sign in language is tamed by objectivism.

3. The paradigm of intersubjectivity in social science

The deep significance of Husserl's phenomenology for social science and studies of culture and interaction was recognized by Alfred Schütz in *Der sinnhafte Aufbau der sozialen Welt* (originally 1940 and translated as *The Phenomenology of the Social World*). For Schütz, the everyday world is an 'intersubjective world of culture' (Schütz, 1972: 180), entailing that *ego* and *alter* are engaged in a reciprocal relationship of lifeworld perspectives and meaning where transcendental and social norms go hand in hand: 'my lifeworld is therefore from the outset not my private world, but intersubjective, the basic structure of its reality is common to us all' (Schütz and Luckmann in Habermas 1992b: 2.131). It was Schütz who sought to integrate Husserlian phenomenology into social science, referring to 'reciprocal acts of positing meaning' as the foundation of a 'social world of mundane intersubjectivity' in which the transcendental basis remains:

> I also know that with segments of my meaningful life I belong to the life-world of Others as Others belong to my life-world, etc. [...] I posit meaningful acts in the expectation that Others will interpret them meaningfully.
>
> (Schütz, 1968: 182)

Schütz distinguishes, as Husserl had done, between signs (*Zeichen*) and indications (*Anzeichen*) where only the latter can be transcendentally apprehended as the indications of someone else's lived experiences. The apprehension is transcendental for the streams of consciousness of two agents are simultaneous in 'flows of duration'. There is in this conceptualization recognition of the contingencies of the understanding of the other: Schütz argues that we can only ever comprehend an 'approximate value' of the other's intended meaning (Schütz, 1972: 109). 'Genuine understanding of the other person', in his words, is however not restricted to the external indications of the other, but rather focuses on 'what lies behind' such indications (Schütz, 1972: 111). In the case of acts with a communicative intent, what lies behind the indication is the speaker's intention. The interpretation of this intention *behind* the other's communications rests on the method of self-explication in a manner reminiscent of Husserl's phenomenological reduction. Schütz also follows Husserl's insight in the *Logical Investigations* that the relation between the sign and its indication exists solely in the mind of the interpreter. Thus Schütz raises a fundamental question in the epistemology of understanding – namely the layer at which understanding takes place between two or more subjects. An understanding of intentions requires much effort in assumptions, inferencing and presupposition on the part of the subject and is therefore necessarily *uncertain*. In understanding the conscious act of the other, the 'interpreter puts himself in the place of the other person and imagines that he himself is selecting and using the signs. He interprets the other person's subjective meaning as if it were his own' (Schütz, 1972: 127).

The tensions between this interpretive leap and the uncertainty that Schütz is quite prepared to recognize in the work of the interpreter are manifest and possibly irreconcilable. At the same time, he is not prepared to concede much space to considerations of such uncertainties as constitutive processes of the construction of society for here he maintains a normative distinction between 'general and objective meaning' and 'occasional and subjective meaning'. Signs have objective meanings within existing sign systems such as cultures at the most complex level where such sign systems are prior 'interpretive schemes'. By contrast, subjective meanings are linked to the expressive functions of the sign. There is certainly significant reflection in this work on the uncertainties of understanding, the work of the interpreter in projecting into the other what could termed inferential processes or processes 'only in fancy' (Schütz, 1972: 114). And yet, the phenomenological assumptions Schütz shares with Husserl induce a resolution of the uncertainty of understanding by virtue of the presumed ability of the ego to access the subjective meaning of the other's act and 'to run over in our own minds in simultaneity or quasi-simultaneity the polythetic Acts which constituted the experience of the producer' (Schütz, 1972: 133). In other words, then, the intermonadological fallacy is not resolved.

In Schütz's *Structures of the Life-world*, written with Thomas Luckmann, the life-world is defined as reality in the natural attitude, where the natural attitude adopted by the social subject is based on the assumption of the givenness of others (Schütz and Luckmann, 1974: 61). The natural attitude is a normative construct which assumes that 'we "know" what it is another is doing, why he does it, and why he does it now and under these circumstances' (Schütz and Luckmann, 1974: 15). We are dealing here with an assumption about understanding and social relations which needs to be tested. The social life-world is in reality the 'wide-awake, normal, mature person finds given straightforwardly' in the natural attitude. Since the natural attitude assumes a relation from the ego to the other and back again, as it were, it can be held to be fundamentally intersubjective for here actors make assumptions about each other and thus enter into a relationship of a reciprocal 'we-relation' ('All experience of social reality is founded on the fundamental axiom positing the existence of other beings "like me"' [Schütz and Luckmann, 1974: 61].) The life-world can be considered intersubjective since actors make assumptions about each other which guarantee the reciprocity of social expectations and assumptions. This *'general thesis of reciprocity'*, as Schütz and Luckmann put it, makes strong cognitive and cultural claims for it assumes that understanding is reciprocal and that the reference frame-works of actors converge provided that non-standard communications are left to one side (Schütz and Luckmann, 1974: 21). Thus the inter-subjective reciprocity of understanding rests on two idealizations – that of the 'interchangeability of standpoints' and that of the 'congruence of relevance systems'.[2] The intermonadological fallacy emerges once more in the belief that the lifeworld is inherently intersubjective, such that 'I know that he knows that I know' (Schütz and Luckmann, 1974: 16).

Similarly, in 'Foundations of a Theory of Intersubjective Under-standing', Schütz portentously warns that the 'notoriously difficult problems which surround the constitution of the Thou within the subjectivity of private experience' and 'how universally valid inter-subjective knowledge is possible' must be left unresolved (Schütz, 1972: 98). The qualification is significant when one considers some of the rather mechanistic models of intersubjectivity which have become popularized in recent decades (see, for example, Crossley, 1996; Feather, 1999; Mintz, 2003 and a substantial body of works in social psychology). The leap from subjectivity to a somehow universal intersubjectivity remains a wishful one.

Of course, Schütz's thesis of reciprocity is perhaps most famously taken up in social theory by Jürgen Habermas in *The Theory of Communicative Action* in which he applies Husserl's concept of a hori-zon of expectation rooted in consciousness to a world which is inter-subjectively shared by communication. Communicating social actors, if one leaves aside pathological communication, stake claims to truth, sincerity and authenticity which protect the lifeworld of shared expe-riences from the clutches of a manipulative reason oriented solely towards its own survival. Husserl had viewed the lifeworld as the forgotten sediment of meaning of natural science, however, this life-world would also mean that social actors 'are vitally immersed in *a concrete surrounding world*' (Husserl, 1960: 135 – my emphasis). The lifeworld concept therefore oscillates between the world as it is perceived by the subject and the world that transcends the restrictions of subjective perception, turning it into a community of 'an essentially unique connectedness'. To the extent that the subject constitutes the importance of the phenomena around him, it relates itself to a perception of the phenomenon in its character as the other. Mead (1913: 376–7) wrote in similar vein that the vocal gestures we use in addressing others 'call out or tend to call out responses' from us.

Within the shadow of phenomenological intersubjectivity theories, Linell's discourse-theoretical framework for a 'dialogical theory of misunderstanding and miscommunication' also reveals much about the difficulty facing dialogical interaction theory in resolving the uncertainty between subjectivity and sociality. His dialogical model is intended to stand in opposition to the 'monological' model which is based on a model of communication as transmission via a conduit. Since such monological communication models were outdated and in need of revision, the dialogical approach certainly introduced much-needed plausibility. However, the dialogical interaction concept has succumbed to its own type of conservatism in replacing one communication model with another based on strong intuitive claims. Here, the use of the concept of intersubjectivity renders dialogism blind to deeper implications of communication as an unstable process: 'Understanding and misunderstanding (in discourse) concern degrees of intersubjectivity and are therefore pertinent to mutualities in dialogue' (Linell, 1995: 177); and 'misunderstanding clearly presupposes some (lack of) intersubjectivity' (Linell, 1995: 208).

Admittedly, the loose association of the concepts intersubjectivity, mutuality, shared knowledge and understanding may be politically attractive in the name of inclusionary politics, but too often such theoretical models dissolve into normative intuition. As a result, where the monological approach is rightly criticized for its simplifications, the dialogical model proposed in its place is oversimplified on a series of cognitive and communicative grounds and its core concepts – dialogism, intersubjectivity, reciprocity – are easily reified:

> The speaker is assigned the status of interpretive authority when it comes to the meaning of his/her own utterances. But this holds most unambiguously for reference, not necessarily for descriptive (or other aspects) of meaning. In other words, the speaker knows

what the intended referents are, but s/he may be mistaken in her/ his choice of words for describing them.

(Linell, 1995: 180)

Despite references to asymmetries, the dialogism paradigm tends to *anticipate* the resolution of communication in the form of shared meaning. If understanding is the grasp of intentions, this model is plausible. However, meaning is unstable – it is neither dependent on the form of the utterance nor on the intentions of the speaker. It is inferred, and thus always subject to a process of selection. In addition, the notion of shared knowledge can be seen in terms of the separateness of minds and as an operative social fiction (see Schmidt, e.g. 1994b, 2001). Kant had solved the problem of the connection between empirical (in the sense of subjectively experiential) and transcendent worlds by referring to the role played by heuristic fictions. Such fictions set up regulatory principles of the systematic use of reason used in the problematic conceptualization of objects considered possible. They operate here as the discourses in society that enable subjects or actors or individuals to communicate their constructions (Schmidt, 1994b).

4. Rethinking dialogism

It is an anomaly of the history of communication science and communication studies that the work of Mikhail Bakhtin has remained underexplored.[3] This neglect is all the more surprising when one considers how significant his influence has been in other areas of the human and social sciences. Theories of the dialogical self, dialogism, intertextuality and intercultural communication have been integrating his work in various ways for over two decades now. Hubert Hermans's and Harry Kempen's *The Dialogical Self: Meaning as Movement* (1993), Ivana Marková's *Representations of Dialogicality* (2004) and Per Linell's *Approaching Dialogue* (1998) are just some noteworthy examples. However, Julia Kristeva's *Desire in Language* (1980) and Tzvetan Todorov's *Le Principe Dialogique* (1981) were primarily responsible for easing the reception of Bakhtin's work in theories of intertextuality which found their way into literary and translation theories in the course of the 1980s and 1990s. By contrast, Bakhtin's intricate and extremely innovative work is almost entirely absent from the great communication philosophies of Habermas and Luhmann in the

1980s. The integration of dialogical theories into a theory of communication has doubtless been impeded by the well-acknowledged uncertainty about the authorial identity of some publications in the Bakhtin canon. Recently published work tends to support the view that his collaborators V.N. Voloshinov and P.V. Medvedev were actually the signatories of their own works and not, as had previously been assumed, the works of Bakhtin. Further confusion arises from the internal political difficulties which resulted in his banishment from Moscow and timelags in translating his work from his native Russian. And yet while many of his works have been available in various European languages since the 1980s, social communication theory persists in its neglect. This fragmented and incomplete reception ignores the fact that he can be considered, in the words of Todorov, the 'modern founder' of pragmatics (Todorov, 1984: 26).

It is no exaggeration to state that the work of the Bakhtin 'circle' occupies a central position in early twentieth century debates on linguistics, aesthetics and the novel. Voloshinov's *Marxisme et la Philosophie du Langage,* published in 1929, offered a detailed and systematic critique of Saussure and engaged directly with the phenom enological tradition, notably Husserl – although Brandist (2005: 27) comments that this is not true of Husserl's work after the *Logical Investigations* – and Ernst Cassirer and Hermann Cohen. The innovative theoretical architecture of the work of Bakhtin and his direct and indirect collaborators demonstrates critically how serious the neglect of his work has been for a theory of uncertainty and communication.[4] Its reception outside literary and translation studies has tended to focus on theories of multivoicedness or *heteroglossia* and has been fed back into educational theories of autonomy and social interaction.

In the 1930s and 1940s Bakhtin's strangely displaced voice was amongst the first to challenge the deterministic linguistic orthodoxy that the arbitrariness of the linguistic sign 'should *not* suggest that the signifier depends on the free choice of the speaking subject' (Saussure, 1968: 101 – my emphasis) and that the language system – *langue* – constitutes a 'sum of impressions deposited in each brain' (Saussure, 1968: 38). Whereas for Saussure '[l]anguage is not a function of the speaking subject, it is the product which the individual registers passively' (Saussure, 1968: 30), Bakhtin argued that there is no trace of a 'system of immutable norms' but the 'uninterrupted development of language norms' (Bakhtin/Voloshinov, 1977: 96–7).

For Bakhtin, then, any language 'system' is necessarily a dynamic process – 'There is no meaning outside the social communication of understanding, i.e. outside the united and mutually co-ordinated reactions of people to a given sign' (Medvedev, Bakhtin, 1978: 8). This approach to understanding suggests duality and relationality and characterizes everyday expectations of the dialogical character of communication – or, as George Herbert Mead put it, '[m]eaning arises and lies within the field of the relation between the gesture of a given human organism and the subsequent behaviour of this organism as indicated to another human organism by that gesture' (Mead, 1967: 75–6). Indeed, Mead himself (1913: 377) offered a radical insight into the contingencies of the self in communication where the self is 'a fusion of the remembered actor and this accompanying chorus' of others in society. This chorus is less harmonic than cacophonous, however and indeed Mead describes it (1913: 378) as 'different voices in conflict with each other' (Mead, 1913: 379–80).

Although Bakhtin proceeds from a phenomenologically informed theory (the early Husserl is a 'key influence') of what could be termed *utterance relations*, his attention to the multiplicity of voices (*vyskazy-vanie*) challenges a view of communication based on rationality, stressing the importance of the event and not the 'fusing of consciousness' (cf. also Koczanowicz, 2000: 64).[5] This move is significant, for Bakhtin is one of the first thinkers to have sought to develop a theory of utterance relations where contingencies of voices and subjects do not appear to merge transcendentally. As noted above, the distinctiveness of Bakhtin's reading of phenomenology, which greatly influenced him, lies in the fact that he emerges from it with strong accounts of subjectivity and tends to avoid transcendental solutions. The shift to an account of discursive relations (Brandist, 2004: 145) was in turn influenced by the work of Voloshinov who had been influenced by Bühler's theory of semiotics. Other influences include scientists at the Institute for the Comparative History of Eastern and Western Literatures and Languages (ILIaZV) who worked on a sociology of linguistic pluralism in major Soviet cities and Iakubinski's 1923 essay 'O dialogicheskoi rechi', this last work heavily influenced by Cassirer's *Symbolic Forms* (Koczanowicz, 2000).

As noted above, possibly under the influence of Marxism, Bakhtin rejected the 'abstract objectivism' of Saussure with its emphasis on the immutable norms of *langue* as a system. He gave vent to a deep-seated conviction that although signs are marked by social circumstances the notion that the connection between signs and signifiers is indispensable is in fact based on a 'lie' (Bakhtin/Voloshinov, 1977: 49). At this juncture, Bakhtin invokes Husserl who had offered a corrective of objectivist views in insisting that 'all ideological signs [...] are marked by the social horizon of a given epoch or social group' (Bakhtin/Voloshinov, 1977: 41). The appeal of the Husserlian view lay in its apparent capacity to reconcile the social situatedness of language and the dynamic process without which language norms cannot come into being.

From these diverse historical roots Bakhtin/Voloshinov proceeded to an account of the linguistic sign. On the one hand, a minimal Marxist position is maintained in the acknowledgement that reality 'determines the sign', meaning that Bakhtin was no early constructivist. His concern with the situatedness of beings in concrete environments is clear:

> It is precisely by having an opportunity to complement our individual perspective in a dialogue with another, that it becomes possible to see wholes instead of fragmented and separate individual identities.
>
> (Dufva, 2005: 140)

However, the Bakhtin circle introduced a significant shift in which the construction of reality is nonetheless considered to be a process in which the sign cannot be static but instead reflects and refracts a reality that is in the process of development. Illustrating his critique of correspondence theories of language in both pragmatic and epistemic terms by referring to the non-identical speech production of plosives under the influence of a neo-Kantian age of 'non-coincidence' or the 'non-identity of mind and world' (Holquist, 1990: 17), Bakhtin sought to distinguish between factual identity or correspondence among several language users and normative correspondence[6] in myth or other social codes. Here, correspondence of meaning in the narrow sense of factual identity is 'non-existent' (Voloshinov/Bakhtin, 1973 in Morris, 1997: 27). Bakhtin's theory of semiotics is a dynamic one: 'What is important for the speaker about a linguistic form is not that it is a stable and always self-equivalent signal, but that it is an always changeable and adaptable sign.' The work of

Cohen had already influenced Bakhtin's work in this context with its emphasis on the 'loopholes of existence'; dialogism, Holquist observes, 'is ultimately an epistemology founded on a loophole [...]' (Holquist, 1990: 7; 39):

> [The] task of understanding does not basically amount to recognizing the form used, but rather to understanding it in a particular, concrete context, to understanding its meaning in a particular utterance, i.e. it amounts to understanding its novelty and not to recognizing its identity.
>
> (Voloshinov/Bakhtin, 1973 in Morris, 1994: 33)

Despite the foregoing, Bakhtin scholars tend to emphasize the universalistic premises of his work where the integration of meaning at the interface of the emergent and socially rooted aspects 'implies a universal epistemological orientation toward wholeness' (Brandist, 2005: 2). This emphasis, a reaction to Michael Holquist's earlier, relativistic view of dialogism, is typified by Erik Dop's statement – '[...] for an utterance to mean, that is, for an utterance to be understood, it has to "respond" to an "objective judgement": the superaddressee, or the *universal*' (cited by Ongstad, 2005: 67). This new, universalistic consensus further stresses the wholeness at the root of the concept of dialogism – a wholeness determined by the 'semantic exhaustiveness', 'the speaker's plan or will' and 'typical compositional and generic forms of finalization': 'In some spheres [...] this exhaustiveness [...] is almost complete, while in others it is only relative, depending among others on the authorial *intent* of the utterer' (Ongstad, 2005: 70). Here, the quest for a universal theory of understanding or meaning not only conjures up a significantly distorted view of semantic saturation or the capacity of utterances to leave no meaning unmarked; it is also independent of intent. Meaning is, in a fundamental sense, contingent on our interpretations:

> Hearers have little access to what people have in mind apart from the interpretation of what they say. So interpretation would be a problem that hearers could not solve if they had to know what a speaker intended in order to identify the content of the context.
>
> (C. Gauker, Zero Tolerance for Pragmatics [MS] 2006: 7–8)

5. Evaluativeness and utterance

Social evaluation plays a highly significant role in Bakhtin's theory of the utterance. In *The Formal Method in Literary Scholarship* written with P.N. Medvedev and first published in 1928, Bakhtin established an understanding of literary scholarship itself as one 'branch in the study of ideologies' where such ideologies are not static and monological but marked by an 'essential plurality' (Medvedev, Bakhtin, 1978: 3); ideology is 'not within us, but between us' (Medvedev, Bakhtin, 1978: 8). Bakhtin was not prepared to explore the emergence of language norms in the context of autonomy but as a socially stabilized environment. This conception of dynamic ideological formation connects with Bakhtin's non-naturalistic semiotics in which ideologies 'signify, reflect and refract reality' (Medvedev, Bakhtin, 1978: 10). Despite these dynamics, the ideological environment is considered to be a horizon which '*determines* the individual consciousness of each member of the collective'. (Medvedev, Bakhtin, 1978: 14 – my emphasis). The ideological environment is at the same time then a reference framework for a collectivity against which meaning is formed as reactions to a given sign. This raises the question as to how certain words acquire certain socially coordinated meanings: 'What, in fact, is the element which unites the material presence of the word with its meaning? We submit that social evaluation is this element' (Medvedev, Bakhtin, 1978: 119). And so, despite the radical implications of his theoretical reflections, Bakhtin sought refuge in determinism. After all, this determinism and the curious tension between an insistence on ideological heteronomies and the dynamics of language processes manifests itself in Bakhtin's views on axiological accentuation, inspired by the philosophical ethics of Nicolai Hartmann. These are also relevant here, particularly in view of the connections between evaluation and the dynamic processes of social communication, or *heteroglossia*:

> [...] in the process of literary creation, languages interanimate each other and objectify precisely that side of one's own (and of the other's) language *that pertains to its world view*, its inner form, the axiologically accentuated system inherent in it.
>
> (Bakhtin, 1998: 65 – emphasis in the original)

Where values are seen as purely socio-cultural foundations the question must be asked as to whether social agents are merely the objects of such values. If so, then values are stable over time when we know them to be mutable (consider the fate of capital punishment, corporal punishment, ecological values, organized religions). And values are mutable – we could say contingent – because they depend on agents who are indeed social, but still agents nonetheless. A more radical axiological theory of evaluation as proposed here seeks to avoid the subject-flattening objectivism of such approaches by acknowledging the autonomy of social agents without reducing such autonomy to solipsism or atomism: autonomy and subjective valuation are con-stitutive social facts. It is worth quoting Bakhtin at length at this stage for the density of his reflections will yield much in these con-siderations. As we have seen, for Bakhtin, languages as social dis-course practices are axiologically accentuated and this accentuation is inevitable. In addition, this axiological accentuation, understood as subjective evaluation, constitutes a belief system which is peculiar to the world view of a language. This language is of course located amidst the tensions of centripetal and centrifugal forces of discourse. The axiological domain can thus be seen as a contingent subjective domain of values and evaluations:

> Alongside the centripetal forces, the centrifugal forces of language carry on their uninterrupted work; alongside verbal-ideological centralization and unification, the uninterrupted processes of decentralization and disunification go forward.
>
> (Bakhtin, 1998: 272)

And yet if the individual utterance is axiologically accented in the sense of Hartmann, and Bakhtin under his influence, then mutual orientation (in Bakhtin's and Medvedev's words), can be nothing more than a temporary stabilization. Indeed, Bakhtin refers to the mutability of social communication codes in speaking of the 'fleet-ing language' (1998: 272) of a day or epoch.

The connection between Bakhtin's critique of formal stylistics and ideological prescriptiveness is more than casual. The monologic utter-ance of the speaking individual is an aporia of traditional philosophy which 'postulated a simple and unmediated relation of the speaker to his unitary and singular "own" language, and [has] postulated as well a simple realization of this language in the monologic utterance of the individual' (Bakhtin, 1998: 269). Unitary language as a force of linguistic centralization operates amidst the dynamics of language development:

> But at the same time it [unitary language] makes its real presence felt as a force for overcoming this heteroglossia, imposing specific limits to it, guaranteeing a certain maximum of mutual understanding and crystallizing into a real, although still relative, unity – the unity of the reigning conversational (everyday) and literary language, 'correct language'.
>
> (Bakhtin, 1998: 270)

The essays in Bakhtin's 'Dialogic Imagination' were first written in 1934–5 but only came to be published in the mid-1970s. Although concerned with literary prose discourse, Bakhtin's extended essay set out to elaborate a critique of models which had come to predominate language understanding, described as being based on various assumptions: that language was a system; that the utterance was monologic and that the level of analysis should be the language of the speaking *individuum*. The orthodoxy of these language philosophies lies in a shared assumption that ideological discourse is in some way unified; a unified language assumes that discourse is subject to *centripetal* forces. According to Bakhtin, this view is distorted for it attempts to close language by imposing stability and order on the 'realities of *heteroglossia*' where the concept heteroglossia captures the centrifugal or uncertain multivoicedness of utterances. A closed, unitary language is not so much based on abstract rules but assumes ideological saturation which in turn ensures maximum mutual understanding in all spheres of ideological life. This conception of language imposes stability on dynamic processes Bakhtin emphasized in his earlier work. Since a unitary language operates in the midst of heteroglossia, any linguistic closure must be seen as relative.[7] The dynamics of heteroglossia are energized by contradictions and tensions which are made more acute by attempts to impose ideological stability on the real life of utterances. Instead, the utterance can be said to be dialogic precisely because there is tension between the meaning of a speaker and the generalized system of language (Holquist, 1990: 60). It is this very tension, the insoluble vagueness of semiosis and the shifting contexts of self and other that transcendental accounts of intersubjectivity or universal truth claims fail to capture. Thus the radical import of Bakhtin's philosophy of communication is less that the radical implications of dialogue preclude the isolation of the subject, as Holquist argues, and more that the dynamics of self and subject meaning and other and social meaning evolve dynamically over time without ever corresponding. Since perceptions involve subjects seeing more of the other than the other sees of himself (the thesis of an 'excess of seeing', as Bakhtin put it in *Author and Hero*), perception is marked by blindspots and radical incompleteness.

Bakhtin sees literary discourse as an exemplar of *heteroglossia*; more specifically, in the range of literary genres the novel is held to be the most *dialogical*. The work of Rabelais, for instance, engages in an interrogation with hegemonic discourse in form of parody and pastiche. It is this interaction with other languages that dialogizes *heteroglossia*. Just as Bakhtin generally sought to challenge a philosophy of language rooted in the speaking individuum, so in his literary essays he challenges the view of literature as flowing from a unified, authorial will since this approach imprisons heteroglossia in the 'dungeon of a single context'. (Bakhtin, 1998: 279). The prose genre, as the dialogized heteroglot literary discourse, is ineluctably interwoven into a fabric of given languages and utterances. Concrete historical human discourse is always embedded in these forms or layers.

It is important to recall in the context of this work on uncertainty and communication that the concept of dialogism is not based on an intuitive, narrowly bilateral understanding, but on the dynamics of multiple voices or, in Bakhtin's terms, multilanguagedness ('We must deal with the life and behavior of discourse in a contradictory and multi-languaged world' [Bakhtin, 1998: 275].) Dialogism is in other words not closed, but innovative and uncertain. The radical significance of these reflections is cast into starker relief in his views on context where, he argues, in an elastic environment of other *alien words*, words become dispersive much like a ray-word (Bakhtin, 1998: 277), spectral and never objective. Indeed, in an anticipation of the work of Kristeva on intertexuality as well as Derrida and Luhmann on polycontextuality, Bakhtin says that words inhabit an *intercontext* (Bakhtin, 1998: 284).

Like Buber and Mead before him, Bakhtin views the utterance as a relational construct which establishes an address in which the 'answer-word' is prefigured; despite a monological composition, the listener orientation is inescapable and 'primacy belongs to the response'. This listener orientation for its part creates a new internal dialogism since the speaker inhabits the listener's horizon before making an utterance; he enters into the 'subjective belief system of the listener'. Bakhtin further argues that the speaking subject is the interface of centrifugal and centripetal forces – a confluence of the individual act ('individualized embodiment') and heteroglossia. Where the tensions of anonymous social language and individual utterances encounter each other, language is 'accented as an individual utterance' (Bakhtin, 1998: 272). Rather than equating intersubjectivity with a universal horizon (which in turn would imply the merger of consciousness of self and other), 'intersubjectivity' can be seen as interstitial – the spaces between utterances (Bernard–Donals) or the open interpretability of an utterance. Social communications are a complex tension between dominant cultures and ideologies and the uniqueness of selves. This uniqueness and the asymmetries between self and others are factors of contingency which generate uncertainty; and if they can be communicated, they are contingent (Grant, 2003a: 104–5).[8] While the speaking subject is not monological but an axiological accent amidst many other voices, contexts are contingent, varying between ideological environment and the non-identity of signs. And yet, a root incommensurability persists and awaits reflection: the assumption of the same socio-ideological horizon (Bakhtin, 1998: 274) and the evaluated attitude of speakers:

> But no living word relates to its object in a singular way: between the word and its object, between the word and the speaking subject, there exists and elastic environment of other, alien words about the same object, the same theme, and this is an environment that is often difficult to penetrate [...].
>
> (Bakhtin, 1998: 276)

3
The Limited Reach of Universal Pragmatics

1. Introduction

This chapter begins with some reconstruction of Habermas's earlier works on the public sphere and legitimacy since a critical theory based on rational communication and democratic contestation clearly prefigures the systematic communications-theoretical work he began in the 1970s. Habermas proposed a theory of communicative rationality derived from an amalgam of the social historiography of ideas and normative theory by which he was able to abstract Kantian pragmatics from their historical situatedness and arrive at a theory of rational use of language as a theory of society and democracy where power is legitimated by the discursive challenges mounted by social subjects. The second part of this chapter is a discussion of some of the epistemological and pragmatic-theoretical problems of communicative action. It starts by considering the normative force and theoretical plausibility of the theory of universal pragmatics before proceeding to a discussion of the sociologically significant concept of the lifeworld and the epistemologically marked concept of intersubjectivity. The third part deals with uncertainty and postmetaphysical thinking in examining some of Habermas's work in the 1990s, primarily *Postmetaphysical Thinking* (1998a) and *Truth and Justification*. It will be argued that a theory of uncertain communication can work with *detranscendentalized* accounts of understanding and interaction. It is further argued that Habermas performs a near-impossible task in seeking to reconcile his postmetaphysical reflections with formal or universal pragmatics and that a truly detranscendentalized account needs to be given considerable epistemological revision. This revision, in turn, is bound to have an impact on theories of communication. Finally, it needs to be recognized that vast amounts of literature have been devoted to these very issues.[1] However, rather less has been said about more recent work from the perspective of a critique of Habermas's epistemology, and it is hoped that the exploration of uncertainty will challenge a complex of epistemological, logical and interactional assumptions in a new way. It is also hoped that new questions will emerge from a discussion of new theories of logic, semantics and pragmatics, which will provide additional underpinning for a theory of uncertain communication and free communication theory from the leaden weight of universal presuppositions.

2. Modernity and critique

Habermas insists on the differences between modernity as a project and current-day administrative and economic modernization whose imperatives 'increasingly infiltrate the ecology of lifeforms, of the internal communication structure of the lifeworld' (Habermas, 1990a: 40 – my translation). It is particularly important to Habermas to recognize the unfinished reserves of modernity by differentiating it from modernization, just as he had distinguished rationality from rationalization. His fundamental argument is that technical-administrative modernization has become uncoupled from aesthetic modernity:

> The multiple motives for ill-feeling and protest emerge where linear modernization, guided by criteria of administrative and economic rationality, penetrates spheres of life which seek out roles of cultural tradition, social integration and education and are therefore guided by different criteria, namely communicative rationality.
>
> (Habermas, 1990a: – my translation)

The innovative potential of modernity is guaranteed by the fact that the project of subject-centred philosophy has taken precisely one route since Hegel. This also means that there is an alternative route which has not yet been explored, and the existence of such an alternative is the proof that modernity contains its own counter-discourse. In view of this, Habermas avoids clinging blindly to the philosophy of the subject and pursues the reconstruction of a rational project which does not confine itself to the rationalization tendencies of technical-administrative action. It is instead a form of intersubjectivity free of constraints on the basis of reciprocal recognition. The social-theoretical concept of communicative action is complemented by an epistemological or cognition-theoretical affirmation of intersubjectivity. This allows actors to make (criticisable) validity claims which can either assert or withdraw legitimation.

Although Habermas first fully developed his theory of social communication in *Theory of Communicative Action* (1992b), the imbrication of rationality and communicative exchange is evident in his much earlier *Structural Transformation of the Public Sphere* (1962). Here, his historiography of the 'bourgeois' public sphere leads him to abstract from historical constraints and establish a normative account of the potential of a public debate unleashed by (or interwoven with) Enlightenment ideals. In this integrated account of counterfactual rationality, and a historical debate which transcends its historical situation, the influence of Kant emerges clearly. Kant's political reformism crystallized in the concept of *Öffentlichkeit* or 'publicness' by which he placed Reason in a social context. Enlightenment depended not only on the use of a subject's own reason, but also on its deployment in a certain public context. Political legitimacy had become increasingly dependent on support from among the learned members of society (such as Kant himself) – a support granted or withdrawn by means of communication (censorship or satire, theatre, philosophy, news reports, etc.).

In other words, Kant was already at least implicitly aware of a tension between the public principle of rational openness and access and the real heteronomies attendant on the public as a locus or principle of communication. The public ideal, without which rationality could not impose itself, entered into conflict with the clergy and new capital classes; vested interests thus confronted the method of rationality. The same conflicts induced a shift from the specious possibility of implementing, as it were, the public sphere to idealizations about the public sphere, which Hegel was later to denounce in the *Philosophy of Right* as the dissolution of publicness into mere public opinion, as Habermas points out. What Hegel observed was the mediatization of the public sphere as a process during which the topography of the public as an accessible space yielded to its status as a communication medium. We shall return to Hegel's critique of Kant's abstract public universalism in due course.

Habermas has mounted a thoroughgoing reflection on the rational potential of western society from the Enlightenment to the present. It is no exaggeration to say that the reconstruction of the rational basis of society underpins his entire critical communication theory to this day and thus also underlines the fundamental unity and continuity in his work. The public sphere is understood as a privileged realm which mediates between civil society and power in which actors use their rational faculties to argue about, and thus also regenerate, social, cultural and political concerns. However, this theoretical emphasis on the irreducibility of the rational content of debate in the public sphere cannot avoid abstracting putative communicative universals from the empirical communication practices which are always embedded in contexts of social control. Normative claims and historical accuracy develop an antagonistic potential.

An example of this antagonism can be seen in the distorting effects of a normative theory of communication whose very normativity means turning a blind eye to a history of social communication where such a history must consider the role of the media as historically changing (means of) communication. Habermas famously neglects the constitutive role played by the media in constructions of what is held to be 'public' – opinion, interest, outcry, unrest, etc. To sacrifice history to normativity is to impose a wilful interpretation on communication which only serves to expose the weakness of the normative claims being made. His more recent revisions (below) do not resolve this dilemma:

> In conjunction with an ever more commercialized and increasingly dense network of communication, with the growing capital requirements and organizational scale of publishing enterprises, the channels of communication became more regulated, and the opportunities for access to public communication became subjected to ever greater selective pressure. Therewith emerged a new sort of influence, i.e., media power, which, used for the purposes of manipulation, once and for all took care of the innocence of the principle of publicity. The public sphere, simultaneously prestructured and dominated by the mass media, developed into an arena infiltrated by power in which, by means of topic selection and topical contributions, a battle is fought not only over influence but over the control of communication flows that affect

behaviour while their strategic intentions are kept hidden as much as possible.

(Habermas in Calhoun ed., 1993: 436–7)

Habermas's normative interpretation induces a dichotomization between a public world which is rationally communicable and the distortions brought about by the media and other instances of power (Adorno's influence is obvious). Moreover, in blaming the media for the channelling and distortion of reality, Habermas maintains his ideal of public contestation as a guarantee of civil society, forgetting that this guarantee is chimerical since these very realities are substantially constructed by the media themselves.[2]

Habermas had identified this amalgam of historical space and normative principle as the basis of modern democracy which flows from a rationally defined dialogical principle of direct face-to-face communication. It is clear that he dislocates the *analysis* of public communication from the empirical study of topographies to a rather more abstract principle which must be counterfactual. Not only can publicness – as communication – more adequately be construed as plural spaces in a fluid landscape in which information flows induce deterritorializations of nation states and public spheres with them (as outlined in the works of Lash and Bauman), but the associated concept of interaction itself should be reconceptualized if rational and normative claims are accepted as uncertainties (cf. Luhmann, 1993). For example, Lash, following Luke, sees the new global information society as consisting of a series of different zones: live zones of heavy information flows, wild zones of low information density, tame zones of high information density and dead zones of light information flows (Lash, 2002: 28; 37). These new information zones make the critical project of a public sphere highly problematic:

Sociations [...] violate the boundary of public and private. They form on the margins, in the 'limit' that separated the public from the private. It is based not so much on rationally choosing individuals or the granting of validity to discursively redeemed speech acts. Its basis instead is affective bonding, the innovation of ritual and shared meanings, it is recognition based on the co-production of horizons. [...] The point is that not civil society and public spheres, but ethical life and immediate and local forms of sociation would seem to be a better basis for a radical political culture under conditions of postmodernity.

(Lash, 2002: 35)

Just as publicness is asymmetrical, so the interaction paradigm – Luhmann's 'semantic of interaction' – also betrays fundamental social hierarchies and cognitive differences. Ideal interaction occupies nothing more than a marginal position in real events which led Luhmann to ask where the social can actually be situated:

[I]n friendship? In salon sociability? And what would offer the sociostructural condition for the fact that sociality appears here at the same time in its actual form and as a model of social rationality? Moreover, the self-realization of the social cannot be fully conceptualized under these extreme conditions. The obstacle quickly appears: every individual must respect the limitations which make it possible for others to bring self-activity into play.

(Luhmann, 1993: 161 – my translation)

It is worthwhile reconsidering the question of the relation between the public sphere and the ideal of legitimacy where legitimacy is communicatively generated. Communications, as the constitutive elements of the public sphere, are today characterized by a far higher degree of dispersion than at the time of Kant's *Conflict of the Faculties*. The 'public sphere' is constituted by mediatizations which introduce turbulence and generate, challenge and renew reality levels with an almost simultaneous speed and intensity. If Kant was able to extrapolate an ideal social dialogue (to which Habermas still subscribes) from a face-to-face communication context, this represented the advent of the interaction paradigm when in fact interaction was undergoing fundamental change from 'direct interaction' to 'mediated interaction'. The timing of such a theory of dialogical interaction in a non-dialogical world, as Luhmann pointed out, is no coincidence. Kant's public theory as a political interaction paradigm was already a wistful recollection of better communication days. If this incompatibility was already present in Kant's day, then it is even more acute with today's world(s).

This approach can be usefully employed in a critique of the public sphere. The belief in the willingness of power to negotiate some of this power (or the discoursal strategy used to communicate this willingness) could, on this new basis, be viewed as the illusion of such willingness. However, not even the simulacrum of the 'public sphere' eliminates all risks from such an operation since the illusion of a hypostatized public sphere able to sustain the simulation – to make it functional – implies the acceptance that some power will have to be yielded. The functional institutionalization of power occurs only when the selection procedure for power decisions remains visible as the 'regulation of contingency'. In this way, and much more convincingly than Foucault's theory of power, Luhmann contrasts the bourgeois ideal of the public sphere with the procedure of visibilization. Visibility, which includes even oppositional communication, is a more elaborate and apparently more legitimate means of control over social subjects than recourse to mere exclusion or destruction of the public. A visible opposition is much easier to neutralize than a clandestine opposition. And visibility means communication.

3. Communicative action: from universal to contextualist pragmatics

The foregoing considered the theoretical-methodological tension between a normative account of rational public communication and a truncated historiography which denies the impact of media from the radio to the blog. It also challenges assumptions about the contestatory power of such communications as a putative source of legitimacy and finally challenges the epistemological premises of an interaction concept based on the semantic of interaction. It is now time to turn more directly to the theory of communicative action and take the development of these criticisms further. First, a brief reconstruction is called for, even if a vast body of literature has dealt with this key work.

The *Theory of Communicative Action* elaborates a theory of social action which links social cohesion to communicative consensus. It is significant that cohesion and consensus coalesce to generate a lifeworld which, although constantly under attack from administrative influence, still offers an overarching horizon of references from which social actors derive their social bearings. Thus Habermas succeeds in uniting social actions and communicative practices by rationality. On an epistemological level therefore the *Theory of Communicative Action* derives from a hermeneutics of rationalism. But this hermeneutic is in itself insufficient to describe what for Habermas are the core elements of social cohesion: speech acts. Since communicative speech acts are, by definition, rational for Habermas, the linguistic basis of his theory must be a form of Apel-inspired universal pragmatics. Communicative action is a form of argumentative ethic based on the (rationally guaranteed) transparency and stability of validity claims even if such transparency is a 'fiction' (cf. Cooke, 1994: 47).

> The intersubjectively shared space of a speech situation is revealed by means of the interpersonal relations into which participants enter when they adopt an attitude to mutual speech act offers and assume illocutionary obligations.
>
> (Habermas, 1992b: 2.436)

The principle of contestation and intersubjective interaction embedded in it remain valid until this day since they offer warranty for the resistance of social actors to the excesses of any involuted entity, such as power:

> The transitory unity which comes about in the poriferous and broken intersubjectivity of a linguistically mediated consensus not only permits, but permeates and accelerates the pluralization of life forms and the individualization of lifestyles.
>
> (Habermas, 1998a: 140)

The same central concept has been increasingly subjected to severe criticisms which tend to be based on accusations that Habermas's theories are idealized at the cost of blindness to reality (e.g., Wellmer, 1992). The *Theory of Communicative Action* privileges communicative action as the sole form of action capable of securing understanding. Whereas simple actions are derived from a prereflexive background, communicative action is the 'explicit knowledge of the given institutional orders to which their speech acts refer' (Habermas, 1992a: 177). Whereas Habermas uncouples teleological (goal-oriented) acts from communicative action oriented towards understanding, Lyotard, for example, observed in language games a constant play of strategic positions. Acts oriented towards reaching an understanding mean that speech actors 'use the reference system of the three worlds – the subjective, objective and intersubjective – as an interpretative frame-work within which they work out their common situation defini-tions' (Habermas, 1992b: 2.120). Communicative reason is both context dependent and context transcendent, and the transcendent power of validity claims are a 'thorn in the flesh of social reality' (Cooke, 1994: 35).

In the preparatory communications-theoretical essay 'What is uni-versal pragmatics?' Habermas had affirmed that the process of com-municative understanding rests on the basis of an intersubjective relation. This grounding of communication – as understanding and social cohesion – acquires especial importance since it holds the status of a paradigm change from the thinking subject and producer to a form of consensual hermeneutics and communication. Universal pragmatics seeks to reconstruct the ideal conditions of speech acts rooted in the inherent rationality of communicative action. The type 'communicative action' is a non-pathological type of action, a type distinct from jokes, irony, pathologies or fictions. Since these patho-logical, or volatile forms of communication are filtered out of the type 'communicative action', it follows that the latter must be char-acterized by stability and transparency. Stability and transparency are inherent in the validity pretensions of a given communicative speech act (that it be true, authentic and correct), referred to as the illocu-tionary binding force of that act. It is at this stage clear that the notion of the norm enacts a crucial function in universal pragmatics. For this reason, the Habermasian concept of language games (which Wittgenstein had set out in the *Philosophical Grammar*) is based on the quest for understanding based on a recognition of difference under a common horizon. In the *Tractatus*, Wittgenstein had attempted to establish the limits of factual language which he saw as a distortion of thought; an understanding of language would thus only come about by means of a minute analysis of the logical propositions of lan-guage. The ontological implications of such an approach mean that it is not suitable for a social theory of communicative interaction. Much more suitable was his later work in the *Philosophical Investigations* and *Philosophical Grammar*.

It must be said that Wittgenstein's concept of grammar does not relate to the syntactic codification of a language, but instead to the complex network of internal relations. Here, the influence of Wittgenstein's language theory on Habermas becomes clear. In the

Philosophical Investigations, Wittgenstein began to investigate language as forms of life and games: language could no longer be seen as an invariable essence; meaning is generated in games amounting to complexes of elements of discourse and other action forms. This is a model of language based heavily on contextualism as opposed to essentialism and yet, despite fears to the contrary, this contextualism is in no way tantamount to arbitrary relativism since speech acts derive from recognized structures (grammars). According to the empirical contextualism of the late Wittgenstein, the success of communication depends on the ratification of the act (which in turn depends on norms) – and this also ultimately means that understanding is a contingent procedure based on recognition. Since the logical basis of the world depends on ratification (understanding), so too, communication must depend on ratification, described by Wittgenstein as a contingency which depends on the reciprocity of the dynamic evaluation of a certain position. It is sustained on the basis of two demands: (a) pragmatic, since the consequences of non-ratification would be disastrous and (b) grammatical: each system of propositions raises its own system of internal rules. In the *Philosophical Grammar*, grammar is defined as a series of agreements (Wittgenstein, 1991: 30 – my translation), meaning being constituted through relations ('Verbindungen') and not effects ('Wirkungen'). Any language rule, therefore, is not constructed according to an external telos, but follows the relational connections of the speakers.

Since language gaming is not aleatory (as Lyotard had suggested with his agonistics concept), contingency can be seen to observe certain norms which serve to enable understanding. The link between normativity and contingency which Wittgenstein makes is flattened by the concept of agonistics. As Wittgenstein himself states, a grammar consists of a package of pragmatic norms ('Vereinbarungen'). By virtue of the force of such pragmatic agreements, meaning is constituted not in terms of the 'impact' of an utterance, but in terms of the possibilities of its connections: 'The rules of grammar may be called 'arbitrary', if that is to mean that the *aim* of the grammar is nothing but that of the language' (Wittgenstein, 1968: 138e). Wittgenstein sees the sign in its quality as a sign *for* someone. The living being is always defined by the fact that it possesses the faculty to use a language of signs (Wittgenstein, 1991: 192) in the language game. In consequence, it could be said that understanding is immanent to language; the chess game is a careful calculation:

> Where does meaning in language come from? Might one say: 'Without language we could not reach an agreement with each other?' No. This case is not analogous to the following: without the telephone we would not be able to talk to America from Europe. It can however certainly also be said: 'without a mouth people could not make themselves understood.' The concept of language lies in the concept of understanding.
>
> (Wittgenstein, 1991: 193 – my translation)

Contingency is therefore never a synonym of arbitrariness, since language, as a sign system, always appeals to a 'live being', defined as being capable of using semiological language (Wittgenstein, 1991: 192). If the rules of language – or chess – were arbitrary, then contingency would be separated from the exigencies of ratification and understanding:

> The clear articulation of thoughts and intentions is made possible only through grammatical language, which forms a reality of its own kind and with its own dignity; states of affairs can only be mirrored by sentences.
>
> (Habermas, 1998a: 66).

Grammar is a contingent form as evidenced by the multiplicity of different grammars for different languages and the levels of formality of different grammars – oral grammars, informal grammars, formal grammars. There is no guarantee that a grammatically 'perfectly formed' sentence should be any less uncertain in its appeal than a grammatically impure statement. Despite the many criticisms his distinction of communicative action from other 'marginal' forms of communication has elicited, Habermas contends that the only way by which to reach the normative force of social understanding processes or '*Diskurs*' is through the universal validity of understanding, since its absence – even if only in the form of a remote, almost forgotten counterfactual ideal – 'would mean regressing into the monadic isolation of strategic action, or schizophrenia and suicide' (Habermas, 1998a: 102). The normative content of the concept of communicative action acquires even greater clarity when Habermas connects his normative reconstruction of communicative rationality to ethics:

> To that extent the rules of discourse themselves have a normative quality, for they neutralize any imbalances of power and provide for equal opportunities to realize one's own interests. The form of argumentation thus arises out of the need for participation and the need for an *equalization of power.*
>
> (Habermas, 1998b: 71 – my translation)

In *Postmetaphysical Thinking* (1998a), Habermas set out his understanding of the linguistic turn which brought to an end the philosophy of consciousness, where the erstwhile view of linguistic signs as instruments of perceptions in a transcendental subjectivity is replaced by the 'world-producing performance' of grammatical structures. Presuppositions are counterfactual and unavoidably so: this applies to the assumption that speakers use terms as if they had identical points of reference:

> Certainly, grammatical rules guarantee an identity of meaning for linguistic expressions. But at the same time, they must leave room for a individual nuances and innovative unpredictability in the use of these expressions, whose identity of meaning is only presumed.
>
> (Habermas, 1998a: 47)

While Habermas overstates the former rules and understates the latter, he also recognizes that the 'intersubjectivity of linguistically achieved understanding is by nature porous' (Habermas, 1998a: 48). He is also not entirely apologetic about Bühler and suggests that the organon model needs to be expanded by releasing it from a certain language psychology, and also by extending further the semiotic dimension. It is therefore unsurprising that he is more open to the questions of Mead and Peirce than intentionalist semantics (based on the intentions of speakers). Action theory is concerned primarily with the interactive effects on the hearer:

> The effect *r*, which is produced by [the utterance] '*x*' and triggered in *H* by *S*, is a particular belief or the intent to carry out a particular action. Two functions of signs that Bühler had separated, namely

the presentation of self and the appeal to an addressee, thus fuse here into one and the same accomplishment: to bring a hearer to infer the communicative intention of the speaker and to motivate him in this way to form the corresponding belief or intent.

(Habermas, 1998a: 59–60)

This is a significant passage in Habermas's understanding of pragmatic action. Not unexpectedly, two normative assumptions are made from the outset and both can be criticized. The first assumption is that there is a quasi-linear causal transmission of an effect intended by the speaker and triggered in the hearer. And yet, bearing in mind constructivist accounts of knowledge and the development of schemata as proposed by Piaget, the 'effect' cannot simply be considered the end product of an intention. Rather, the effect is a cognitive- communicative construction by the hearer; intentions are not 'there' to be inferred. The second assumption is that the opinion or intention to trigger an action are determinate, precise and defined. Even in the framework of formal pragmatics, the determinateness can only be presupposed at a price, for determinateness depends on the hearer and at least three different contexts, namely that of speaker, hearer and situation. These contexts are not coterminous, and as polycontexts (cf. Derrida, 2000; Luhmann, 1997), render any intention or opinion uncertain. A case could even be made for a formal pragmatic account of such uncertainty, although this is not yet the place to do so.

Whereas for Habermas the inherent telos of language is *Verständigung*, from within the realist tradition there are more radical accounts. For example, complex pragmatic processes, described by François Recanati as loosening, enrichment and semantic transfer, go beyond the concept of linguistic trigger function (Recanati, 2004: 21). Here, derived interpretations are not inferentially derived, but are parallel processes whose appeal can lead to multiple activation (Recanati, 2004: 30). Here, Recanati builds on his theory that a referentialist conception of semantic potential argues that expressions can be applied to a 'collection of real situations' (Recanati, 2001: 202). His criticism of Friedrich Waismann's conception of the open texture of concepts (see Grant, 2001: 45–6) stems from the belief that the real 'source situations' underlying 'semantic potential' act as an 'input for the contextual construction of sense' (Recanati, 2001: 204). True, this model can contribute to a theory of uncertainty in communication by virtue of the concepts of polysemy and semantic potential. On the other hand, it affirms the 'reality' of 'real' situations without investigating the construction of that reality.

As observed above, leaving aside the epistemological questions of realism, Recanati offers a more complex view of pragmatic processes. Pragmatic enrichment is understood here as an expression of uncertainty and is contrasted with saturation, which is a 'mandatory contextual process' from a semantic point of view – 'the process whereby the meaning of the sentence is completed and made propositional through the contextual assignment of semantic values to the constituents of the sentence whose interpretation is context-dependent' (Recanati, 2004: 7). Recanati takes the example of a comment by a restaurant worker on a man who has ordered a ham sandwich and left without paying, which is contracted to the form 'the ham sandwich has left without paying'. Recanati's interpretation of this elision is as follows: 'The interpreter does not go from the concept of the ham sandwich to that of the ham-sandwich orderer after having entertained the absurd literal position' (Recanati, 2004: 33). An alternative reading of this communicative act is that the interpreter does indeed entertain the literal interpretation, *albeit momentarily prior to rejection.* He suspends this literal interpretation where contextual cues make it clear that a literal reading is contextually irrelevant. The point is that these suspended interpretations remain in the background as a tacit, latent understanding that in this interpretation community, food is anthropomorphized. Interpretation is an imperfect filter which leaves literal and derived, or enriched interpretations in its wake without obliterating them. *So we can say that the inherent telos of language is communication of which understanding is an uncertain, dynamic and multivalued outcome.*

Despite these misgivings, it is plausible, even from within a theory of uncertain communications, to intertwine the expressive and appellative functions Habermas has derived from Bühler, albeit not without caveats. In view of the uncertainties which a predetermined realist epistemology and predetermined formal pragmatics neglect, the appellative function can be given a more radical interpretation as an acceptance of the contingency of the communicative act of the speaker and the contingency of the response of the hearer (cf. Grant, 2004). These tensions are not resolved by the concession that what is meant is not determined by what is said since the speaker's intention is part-constitutive of the meaning content of an expression. This approach is quite distinct from the formal semantic approach which abstracts the linguistic system of rules from acts. Habermas tries to reconcile both in order to correct the semiotic narrowness of Bühler's model and include the referential, representational function. Moreover, truth semantics remains crucial for rationality, leading to the conclusion that there is a pragmatic distinction between truth and assertibility, and yet Habermas recognizes that the 'variety of illocutionary forces cannot be ordered from the viewpoint of truth-semantic' (Habermas, 1998a: 72). An assertoric sentence requires that the listener understand the grounds on which the assertion is made. It then becomes a question of justifying the assertion.

Habermas proposes enriching Bühler's functional model with an interpretation derived from value theory thus resolving the limitations of formal and intentionalist semantics. The advantage of value is that it is not limited to isolated speakers since the validity claims we make depend on intersubjective recognition in which validity claims relate to truth-analogous conditions, subjective authenticity and normative adequacy. While this recognition of the communicative dynamic is useful, a problem persists in the way in which it is conceived. For Habermas, the attempt of the speaker to reach an understanding about something in the world with a hearer terminates (*terminiert*) in an understanding between them (Habermas, 1998a: 73–4). Leaving aside Habermas's rather too one-dimensional use of Bühler, a reinterpretation of validity theory implies that the speaker refers simultaneously to something in the subjective, objective world and something in the shared social world. There is a need for a critique here on epistemological and methodological grounds. With the interrogation on constructivist epistemology and the methodological focus on the pragmatic ambiguities, syntactic paradoxes and the fuzzy frontier between enrichment and inference of communications, it is possible to follow Dummett's view that we understand a speech act only when we understand what makes it acceptable, and this requires great contextual sensitivity.

While Habermas does argue that to lead someone to think indirectly is a marginal case, his only grounds for taking this position are to be found in a normative understanding of the forms of pragmatic actions.

And yet, not only are the contexts of communication multiple, direct utterances can only be inferred from a form which has been purified of its uncertainties. Since linguistic forms exist in contexts and these contexts are complex dynamics of uncertainties, directness of utterance necessarily becomes problematic. Frequently, even the most everyday communicative exchanges are hybrid constructions since triggering a response, persuading someone and so on are appellative acts in the radical sense proposed above. Communicability is not so much a counterfactual, with connotations of a clear, determinate counterfactuality *vis-à-vis* the facts, but rather a precarious, uncertain undertaking, or, to modify Davidson, an uncertain appeal of interpretability. Whether one is talking about a regulation, resolution, essay or law, uncertainty is never actually removed; all communications are appellative, that is, subject to interpretation, reflexivity, revision, enrichment and critique.[3] Anything else makes the communicator a mere function of rationality.

4. Social contexts

In terms of social theory, the integration of social actors by means of relationality presupposes a common network of references. This network facilitates the meeting of social actors in situations of intersubjective reciprocity as set out in *The Theory of Communicative Action*. For it is here that Habermas places Husserl's horizon of expectation grounded in the lifeworld in the social sphere (by dropping the phenomenological method) and thus recontextualizes the concept as a social lifeworld:

> If we now relinquish the basic concepts of the philosophy of consciousness in which Husserl dealt with the problem of the lifeworld, we can think of the lifeworld as represented as a culturally transmitted and linguistically organized stock of interpretative patterns.
>
> (Habermas, 1992b: 2.124)

There is indeed an ethical desideratum despite the criticism this study makes of intersubjectivity: the recognition of human vulnerability (Habermas, 1992a: 200ff.) is an instance of common ground. A theory of uncertain communication accepts such vulnerability in a way which establishes connections with existentialism, for this is the dynamic at the core of the communication paradox:

> [...] the same medium, linguistically mediated interaction, is both the reason for the vulnerability of socialized individuals and the key resource they possess to compensate for that vulnerability.
>
> (Habermas, 1992a: 201)

In this way, Habermas can refer to the 'factual force of counterfactual presuppositions' (Habermas, 1998a: 203) as part of the 'universalization principle' of argumentation. *Diskurs* is reflective interaction which presupposes 'reversible' speaker perspectives based on the 'intersubjective authority of a common will' (Habermas, 1992a: 160):

> Here too the perspectives interlock in an interpersonal framework of communication whose presuppositions are *improbable*: world perspectives that have been refracted by reflection are linked up with the roles of opponents and proponents who criticize and defend validity claims.
>
> (Habermas, 1992a: 159–60 – emphasis added)

The society of social lifeworlds rests on communications in which opinions and standpoints can be contested. When shorn of phenomenological premises, the lifeworld as a concept acquires the character of background knowledge on which all actors may draw. Each communicative speech act accordingly raises three ideal validity claims: (1) truth, (2) truthfulness and (3) correctness, and in so doing creates a three-fold relationship consisting of subjective dimension (of the speaker), an objective dimension (of the listener) and an intersubjective dimension (of society): '[...] The interpreter who understands meaning is experiencing fundamentally as a participant in communication, on the basis of a symbolically established intersubjective relationship' (Habermas, 1998a: 152). Despite the range of Habermas's programme of universal pragmatics, the treatment of the uncertainties of social communication tends to eschew some of the more radical points sketched here:

> To be sure, the rational motivation based on each person's ability to say no has the advantage of stabilizing behavioral expectations

non-coercively. But the risks of dissension, which are continually fuelled by disappointing experiences and surprising *contingencies*, are high. If communicative action were not embedded in lifeworld contexts that provide the backing of a massive background consensus, such risks would make the use of language oriented to mutual understanding an unlikely route to social integration [...]. The constant upset of disappointment and contradiction, contingency and critique in everyday life crashes against a sprawling, deeply set, and unshakable rock of background assumptions, loyalties and skills.

(Habermas, 1996: 21–2 – my emphasis).

Rational lifeworld communicative practices have the capacity for communicative renovation 'in a communication threatened by entropy' (Habermas, 1995a: 552 – my emphasis) where entropy is considered to be the opposite of a rational communication which is inclusive on account of its very rationality. However, as Shannon and Weaver argued, entropy means uncertainty in communication and this uncertainty cannot be subtracted from multiple pragmatic contexts and enrichments. Habermas's pragmatics of social integration seriously neglects the fact that this factor of contingency is essential to social functioning and the complex reality constructions (S.J. Schmidt) used to communicate over this are an essential part of communication and therefore society.

An ideal communication community, the related normative concept of consensus or dialogical mutuality rely heavily on counterfactual ideals that can be invoked in order to challenge the growing gulf between self-referential media and financial systems, abuse of power and 'violations' of language games on the one hand and our subjective communicative experiences on the other. Habermas himself makes explicit the universal pragmatic premises of his communication theory and thereby places it at such a distance from everyday language that its plausibility can be rightly criticized:

[... Under] the microscope every understanding proves to be occasional and fragile. By contrast, philosophical hermeneutics investigates the interpretative competence of adult speakers from the perspective of how speaking and acting subjects make incomprehensible utterances in an alien environment comprehensible.

> Hermeneutics is concerned with interpretation as an *exceptional accomplishment*, which becomes necessary only when the relevant segments of the lifeworld become problematic [...].
>
> (Habermas, 1992b: 1.130–1 – emphasis in original)

The reconstruction of the ideal conditions of communicative action shift the perspective from the invariables of (phenomenologically defined) consciousness to the pragmatics of contexts of reference. Husserl's phenomenological method is incapable of escaping the aporias of the philosophy of the subject and only a critical-pragmatic social philosophy can grasp the context of reference as a context of meaning. These contexts possess their own grammars (in Wittgenstein's sense of the term) and operate as forms of the organization of knowledge or epistemic orders (Michel Foucault). This means that a lifeworld without grammar – norms, rules, ideals – is inconceivable. The lifeworld is composed of a 'context which constitutes the horizon and processes of understanding among social actors, a reservoir of assumptions and organized cultural values' (Habermas, 1995b: 590–1 – my translation). Actors in the lifeworld, unlike actors in the system, communicate rationally, without seeking to impose their views.

On Habermas's account, when Luckmann perceived the lifeworld as a social *a priori* which cannot be problematized, but at best destroyed, then it follows that he was abandoning the connection between intersubjectivity and communicative practice. Once the lifeworld is blinded to the enactment of dissent on a rational basis the loss of the legitimation basis of modern societies is inevitable. The ideal reader communities of Kant's time have given way to the extensively fragmented and mediatized, and therefore diffuse, network communications, the porosity of these communications making resistance to the autism of system imperatives possible. This strangely *porous* character of communication, as will be explored at greater length in chapters five and six, cannot be grasped by the stable concept of the lifeworld proposed by Luckmann:

> The one-sidedness of the culturalistic concept of the lifeworld becomes clear when we consider that communicative action is not only a process of reaching understanding; in coming to an understanding about something in the world, actors are at the same time taking part in interactions through which they develop, confirm

and renew their memberships in social groups and their own identities. Communicative actions are not only processes of interpretation in which cultural knowledge is 'tested against the world'; they
are at the same time processes of social integration and socialization.
(Habermas, 1992b: 2.139)

5. Uncertain counterfactuals and the limits of realism

Habermas provides a subtle account of his consensus theory as a normative ideal which is intimately interwoven with the constant possibility of negation and whose 'existence' is contingent; consensus
appears as a *disruptive mechanism* (Habermas, 1998a). It would fall
outside the scope of this chapter to reconstruct the various critiques
of Habermas's counterfactual ideality in their entirety. Suffice it to say
that many quite simply ignore the subtlety and critical intent of the
role of counterfactuals in communication processes. One of the
exceptions to this group of critics is Manfred Frank, who is concerned
that the concept of intersubjectivity can be used as a camouflage to
sweep away any notion of subjectivity. Following Sartre, his alternative proposal is to locate all subjective energies in the subject and not
in the abstraction of intersubjectivity, which serves merely to neutralize the subject:

> All socialization must – this was the correct intuition of Sartre's
> social philosophy – start from the individual: it is the source of all
> understanding, and an understanding of social relations is meas-
> ured by the self-knowledge of the subject. Rather than presuming
> to accuse the subject of being unable as a point of (allegedly unac-
> knowledged) self-transparency to make the transition to intersub-
> jectivity transparent, intersubjectivism appears to be beset by the
> converse problem, that of failing to move from the presupposition
> of a social apriori to the individual which is merely assumed and
> not explicated in the expression 'inter-individuality'.
> (Frank, 1995: 528 – my translation)

It is doubtlessly defensible to challenge the irreducibility of the subject and to undertake the productive attempt to place the relations of
various social subjects on a pragmatic communicative footing. At the

same time, the success of this attempt remains determined by the premises established in *The Theory of Communicative Action*. This means that the attempt to escape the philosophy of the subject by means of a theory of intersubjectivity can only be understood in the confines of the philosophy of the subject. The 'reality guarantee' of intersubjectivity, even as a counterfactual ideal, stands and falls with the assumption of the rational subject itself. Intersubjectivity compromises the subject and itself.

From within the critical realist paradigm, without abandoning the theory of universal pragmatics, Habermas has more recently appealed for a revised concept of linguistic reference without abandoning realist foundations. Accepting that there is no representational correspondence between language and facts, he argues for a new concept of reference which will be able to explain how it is that speakers can refer to the same object (Habermas, 1999b: 18 – my translation). In realist terms, the 'objective world' is still held to be the backdrop for our assertions or 'a system for possible references' in which reference can be made to the same object: 'The presence of possible alternatives expresses the realist intuition that we refer provisionally to an extension of the concept which is assumed to be independent of language' (Habermas, 1999b: 37 – my translations). Habermas appeals for a revised concept of reference within a dynamic realist framework ('a system for possible references'). Conceding that his earlier work on a formal pragmatic framework had resulted in a narrow focus driven by his theoretical strategy (*theoriestrategische Einseitigkeit*) (1999b: 7 – my translation), *Truth and Justification* focuses on two principal questions: ontological naturalism and epistemological realism. The former relates to a possible reconciliation between the 'unavoidable normativity' of a linguistically structured lifeworld which predates our birth on the one hand and the 'contingency of the natural development of socio-cultural life forms' on the other. The latter epistemological question explores the reconcilability of the 'assumption of an identical world independent of our descriptions' with the fact that there is no possibility of any direct, unmediated access to 'pure reality'. This is clearly an example of revised philosophical realism rooted nonetheless in strong claims – the normativity of the lifeworld or the assumption of a world beyond our contingent descriptions. The same realism emerges from the sustained belief in the complementarity (Habermas, 1999b: 15 – my translation) of an intersubjectively shared lifeworld and the pragmatic assumption of an objective world. A different epistemological architecture would, naturally enough, produce a different set of premises. Even after abandoning Kantian pragmatism a case can still be made for 'transcendental analysis' as the 'quest for the presumably general, but only de facto unavoidable conditions' for social and communicative action. There is also evidence of attempts at further, perhaps rather unexpected reconciliation when Habermas reapproximates the Erlangen school of constructivism: self-reference is seen as a 'precondition for the rationality of persons' (Habermas, 1999b: 105 – my translation).

Habermas proclaims that the philosophy of consciousness is exhausted and in this case 'the symptoms of this exhaustion should dissolve in the transition to the paradigm of mutual understanding' (Habermas, 1990b: 296). Several influences coalesce in this theory of a post-subjective mutual understanding. Habermas's normative dichotomies need to be dropped but without sacrificing the enterprise of critical theory. Background knowledge is not immune (Habermas, 1992a: 90–1) to the 'problematization pressure of contingency-generating experiences' and only becomes fallible when it is communicated. It is still important to note, however, that such fallibilism in no way atomizes the subject (Habermas, 1999b: 158 – my translation).

Habermas further insists on the importance of the social in that the 'public practice of a language community comes before the epistemic authority of a subject' (Habermas, 1999b: 141 – my translation). Similarly, his reception of the work of Robert Brandom seems to suggest a willingness to consider more carefully the construction processes of understanding which, potentially at least, make the idea of a universal pragmatics unstable. For instance, in a personal communication to Habermas Brandom wrote:

> I have in mind thinking of communication as somewhat like Fred Astaire and Ginger Rogers: they are doing very different things – at least moving in different ways – but are coordinating, adjusting, and making up one dance. The dance is all they share and it is not independent or antecedent to what they are doing.
> (Brandom cited in Habermas, 1999b: 176–7)

In the course of this a mutual coordination exercise, we become aware of the autonomous moves of each partner, governed only by two separate contexts and the uncertain dynamic of a shared move.

It is worth returning to Recanati at this point, for he argues that normally we do not have to reason to understand what others are saying since communication, in its most basic form, is 'not constitutively inferential' (Recanati, 2004: 38). For Recanati, there are two forms of conscious inference: effortful, explicit reasoning and primary, spontaneous inference. And the porous nature of contexts means that there is no limit to the amount of contextual information that can affect pragmatic interpretation (Recanati, 2004: 54). It is this elasticity of context that makes formal universal pragmatics at best only a half-answer. However, Recanati, too, offers a simplistic cognitive-communicative account of what 'successful communication' could look like. It is worth reconstructing this view at some length:

> To communicate that *p* is therefore to act in such a way that the addressee will explain one's action by ascribing to the agent the intention to communicate that *p*. For communication to succeed, the addressee must not only understand *that* the agent does what he does in order to communicate something to her; she must also understand *what* the agent tries to communicate. To secure that effect the communicator will do something which will evoke in the addressee's mind that which he wants to communicate.
>
> (Recanati, 2004: 54)

Similarly, Recanati argues that semantic interpretation does not deliver complete propositions: it delivers only semantic schemata: 'Either semantic interpretation delivers something gappy, and pragmatic interpretation must fill the gaps until we reach a complete proposition' (Recanati, 2004: 54). The theory of universal communication rests on such semantic porosity ('gappiness'), semiotics, radical interpretability, cognitive enrichments and multiple contexts.

Accepting that there is no representational correspondence between language and facts, Habermas also argues for a new concept of reference by means of which it can be explained how speakers refer to the same object. In realist terms, the 'presence of possible alternatives expresses the realist intuition that we refer provisionally to an extension of the concept which is assumed to be independent of language' (Habermas, 1999b: 37 – my translation). And yet once residual transcendental claims are dropped and uncertainty considered in relation to the communicative interactions between selves and society, it becomes clear that there is no guarantee that our references transcend language in making reference to an external reality.

There is some sense then that his revised realism after the pragmatic turn and these elements of constructivism as being pursued towards some kind of synthesis in which the real enemy is a mentalism which mythologizes the given (Habermas, 1999b: 21 – my translation). This shift towards a constructivist realism (as Mitterer might put it) accepts the end of the immediacy of sensorial impressions and the need for an acceptance of second-order experience. However, even here this constructivist *move* is embedded in action theory since only acting subjects are capable of such second-order experience. Habermas recognizes that our 'truth claims' are confronted with those of others – thus opening up the possibility of inquiry into logics which take diversity and multivoicedness seriously, for everyday communicative practice is not otherwordly:

> Transcendental consciousness loses the connotations of the 'other-wordly' – it has come down to earth in the desublimated from of everyday communicative practice. The profane lifeworld has taken in the transmundane space of the noumenal.
>
> (Habermas, 1999b: 26)

Even so, in the desublimated or *profane* lifeworld of communications tensions persist between idealized or *counterfactual* claims and the *facticity* of everyday life. Understanding and communication cannot avoid producing idealizations if the lifeworld is to sustain itself as a communicative social sphere. The 'normative gap' so characteristic of society is thus also marked by ambiguity (a 'Doppelbödigkeit eines normativen Gefälles') – the idealized counterfactuals of communicative communities and the facts of the uncertainties of their communications.

Despite his recognition of the tension between the contingencies of subjective communicative practice and lifeworld idealizations, Habermas argues that linguistic pluralism does not actually induce a plurality of incommensurable language worlds.[4] The counterfactual force, which requires constant revision precisely because of its counterfactuality, of a transcendental communication community interrupts the contingencies of self and communication in such a way that the:

> detranscendentalized constitution of a world-generating spontaneity is at least reconcilable with the expectation that we discover

generally distributed characteristics which characterize the very constitution of sociocultural forms of life.

(Habermas, 1999b: 29 – my translation)

As part of a commitment to what he terms 'weak naturalism' Habermas argues that representationalism ('realism without representation') cannot account for our communication of reality. Instead, reality only emerges in resistance, the 'facticity of constraint' (Habermas, 1999b: 37) which confronts our attempts at problem solving and learning. In this sense, an objective world is an operative assumption (*Annahme*) as a system of possible references of objects (*Gegenstände*) and not facts (*Tatsachen*). Weak naturalism, then, suggests that our organic constitution and cultural forms of life have a 'natural origin' which is amenable to an evolution-theoretical approach. There are strong connections between weak naturalism and the facticity of constraints to which we are all ontogenetically exposed in the processes of adaptation and construction (Habermas, 1999b) which mean that the contingency of community is not reducible to an aleatory process. However, although the abandonment of the principle of the transcendental subjectivity of consciousness is plausible and indeed necessary, its replacement category – the *detranscendentalized intersubjectivity* of the lifeworld (Habermas, 1999b: 40) is a logical contradiction. *Intersubjectivity, once shorn of its transcendental counterfactuality, is no longer intersubjective.*

Ultimately, whether or not Habermas is able to reconcile his realism with his own constructivist admission that we make assumptions about reality, objectivity, truth and others is open to some sceptical questioning. Although it is unproblematic to say that ideal truth assertions are contingent on language, this relates to only one aspect of the multiple contingency of communication. The other aspect of contingency is that there is no guarantee that our references transcend language in establishing a reference to a 'reality' outside our own reality constructions; and if they do, it is only by means of imputations (Von Glasersfeld, 1996) of other possible worlds. These imputations are also constructions, and, therefore, contingent. In other words, the notion of reference does not imply the certainty of semantic mapping of an object in the sense proposed by Putnam, but instead assumptions about temporary the social stabilization of 'objects'. These assumptions are uncertain and thus unavoidably dynamic and socially constitutive.

For Habermas, reference must remain epistemologically realistic in the sense that the concept of reference to an objective world is retained. His proposal makes use of a 'detranscendentalized intersubjectivity of understanding' which eschews a monadological understanding of language universes (Habermas, 1999b: 29): 'By orienting themselves to unconditional validity claims and imputing accountability to each other speakers aim beyond all contingent and purely local contexts' (Habermas, 1999b: 25 – my translation). In other words, society is cohesive because speakers are embedded into common contexts of reference which in turn make shared knowledge and consensus as a counterfactual ideal a possibility and remove the danger of social disintegration. Is it however the case that speakers overcome – 'transcend' – the contingency or locality of their experiences by raising validity claims, however counterfactual or, as Habermas argues, imputational, these may be? While it is certainly a fact that society resolves contingency by recursive redundancies (codes) in order to operate, there is a dualism implied in counterfactuality as an alternative to factuality. Communicative interaction, in other words, should not be taken as resolved by or in intersubjectivity. Equally, it should not be superficially denied or comfortably dismissed either as monologues or as an intersubjectively constrained dialogism for neither understanding of interaction offers an adequate account of the uncertainties of communication.

4
The Limited Reach of Communication Systems

> One should remember that every either/or
> must be introduced artificially
> above a substratum
> where it does not apply.
> —Niklas Luhmann, 1995: 209[1]

1. Systems, differences and communications and Luhmann's critique of the 'the semantics of interaction'

It must be said that Luhmann's systems theory has produced highly significant gains for communication theory. It has enabled a plausible critique of some rather tenacious interaction theories with their concepts of mutuality, commonality and dialogue bequeathed by the 'semantic of interaction' (see Social Structure and Semantics – *Gesellschaftsstruktur und Semantik*). It has also facilitated a salutary counter-intuitive analysis of the role of Reason, morality and other assumed aprioris such as the distinction between the general and the specific and a critique of Habermas's *Theory of Communicative Action* even if this critique has regrettably remained little-explored by English-speaking scholars.

Systems theory is described as an observer-dependent theory. The importance of observer dependency lies precisely in the fact that it is in the observer that observations form as the difference between endogenous and exogenous information. The observer is thus also a self-referential system. This means that Luhmann bids farewell to traditional epistemology with its emphasis on the subject–object dualism. It needs to be recalled that his conception of the system is not restricted to historically verifiable institutions, but rather possesses a fundamental epistemological and methodological value. Here, every social contact is conceptualized as a system (Luhmann, 1995).

The principles of this theory are as follows: (1) The difference between system and environment. Since logically the system cannot be defined without relation to its environment, the two can be said to entertain a relation of interdependence. (2) The paradigm of the difference between the whole and its parts is replaced by the paradigm of internal system differentiation. In this process, the general system acquires the function of internal environment of sub-systems. (3) As a corollary of system–environment interdependence, the concept of causality itself must be reviewed in terms of recursive processes and internal reproduction. (4) Within a system, the basic system–environment distinction must be complemented by the distinction between element and relation. There cannot be elements without relations and there cannot be a relation without elements. (5) The relation between elements is defined by conditioning. One of the conditioning principles of the regulation of the relations between elements is inclusion/exclusion. (6) Complexity is the pressure of selection. This pressure for selection also induces contingency and risk. (7) System frontiers operate sui generis: frontiers are inconceivable without a sense of what lies beyond them; they thus enact a specific dual role in dividing and connecting. (8) Systems are distinct from complexity in the sense that complexity is not defined by the system–environment difference. (9) The concept of self-reference relates to the unity which an element or system constitutes for itself. This means that self-reference presupposes operational closure. (10) Self-reference also presupposes the principle of 'multiple constitution'. (11) Self-reference enhances operationality which in turn requires the greatest possible degree of homogeneity. (12) Self-reference also expands the scope for structural coupling and internal system communication (Luhmann, 1995).

In terms of specific types of system, both the biological system and the social system can only ever be conceptualized as systems within environments. The human body as an organic system can only function under certain ecological conditions, becoming dysfunctional at temperatures above 50 degrees celsius, for example. To a certain extent, the social system obeys the same functional necessities: the educational system would become dysfunctional without an environment populated by the economic or religious systems, for example. Attempts to bring biological theory into contact with social theory have long provoked unease and immediate accusations of creeping social darwinism. However, the accusation does not apply here, for Luhmann is extremely careful not to reduce social complexity to biological impulse.

Luhmann's systems theory is based on a series of core operations: the distinction between system and environment and the distinction between closed and open systems (where open systems are described as being non-trivial). According to the new paradigm, 'System differentiation is nothing other than the repetition within systems of the difference between system and environment' (Luhmann, 1995: 7). For instance, in order to preserve dynamic relations and performance between itself and a constantly changing environment, a system will differentiate to produce different types of interaction (multiple or flexible geometry); these differences are marked by communications. The emphasis is placed clearly on social systems which are open, and in such open relations communications play a key role. Social systems theory builds on self-referential conceptions of systems where self-reference is the precondition for the differentiation of systems. Since this type of self-referential closure is only possible in an environment, the question becomes 'how can self-referential closure create openness?' Or, alternatively, how can a system define itself and interact with the 'wider world'? (Luhmann, 1995: 9). The consequence of self-reference is that systems operate between identity (with their own self-referential procedures) and difference (vis-à-vis the environment). Systems generate themselves, self-referentially, in autopoietic, that is, self-generating, fashion (following the concept of Humberto Maturana). This shift from reference (say, to objective reality) to self-reference is crucial to an understanding of Luhmann's work and has clear implications for the theory of communication.

If systems operate by means of self-referential closure in the sense that in order to be defined as systems they require a sense of 'self' then, in order to sustain their identity as systems, they need to define the boundary between 'systematicity' (their character as systems) and the environment:

> Without difference from an environment there would not even be self-reference because difference is the functional premise of self-referential operations. In this sense, boundary maintenance is system maintenance.
>
> (Luhmann, 1995: 17)

Within a system as an epistemological category, relations between the elements (components of a system) are said to be *complex* when the coupling capacity of the elements cannot guarantee couplings with other elements at all times. Society is thus clearly a complex system since its elements cannot couple with other elements at all times – blind spots, and, one might say, ignorance, as generalized blind spots, are part of the dynamic uncertainty in our interactions. In this way then, complexity induces selection. Indeed, 'Complexity [...] means being forced to select; being forced to select means contingency; and contingency means risk' (Luhmann, 1995: 25). Where the environment is perceived as a system's resource, contingency is absorbed as a relation of dependence; where the environment is perceived as Shannon-inspired information, contingency is interpreted as uncertainty. In another formulation, complexity is the *missing information in the system* which would enable it to grasp its environment. Without complete knowledge, the system–environment relation must be dynamic and involve *uncertainty coping strategies*. This is true of cognitive systems, institutions and organizations. In the case of social systems this completeness of knowledge is a chimera. Formally, it is proposed here to describe open systems as *porous systems*. This means that the system reacts to a 'vague picture of itself': if it cannot fully grasp complexity (and if it could, it would merge with its environment), then it can maintain awareness of that failure (as societies do, most recently in the case of debates about terror and security). In his earlier collaboration with Habermas (*Theory of Society or Social Technology*, 1972), Luhmann wrote that society was the social system which 'institutionalizes ultimate, fundamental reductions [of complexity]' (Habermas, Luhmann, 1972: 16).

The frontier between system and environment referred to above is dynamic and Luhmann does indeed acknowledge boundary-crossing traffic, such as information. Boundaries enact the 'double function' of separating and connecting systems and environments (Luhmann, 1995: 28). Boundaries are 'self-generated' in the manner of 'membranes, skins, walls and doors, boundary posts and points of contact' (Luhmann, 1995: 29). This conception of boundaries represents a refinement of Luhmann's earlier position in which complex systems tend to produce ever more abstract boundaries which mark the exclusion point of indeterminacies. These indeterminacies are then interpreted as reducible complexity (Habermas, Luhmann, 1972: 19): 'The social exclusion of the indeterminate changes the forms of coping with fear' (Habermas, Luhmann, 1972: 20). The contemporary example of the security risks emanating from diffused terrorist groups offers an illustration of this earlier formulation. This organization is often schematized as irrational (despite its 'rational', albeit loose organization) and thus placed beyond socially recognized groups. This in turn can legitimate forms of state-sanctioned violence (assassinations) and perhaps reduce citizens' fears. And yet, the exclusion depends on precisely such a schematization and the forms of this schematization are communications. Luhmann notes that the magnetic field of the world is relevant to organisms although they do not 'notice' this field as the frontier between organism and environment:

> A communicative social system arranges everything in its own communication as either internal or external and practices its own system/environment distinction as something universally valid, insofar as its own communication is concerned.
>
> (Luhmann, 1995: 178–9)

Thus religious systems distinguish the profane from the sacred, the theological from the secular-political, the eternal from the contingent. Despite this distinction, Luhmann concedes that 'physical, chemical, organic and psychic realities' (e.g. heat) run through this difference. Instead, 'communicative action is especially suited for the operative execution within the system of the difference between system and environment in the system' (Luhmann, 1995: 180). It is above all with Luhmann, following Shannon and Weaver, that the relation between communication and uncertainty is made tangible for a social theory in which uncertainty is significant. It is striking here that Luhmann does not see communications in general as having the capacity to cross frontiers between systems and environment, as noted above:

> However complex its linguistic possibilities and however subtle the structure of its themes society can never make possible communication about everything that occurs in its environment on all levels of system formation for all systems [...]'.
>
> (Luhmann, 1995: 182)

Perhaps the most striking example of the gap between the complexity of Luhmann's systems theoretical architecture and his theory of communication is demonstrated by his description of ritualizations:

> Ritualizations, religious and otherwise, possess a similar function. They translate external uncertainties into an internal schematic that either happens or not, but cannot be varied and therefore neutralize the capacity for deception, lies and deviant behaviour. Ritualizations make little claim on the system's complexity.
>
> (Luhmann, 1995: 185)

Here there is a *complexity gap* between Luhmann's theory of systems and his theory of communication, for the latter is inadequate compared to the complexity of his systems theory. True, communication ritualizations make few claims on the way in which a system deals with complexity. However, there is an increasing awareness in society of the precariousness of rituals – an awareness which arguably assumes at least two forms: (1) retraditionalization or the renaissance of religious fundamentalisms (the paradox which is often the need for redundancy or incantations of truth-value); (2) the de-traditionalization of society. This is a moment where the reflexivity of our communicative practices and awareness of such paradoxes clashes against the self-referential closure of communications systems and this clash unveils the contingency of systems which observe themselves as being permanent. In other words, actors in society are (reflexively and therefore contingently) aware of the plurality of rituals and their diversification (the rituals of law, celebrity, politics, the arts). Every system assumes the existence of other systems in its environment: 'Depending on the depth with which the environment can be perceived, more systems and more different kinds of systems appear in it' (Luhmann, 1995: 187). The emphasis here is on a more general modelling of the uncertainties of communication processes in society rather than the structures of repeatable texts. Here, context and communication must be enhanced by cognition-theoretical questions such as cognitive autonomy. As noted above, this does not mean logical vagueness or the impossibility of distinguishing between true and false (bivalence), but the theoretical approach to social communication as a system of *vague signs appealing to someone somewhere sometime* (multivalence) (Grant, 2003a: 105). As Derrida put it, 'Every sign, linguistic or non-linguistic, spoken or written [...] can break with every given context, engendering an infinity of new contexts in a manner which is absolutely illimitable' (Derrida, 2000: 12).

A complex system, such as the cognitive system which is capable of understanding, can apprehend the systems in its environment from the perspective of their environments, thus replacing the *units* of its environment with complex *relations* between systems in an environment. With the plausible abstract theories of relations and units, it is easy to overlook the innocuous qualifying statement at the outset of these ideas: everything depends on the sharpness of the definitions a system can make of its environment. In terms of first-level systems heuristics (machines etc.) this is not problematic, but in terms of cognitive or social systems the issues become rather more complex and *blurred*, not least because:

> There are no social systems which are entirely regulated or controlled. Individual or collective actors can never be reduced to abstract and disembodied functions.
> (Crozier and Friedberg, 2001: 29 – my translation)

Attention will return to Luhmann's neglect of the agent/actor in subsequent chapters. For the time being, it is worth noting that the 'paradigm shift' in systems theory, as Luhmann puts it in *Social Systems*, takes place on three levels: (1) the foundational level of systems as conceptualizations; (2) machines, social and psychic systems and finally, (3) interactions, organizations and societies (Luhmann, 1995: 2). So systems theory is a super-theory in the sense that it enables the formation of *differences* to be 'centralized'. As we shall see, this emphasis on a supertheory as a theory of difference is, in part at least, already problematic. Some (perhaps rather too many) critics have accused Luhmann of reifying his system concept. And yet it is important to repeat, as Luhmann himself was compelled to do, that systems do not correspond to putatively objective realities – they are categories of observation and selection. Thus, as Luhmann himself argued, the very critics who accuse him are themselves producing the reification. Systems 'organize' systems in their environments by the communicative means of 'differentiation schemata'. Complex systems, such as cognitive systems, remain aware of the contingency of such schemata in view of the blind spots of observation and the selectivity of perception (cf. Bakhtin's concept of the 'excess of seeing'). This awareness is a form of reflexivity. Here, then, complexity means that 'both possibilities [self-reference and other-reference] simultaneously and/or alternatively are at one's disposal' (Luhmann, 1995: 188). Despite Luhmann's attempts to couple differentiation schemata or difference-formation to complexity (the schematic of differentiation 'does not lie in knowledge schematized as a binary right/wrong' [Luhmann, 1995: 542]), a core epistemological principle remains in force. The complex character of differentiations means that difference is a 'gradual phenomenon' which is mediated by *Sinngrenzen* (meaning boundaries). These meaning boundaries are measured against communication (Luhmann, 1995: 196):

> Conversely, representations of boundaries serve to order the constitution of elements; they make it possible to assess which elements form in the system and which communications can be risked.
>
> (Luhmann, 1995: 195)

It should be recalled that Luhmann sees the differentiation of systems as a source of indeterminacies which can be manipulated by a system. It could even be argued that communications which cross internal meaning frontiers (Luhmann, 1997: 2.607) are crucial in the generation and control of such indeterminacies and account for the way in which systems 'drift' dynamically between integration and disintegration (Luhmann, 1997: 2.605). Although 'the system of society can only use communications as systems-internal operations and thus cannot communicate with the environment external to society' (Luhmann, 1997: 2.607), it could be contended that the capacity for communication complexity means that communications constantly cross systems frontiers. In this way, communications actually challenge the internality of systems reference and induce a much stronger form of systems drift. Systems, in other words, are at the mercy of communications, and, *pace*

Luhmann, the agents who make them. This is true of NGOs, government departments and agencies and terrorist networks. Systems theory thus makes a break with the presuppositions of theories of rational perfectibility by means of a fundamental epistemological shift. As a theory based on the formation of differences in scientific observations, it provides useful incisions in part informed by Gestalt theories of schemata-formation. Rather less plausibly, the concept of the subject is discarded, as we have seen above, by the concept of the self-referential system whose identity with itself is located in its difference vis-à-vis its environment:

> The theory of self-referential systems affirms that the differentiation of systems can only occur through systemic reference, i.e. through the fact that systems refer to themselves in the constitution of their elements [...]. Self-referential closure is therefore only possible in an environment under ecological conditions. The environment is the necessary correlate of self-referential operations [...].
> (Luhmann, 1995: 7)

It is well-known that the richness and controversy of Luhmann's theory derives as much from its epistemology as from its sociology. However opaque it might appear at first glance, it is a theory which is an attempt to respond to a process of detranscendentalization or the eclipse or competition of the grand narratives, despite its super-theory ambitions. Its applicability to cognitive and social systems does allow for consistency and responds to the crisis of transcendence. For Luhmann, Kant's invocation of the public sphere as a locus and ideal for social interaction is merely a self-interpretation of society and offers no reality guarantee. To describe society in terms of dialogue or interaction in the face of the multiple fragmentations of a cognitive and social order is to perpetuate metaphysics and fail in the task of creating a sociology disabused of illusions (Luhmann, 1995):

> In its long history the description of the social life of man [...] was guided by ideals which reality did not satisfy. This was as true of the tradition of ancient Europe with its ethos of the natural perfection of man as it was for its efforts to educate and forgive sins. But this is also true of modern Europe, for the Enlightenment with its double deity

Reason and Critique. And well into this century the consciousness of imperfection is retained – consider Husserl or Habermas.

(Luhmann, 1997: 1.21–2 – my translation)

In *Gesellschaftsstruktur und Semantik* (1993) Luhmann reflected on the relationship between self-referential systems and bivalent codes or, in his words, *binary schematisms*. The theory of self-reference relied on its extrication from the dual order of binary realities, but equally, these very dual orders are used in self-referential systems. Binary schematisms are made operational for the self-reference of systems in a general sense as 'forms of securing coupling capacity'. 'Self-reference is on the one hand synthesized into dual form: Truth refers to Untruth and Untruth refers to Truth' (1993: 311). However, couplings require that the short-circuitry of binary schematisms can be interrupted to allow complex integration into a system. The relevance of binary schematisms is that they are functional derivations of bivalent logic. Indeed, Luhmann expressly refers to the need for a multivalent logic since a bivalent logic is not adequate to the complexities of social life.[3]

In *Gesellschaft der Gesellschaft* ('The Society of Society', 1997) Luhmann sought to make a distinction between his theory of the two sides of a form and classical bivalent logic based on the formal logic of George Spencer Brown set out in *Laws of Form*. With its distinction between true and false, bivalent logic offers a particular perspective of the observer and, according to Luhmann, 'simplifies descriptions of the world and society and thus corresponds to the realities of pre-modern society' (Luhmann, 1997: 2.905). His critique of bivalence is pertinent in view of the uncertainties of reference and communication (Grant, 2003b):

> It is noteworthy in sociological analysis that a logical-bivalent form of observation correlates to a social structure which envisages an unchallenged position for descriptions of world and society.
>
> (Luhmann, 1997: 2.928)

2. Communication and contingency beyond systems

Information, according to Luhmann, is generated when a selective event operates selectively in the system. This selective operation in turn presupposes the capacity for the formation of differences (e.g. the irruption of the fatwa which followed the publication of the *Satanic Verses*). In this way, information comes to be viewed as the experience of difference. Clearly, information is not synonymous with communication, let alone meaning. As Warren Weaver pointed out in 1964, 'information is a measure of one's freedom of choice when one selects a message' (Shannon and Weaver, 1964: 9). As the selection of elements, information is uncoupled from classical notions of meaning and is closely related to freedom and entropy. At the same time, information marks selection and reduces complexity by excluding possibilities (Shannon and Weaver, 1964: 103).

It can be argued with Luhmann at this point that communication is not a symptom of some transcendental community, but it rather simply discharges the function of continuing communication which, in turn, must be self-referential:

> The social system [...] is no longer characterized by a defined 'essence' or even by a determined morality (dissemination of happiness, approximation of quality of life, rational-consensual integration, etc.), but only by the operation which produces and reproduces society. And that is communication.
>
> (Luhmann, 1995: 70)

Since there is no possibility of ascertaining the correspondence of communication and a putative external reality, the 'referent' as it might be called, can never be anything more than a self-thematization or fictionalization – albeit endowed with heuristic properties. Since society, as part of a putative external reality, cannot be known outside communication, it can only be known inside communication. Society therefore can be said to consist of communication about communication.

With the abandonment of correspondence claims (to which attention will return in the next chapter), and the recognition of the recursive functioning of communication, it is possible to move to an understanding of social communication, and the notion of shared realities emerge more clearly as construction-dependent. In the same way, theories which seek to resolve the question of solipsism by recourse to theories of consensus or intersubjectivity, do so by recourse to the same fictions, which are accompanied by unacknowledged truth claims. By contrast, the models of intersubjectivity and consensus should be seen as the products of centuries of social self-thematization which have sought to overcome the isolation of the subject or monad:

> Certain problems of the philosophy of the subject can be [...] resolved, especially the problem of intersubjectivity. Contrary to what is frequently presumed, the functioning of social relations – that means here the autopoiesis of society – does not depend on 'intersubjectivity' or even 'consensus'. Intersubjectivity is neither always given nor can it be generated [...]. The premises of 'intersubjectivity' or consensus can simply be abandoned.
>
> (Luhmann, 1997: 2.874–5)

In revealing the fictional content of the theory of intersubjectivity in this way, Luhmann broke for good with the tradition of the philosophy of dialogue. And yet the concept remains in Luhmann's theory, revealing that systems theory is good at conceptualizing differences, but rather poor when it comes to conceptualizing interactivity. Expectation is the result of a symbolic generalization which condenses a referential structure. Social systems operate with various types of expectation which are essential for a series of simple and complex functions. A referential condensation is essential since it regulates action with a view to a result. Expectation thus regulates, reduces and selects the possibilities for a particular action. Moreover, these expectations sustain themselves even when the original expectation context (for a certain type of action) has been displaced, for it performs a dual function: firstly, it is a cognitive selection procedure; secondly, it connects discontinuities so that norms may guarantee social cohesion. In terms of the consciousness of the psychic system, expectation is the form by which an individual psychic system avoids the terminology of the subject by exposing itself to its environment – that is, all that which is not part of its own psychic system:

> An expectation reconnoitres unknown terrain using a difference it can experience within itself: it can be fulfilled or disappointed, and this does not depend on itself alone.
>
> (Luhmann, 1995: 268)

In terms of expectation theory, the individual actor seen as a self-referential system is faced with the constant risk of observing so many expectations in so many polycontexts that history or society exclude the actor and his power over expectations guaranteed by his cognitive autonomy. This excess may be corrected by returning to the action concept in conjunction with expectation theory.

Luhmann unmasks the dialogical pretensions of the Enlightenment and its self-thematizations. The impulse for the discourse of action, reason and emancipation stems from a recognition of the increasing decentering or desperate recentering of the modern world: the resurgence of faith and fundamentalism, the loss of myths and centralization of world views. The new paradigms can be interpreted as self-thematizing compensations for a loss of stability or a desire to create stability and a rational centre in a world which, taken to its radical rational conclusions, is based on 'heuristic fictions' (Kant, 1983b: B 799). Uncertainty could in effect only be remedied by bringing rational subjects back into the fold:

> The answer was sought in the concept of Reason, the moral law, or similar apriorisms, in the concept of education, or in the concept of the state. The old sense of the insufficiency, of the corruptibility, of all things beneath the moon, was overcome by idealization. Thus one could to the greatest extent from social phenomena, postulating eventually even 'freedom from domination' as the basic condition of the unrestricted presence of the universal in man. The universal was conceive as pure, free of risk, and in no need of compensation – and this in spite of all the counterevidence the French Revolution offered. The universal could appear with a claim to realization. Spirit or Matter would have to take the long route of realizing the universal in the particular.
>
> (Luhmann, 1995: 6)

Leaving aside the question of the utility of the lifeworld–system distinction proposed by Habermas, both lifeworld and system discourses are stabilization operations in the formation of consensus in the pragmatics of everyday conventionalizations but also in self-referential institutional settings. Without conventions, rules, genres, text forms in both spheres (if indeed the frontier between the two is meaningful), it could be said that communication would not so much *break down* (in the sense of communication failure), but *break out* (in the sense of anarchy). As Parsons argues in his discussion of the central status of language in social systems:

> A social system which leads to too drastic a disruption of its culture, for example through blocking the processes of its acquisition, would be exposed to social as well as cultural disintegration.
>
> (Parsons, 1967: 34)

Any system which tends to produce more disruption than order will disintegrate. Thus, disruption in social terms – contestation, dissent, opposition and so on – can be taken as the informational entropy (fictionalized as the freedom of expression) of the social system while order can be taken as the redundancy of the social system: stabilized semantics based on codes, conventions, rules, stereotypes, discourses, ideologies, theologies and beliefs which seems to escape individual or social volition. However controlled the disruption of the stabilized semantic-semiotic orders of societies may be, however onerous representational hegemonics remain, the fact is that all rules are subject to disruption since language users are *reflective agents in communication*. There is therefore a constant tension between stabilized convention (semantics) and information, understood as a factor of uncertainty. But this is a trivial statement. A social communication-theoretical approach must take account of the uncertainty and certainty or – in short, of the complex form of communication:

> The everyday hermeneutics of mass communication are indeed a melting pot permeated by subcultural value orientations and in which the evaluative vocabularies of public speech are constantly subjected to revision [...]. Public speech remains *porous* to innovative stimuli to the extent that it is not moulded in the deformed communicative structures of a network of autonomous publicness.
>
> (Habermas, 1995a: 558 – emphasis in the original; my translation)

Habermas has never formulated in detailed theoretical terms what porous speech might be. In this reference it is evaluated positively as openness to innovation or contestation of everyday mass communication suffused with sub-cultural value orientations. This means that the conception of openness is normatively constrained and associated with an emancipatory discourse which is not neutralized by 'deformed communicative structures' (n.b. deformed *and* communicative structures!). However, there is no ontological precondition according to which openness operates in one way only. Porosity is a property of all communications and implies that communication structures (from syntax to ideologies) are always permeable. The communication dynamic born of undertone and overtone, sincerity and ulterior motive, exposure and concealment – the crashes of contradiction and disappointment – cannot be reconciled simply by recourse to counter-factual ideals and ontologically determined consensus or shared knowledge. Communication is porous – contingent on communication media and cognitive autonomy and this contingency makes the self-reference of systems, institutions and even discourses precarious. Signs are given and systemically stablized, but remain uncertain as appeals to readers and can be infinitely iterated and subverted not only in contexts but in the act of communication itself.

Communication uncertainty is a result of complex relations between speaker and speaker, speaker and worlds and also of the fact that meanings of communication do not correlate with the semantic processing of the simultaneous cognition operations of social actors (as Luhmann argued, consciousness processes cannot be controlled by communication [see Luhmann, 1997: 2.814]). Dirk Baecker makes a similar point in his reflections on the inescapable ambivalence of communication when he argues that ambivalence is the precondition for the fact that participants in communication are not determined by communication but gain selection opportunities through communication (Baecker, 1999b: 54). In a more complex human communication model, which goes beyond the discrete characters Shannon had in mind, semantics cannot be ignored. Equally, communication as a social operation cannot be reduced to semantic or semanticist models and it must integrate the uncertainties of semiotic and pragmatic dimensions of communication agents. By contrast, the emphasis here is on a more general modelling of the dynamic uncertainties of communication processes in society rather than the structures of repeatable texts. Here, context and communication must be enhanced by cognition-theoretical and indeed ethical questions such as the status of the autonomous subject. As noted above, this does not mean logical vagueness or the impossibility of distinguishing between true and false (bivalence), but the theoretical approach to social communication as a system of multiple contingencies and many-valued dynamics.

For the concept of porosity the role of the agents of communicative uncertainty is crucial. In terms of social communication theory, the use of the entropy concept – the uncertainty in communication as a source of information – implies that society builds on unstable or, in Derrida's terms, polycontextual structures:

> Meaning [...] is a completely open structure, excluding nothing, not even the negation of meanings. As systems of meaning-based communication societies are closed and open systems. They gain their openness by closure.
>
> (Luhmann, 1990: 146–7)

3. System-agent dynamics: ambivalence, noise, complexity

Almost 20 years have passed since the publication of *Social Systems* – Luhmann's first systematic account of his super-theory. Even after his death his works continue to be published, and yet it is conceivable that the epistemological and methodological radicalism of his theory has, to some extent, been absorbed in the human and social sciences and that a critical re-evaluation is beginning in some of the most recent discussions. Such a shift would be unsurprising given the natural course taken by the history of ideas and the capacity for the academic system to integrate what was once considered to be marginal. There have indeed been clear signs that Luhmann's social systems theory is being challenged in such a way as to introduce a greater measure of complexity into the concept of the system. Suffice it to point to some recent examples: in *Histories and Discourses*, Siegfried J. Schmidt (2003a) seeks to go beyond dualistic epistemology while in *Organization as System* and *Organization and Management*, Dirk Baecker (1999a/b) writes of the distinction between ill-defined and well-defined systems and the inescapable ambivalence of communication. In a different disciplinary tradition, Bauman (2003) argues that there is a growing cleavage between the overall, increasingly rigidified order and cultural subsystems or agencies. The concepts of a radical disengagement, the loose definition of systems and a non-dualistic epistemology offer new points of departure for a critique of systems theory and indeed potentially a critical systems theory.

As argued above, Luhmann's conceptualization of systems is more complex than his conceptualization of communication and, as a result, his theory of systems is arguably less adequate to the complexities of communication. In post-Luhmannian systems theory, there is a growing awareness of this complexity gap. In this way, rather than conferring absolute status on communication (as Luhmann does) and vaporizing the category of the social actor, communication is increasingly seen in social terms as a dynamic of uncertainties. Dirk Baecker sees organizations as more or less loose couplings of order and disorder (Baecker, 1999a: 25), whereas Siegfried J. Schmidt's 'farewell to constructivism' (which is less a farewell and more of a re-encounter) explicitly criticizes constructivism (embraced by Luhmann) for its reluctance to jettison dualistic epistemology. For Schmidt there is no ontological dualism which he describes as a *petitio principii* (2003a: 92). The distinction and separation between truth and utterance, subject and object forecloses a different epistemological approach in which the relationship between speaker and 'object' is a processual and reflexive one. Here, reality can only ever emerge in concrete relations and contexts – 'existential utterances and existential denials are made by actors in concrete communication contexts – where else?' (Schmidt, 2003a: 93). In view of the situatedness of 'ontological' statements, utterances about the existence of tables or chairs are utterances made by an 'I' in a setting. This recognition demonstrates a *'process-specific reality'* without ontological objects which are postulated as being somehow independent of processes (Schmidt, 2003a: 95 – emphasis in original). Schmidt refers to such basic cognitive operations as *'process-bound difference management'* to be explored in the following chapters. Where Schmidt plausibly seeks an epistemological revision of dualism and reintegrates the actor and Baecker plausibly considers the contingencies of organizations in interaction with ill- defined systems, I have argued for a theory of complex communication which takes the contingency of communication in semiotic and pragmatic terms, the communicating subject and social organizations seriously. This complex approach, epistemologically compatible with Schmidt's latest account, is based on a theory of multiple contingencies across agents, media and environments where distinctions between true and false cannot be made, but where such uncertainty is not the result of our ignorance, but the uncertain dynamic of form and non-form.

It is worth recalling that both Habermas and Luhmann stake claims to universality – either on the basis of rationality or on the basis of a radical systems theory. In one sense, both theories, however divergent their conclusions may be, seek a stable purchase on their object. This stability emerges in explicit form in the *Theory of Communicative Action* in the reconstruction of ideal speech acts and implicitly in Luhmann, in the guise of the clear claim to *supertheoretical universality* (Luhmann, 1995). The key construct of heuristic fictions in Radical Constructivism and the specific conception of entropy in *The Mathematical Theory of Communication* and in the concept of porous communication leave greater scope for oscillation and imperfection between ideality and reality, fiction and truth, subject and society, cognition and communication.

As suggested above, the concept of porous communication can be made useful in a study of a general systems theory as a useful epistemological framework and more specifically in the definition of the frontier between system and environment as part of a theoretical modelling of communication at a social level. Parallels have already been established between thermodynamics and systems theory in a modelling of systems in the human and social sciences as open systems. Watzlawick *et al.* drew attention to this very fact in their famous *Pragmatics of Human Communication*:

> The distinction between closed and open systems can be said to have freed the sciences concerned with life phenomena from the shackles of a theoretical model based essentially on classical physics and chemistry: a model of exclusively *closed* systems. Because living systems have crucial dealings with their environments, the theory and methods of analysis appropriate to things which can be reasonably put in 'a sealed insulated container' were significantly obstructive and misleading.
>
> (Watzlawick, Beavin Bavelas, Jackson, 1967: 122)

They conclude that an open system consists of an 'integrated hierarchy of semi-autonomous sub-wholes' in which a dyadic interactional system of human–human interaction can easily be conceptualized in the setting of larger systems such as the family, church etc. The key difference in the conceptualization of uncertain systems lies in the capacity of systems to manage the complexity of communications.

Baecker's distinction between well-defined and ill-defined systems is a useful modification of Luhmann's systems theory. Whereas well-defined systems are like trivial machines in being stable in time, in ill-defined systems transitions between the stages in a system are not known, the probability of transitions is unknown and the system itself is unstable in time. One such system is the human being. The paradox is that the system, in our case, the social system, composed of ill-defined systems and error-prone agents is actually a well-defined system (Baecker, 1999a: 19). Agents interact better with poorly defined systems and do not want to be confronted with overdetermined systems in which their autonomy is denied. Thus organizations are 'more or less manageable mixes of order and disorder, redundancy and variety, loose and firm coupling' (Baecker, 1999a: 25). Or, in a different terminology, organizations and systems are a hybrid of a void space and solid phase – of uncertainty and structure.

Systems theory provides a useful point of departure for establishing connections between complexity and communication systems for it is explicitly concerned with instability and contingency. While an organization is only able to define its frontiers, however contingently over time, by communications, for Baecker, communication is a 'stability condition' of the system (Baecker, 1999a: 29), but it is also a source of instability given its polycontextual contingencies: its vagueness, the closure of its users, the contexts of its use. Thus we can say that communication both deals with contingency and generates contingency. Baecker also refers to ambivalent communication (Baecker, 1999a: 52f.) where message aspects can 'ruin' information aspects. Ambivalence is essential to communication as the guarantee of the 'freedom' of 'heads'. Given that ambivalence cannot be removed from communication, that contingency cannot be neutralized and that the form of communication is porous, how do social systems survive as systems? For Baecker, the answer is that rather then denying ambivalence, systems use it in a process he refers to as 'stochastic resonance' (Baecker, 1999a: 45). According to this process, systems use noise (often regarded as disturbance with a negative connotation) in order to gain information; maintaining a good level of noise ensures that the system retains a level of alertness or sensitivity to contingencies:

> The system reference of communication is no longer that of the 'heads', that is, 'communicating' individuals, but that of a 'social' system which is engaged in nothing more than testing and using ambivalence and, from case to case, deciding in favour of one or other possibility without ever finally committing to one or other possibility.
>
> (Baecker, 1999a: 58 – my translation)

Thus systems do not reduce contingency: they actively seek it out rather than trying to drive it underground. However, additionally, porous communications cannot guarantee the success of the operation of closure unless they rely on brute force (and this is no guarantee either of 'successful' communication as the history of dictatorships demonstrates). Since environmental openness means that (porous) systems rely on communication for their interactions, it also means that such systems are exposed to the risk of the uncertainty of that communication (its entropy) and the independence of cognitively distinct social subjects. As noted above, it remains the case that the semiotic appeal of communications can, ultimately, be rejected:

> Each participant knows for himself and of others that fixed forms of linguistic meaning are selected contingently (thereby continually confirming the fact that it is only a question of 'signs'). What can be perceived acoustically or optically and can therefore also be distinguished, is subjected to a second mode of selection. The 'material' of language itself is so formed and perceptible only in this form; but it is also occupied with references which function independently of their environment and thus permit repeated use. Thus, linguistic signs are and can always be different.
>
> (Luhmann, 1997: 1.211 – my translation)

Systems develop constraints in order to neutralize uncertainties or risk, but even in this case autonomy implies autonomy to reject or amend constraints. It is probably true to say that in the human and social sciences no contemporary theorist seeks to use the closed system model since it would be implausible in view of the complexities and instabilities of communication and cognition. However, conversely, systems theorists also tend to offer a pure conceptualization of the frontier between system and environment which excessively constrains the permeability of social systems. In terms of a theoretical modelling of communication instability Baecker argues that 'a system is a highly precarious *'dance'* of ensuring a distinction between the system and its environment, which is the only way of ensuring the system reproduces itself' (Baecker, 2001: 63 – my emphasis). The introduction of such precariousness into the system concept is essential if hypostatizations are to be avoided and the system concept be rendered dynamic. According to Baecker, two causalities perform in this dance: the external causal influence of the environment on the system and the 'self-determination of the system by the constraints under which it is placed and/or which it is ready to accept' (2001: 63); such 'split causality' is part of the openness of systems. Communication is inscribed into this double causality in the sense that it recursively generates the sets of possibilities (e.g. discourses, genres, conventions, types) for selection of communications and also states that these sets are not given, but require constant recursive generation: 'Therefore, communication indeed means production of redundancy (Bateson, 1972: 406–7). It defines both the message being selected and the set of possibilities from which it is selected' (Baecker, 2001: 66). In terms of social systems, entropy must also be lower than 1, since otherwise a social system would not be distinct from its environment, i.e. would not be definable as a system. Warren Weaver refers in this context to the 'good connotations' of the term information:

> It is therefore possible for the word information to have either good or bad connotations. Uncertainty which arises by virtue of freedom of choice on the part of the sender is desirable uncertainty. Uncertainty which arises because of errors or because of the influence of noise is undesirable uncertainty.
>
> (Shannon and Weaver, 1964: 19)

Porosity makes this normative dichotomy between good and bad noise highly uncertain since noise is inseparable from freedom of choice and the undesirability of uncertainty is not reduced to 'errors' – from undertones, subjects, pragmatic enrichments and semiotic appeals. Where Baecker sees blindspots as an observational feature of an epistemological and methodological category, the concept of porous systems does not assume that the system can absorb its own blindspots but rather conceptualizes the distinction between the system and its environment as porous in itself. Thus the differentiation capacity of systems is always deferred.

Discourses remain embedded in lifeworlds since their function is to repair background knowledge which has been 'disturbed' or fragmented by the rationalization tendencies of the differentiation of social systems. At the same time, discourses are hybrid and porous in terms of communication and cognition. As such, they do not remain solely embedded in or confined to lifeworlds: there is no rigid frontier between lifeworld and system and colonization operates in both directions, not merely as the infiltration of the lifeworld by discourses of 'power', but as the infiltration of the 'system' by a range of other discourses, such as environmentalism, feminism and minority rights at a political level. Indeed, Habermas's model of discursive democracy offers a theoretical model for the capacity of discourses to inform 'systems'. Admittedly, it could always be argued that such *counter-colonization* could constitute little more than a well-defined and systems-driven sphere of communicative tolerance in order to visibilize and thus also neutralize counter-discourses. And yet, given the multiple contingency of communication in terms of social systems and the porosity of that communication in pragmatic, semiotic and cognitive terms, there is no guarantee of system success in maintaining the defining frontier of the area of tolerance.

In certain important respects these critical re-evaluations of systems theory and constructivism are closely related to the concerns of the current study. As noted above, S.J. Schmidt's starting position is the need to replace the ontological dualisms of subject–object relations and their shortcut to stability and resolution with processual theories which challenge logical realism. He still believes that cognition is a question of positing differences (*Differenzsetzung*) but it might be possible to go further beyond this move and challenge the sharpness of the cut, in view of the processuality of knowledge formation. The dynamics of knowledge formation at a social level would indeed need to see difference formation as a temporary 'interruption of contingency', as Schmidt puts it. In this way, any coorientation of actors' values or behaviours can only ever be a temporary and contingent communication which in turn needs to be re-established recursively through social redundancies. Genuine processuality and contingency sits with Schmidt's commitment to reality models in which 'everyone assumes that everyone else possesses the same knowledge' (2003a: 34) because these assumptions operate as operative fictions (cf. Schmidt, 1994 and Grant, 2000). In terms of social formation, processual epistemology connects with latency and emergence – where society is a process in formation in which there is a dialectic between tradition and innovation, autonomy and constraint. Cultural formations achieve stability by 'invisibilizing contingency' or creating the illusion of permanence (2003: 47). And yet, even these invisibilzation strategies remain visible to the communicating agent as autonomous interpreter.

Following his theory of cognitive autonomy (1994b), Schmidt argues that all events relating to consciousness are tied to the context specificity of actors. However, this is not a recipe for 'solipsistic hell', since actors use a semantic system at the social level. This semantic system is referred to as a system of meaning orientations. In this conceptualization, the emphasis is transferred from referential realism (references to reality) to the *functioning* of semantics. Taken as a complex whole, the system of meaning orientations can be described as the 'reality model of a society': 'since there can be no examination of the validity [...] of communication independently of these circumstances, such meaning orientations operate as operative fictions' (cf. also Grant 2000).

5
Uncertainty and Social Communication Theory

1. Introduction

This chapter argues that existing interaction accounts, heavily indebted to the semantic of dialogue, are unable to construct a theory which is both sufficiently sensitive to uncertainty in cognitive and communication terms and is also able to reconcile such uncertainty with theoretical accounts of the social. Taken at a weak, intuitive level of extension, the concept of interaction is unproblematic: people interact all the time. However, the term is more often than not accompanied by strong claims, taken as a synonym for generalized modes of interaction, and often modelled as dialogue, dialogism or exchange of meaning with strong assumptions being made about intentionality, inference and understanding. This chapter examines the point of transition, from intuitive notions of interaction to generalized models, at which problems relating to the theoretical conceptualization of interaction emerge, for it is at this point that intuitive beliefs are all too often reified. The central argument advanced here is that, however defined, the interaction concept has remained within the confines of transcendental theories. Furthermore, despite the more recent diversification of communication theories into theories of dialogism, constructivism and uncertainty, conservative interaction theories display a remarkable resilience and obscure some relevant questions such as how social communication emerges across the deep uncertainties of subject, media and language.

2. Aporias of social interaction theories

As argued in chapters 1–4, part of the problem in the prevailing social communication theories can be found in the tendency to reify notions of dialogue and relate them to transcendentalized accounts of inter-subjectivity or to deny the role of the actor as communicator, suppressing his autonomy.[1] In both cases, actors become discourse functions, and autonomy is compromised. Even for Habermas, there might indeed be greater room for an account of actor autonomy, but this is locked within a counterfactual rationalist communication paradigm. For Luhmann, there is less room for a conceptualization of autonomy, but greater openness to uncertainties in communication. Habermas has argued that by following Husserl, Luckmann[2] for example could not go beyond the phenomenological lifeworld concept, affirming common knowledge without due regard for the communicative practices which construct it. As Habermas sees it, this aporia can be avoided by replacing a phenomenological method with a communication-theoretical method, since the former fails to grasp the regenerative communicative energies of the lifeworld. The theories of intersubjectivity and dialogism and Luckmann's theory of collective knowledge are representative of the dominant interaction paradigm. Communicative interaction, in other words, should not be taken for granted as the correct inference of intentions since intentions cannot be accessed. Equally, we must guard against solipsism or dismiss communication either as monologue or as dialogism, for neither of the understandings of interaction offers an adequate account of the uncertainties communication. Such uncertainty is a result of autonomous enrichments in dynamic interactions of non-corresponding dyads, the fluid contexts of globalization in terms of social organization, semiotic appeal and the appeal we make to be interpreted by others in the complex relations between speaker and speaker, speaker and worlds, and the fact that meanings of communication do not correlate with the semantic processing of the simultaneous cognition operations of social actors (as Luhmann argued, consciousness processes cannot be controlled by communication – see Luhmann, 1997: 2.814 – cf. also Baecker, 1999b: 54).

The tendency to operate with concepts such as dialogue, exchange of meaning, or even dialogism, intersubjectivity or consensus introduces at worst a binary aspect into an understanding of communication processes or at best unproblematic assumptions about cognitive accessing, social relations and social stability itself. Equally, normative or supertheories of innateness or rational predisposition in communication must remain less sensitive to the construction of communication in society and to the role of agents of communication in making and negotiating these communication codes:

> Irrespective of the cultural background, all participants know intuitively too well that a consensus based on conviction is not possible without symmetrical relations between the participants in communication – relations of reciprocal recognition, reciprocal adopting the stance of the other, reciprocal imputed willingness to see one's own traditions with the eyes of an outsider and to learn from each other etc.
>
> (Habermas, 1999b: 332)

If our understanding of communication is revised on the basis of different assumptions about the constitutive role uncertainty plays in communication processes, then these claims can be challenged or reformulated in a way which is still socially meaningful. This point is vital: the critique of the intermonadological fallacy and universal inferentialism (inferring a speaker's true intentions) is not a simplistic appeal for a society of non-communicating self-referential human agents qua black boxes whose data are irretrievable. Rather, the task is to understand communication as inconceivable without uncertainty. If all we communicated were certainties (intentions, sincerity, truthfulness, sharedness, a common horizon of understanding), then, quite possibly, communication would no longer be necessary. In what follows, the interaction concept will be recast with a different theoretical model without recourse to realist philosophy, universal pragmatics, theories of intersubjectivity or a systems theory with no room for the agent. The task is to reconcile agency, uncertainty and society:

> To Searle's appropriate question 'How does it all hang together?', the response will not be an inappropriate (dogmatic) recourse to realism, but to social need. Society 'hangs together' fallibilistically on the basis of functional fictions (in the sense proposed by Schmidt, 1994b, 2001).
>
> (Grant, 2000: 131)[3]

An understanding of social communication processes as complex uncertain negotiations derives from the cognitive autonomy (Schmidt, 1994b) of speakers who clearly cannot gain access to the intentions, beliefs, motives or identities of their communication partners, but rely instead on their communications. Schmidt was at pains not to disconnect such autonomy from the social realm, however, and thus refers to social orientation as the pragmatic environment without which a cognitive system would become involuted – the black box scenario. He resolves the problem of social cohesion by means of the concept of operative fictions of collective knowledge, the cognitive autonomy of social actors is somehow communalized (Schmidt, 1995: 322–3). The equivalent of such an environment in communication theory could be the concept of context:

> Social fictions also operate as complex pragmatic fictions by means of recursively linked communications and thus build stable social orders through culture as a socially obligatory semantic instantiation of world models.
>
> (Schmidt, 2001: 11)

If communication is always a negotiation between uncertainties and the need for organization, then the concepts of identity, understanding or mutuality can only ever be imputations, and yet precarious and necessary imputations all the same. The uncertainties in communication thus need to be reduced by elaborate fictional codes constructed to simulate or impute 'shared knowledge'.

By recognizing social interaction in terms of its functioning and without recourse to the concepts of intersubjectivity, dialogism or consensus, real epistemological, and potentially empirical, gains can be achieved by operating with the fictionality of the constructs of social interaction. In other words, in this conceptualization of social communication using the constructivist concept of cognitive autonomy, solipsism at an individual level or atomism at a social level are not inevitable risks: uncertainties in communication are negotiated for purposes of social interaction by means of extremely complex social semantics, cultural codes and orders of discourse. In none of these complex social epistemes or semantics can uncertainty be removed, but it can be and is managed.

3. Contingency, cognitive autonomy, communication

The work of radical constructivists such as von Glasersfeld and S.J. Schmidt can be made useful in the context of a theory of the interweaving of uncertainty and social organization because they challenge premises inherited by the human and social sciences from certain Enlightenment rationality theories. By placing emphasis on the inescapable contingency of knowing and perceiving, reality can be conceptualized as a construction without recourse to static ontologies. Contingency of perception, which constructivists are at pains to see as socially functional, means the end of the knowability of objective realities as something external to human beings. A theory of porosity in social communication must go beyond the postmodernist jouissance of pure contingency for contingency's sake in the development of a theory of functional contingency. Rather than simply positing, with Lyotard, paralogy (the inventiveness of linguistic games) without rules, a theory of human communication in society enriched by the work of the radical constructivists in the 1980s should consider social communication in terms of the irreducible non-correspondence of uncertain signs – be it with 'reality' or the worlds constructed by other speakers. And in so doing, the intermonadological fallacy can be debunked. As Heinz von Foerster put it in his Declaration to the American Society for Cybernetics delivered in 1983, 'reality is an interactive concept since the observer and the observed constitute a mutually dependent pair'. For some constructivists, operative fictions of collective knowledge enable the cognitive autonomy of social actors to be communalized – and yet the concept of collective knowledge sits uneasily with the concept of cognitive autonomy and tends to undermine the processuality of the construction of social realities. Observer and observed form a mutually dependent pair; 'reality' is interactive since self-regulation can only take place in an environment.

In his approach to a metadisciplinary theory of knowing, von Glasersfeld describes knowledge as being characterized by two distinct operations: action and result. His epistemology problematizes the Platonic dichotomy between knowledge (any cognitive operation means fictionalization) and being. This means that entities such as truth, reality and objectivity are no longer contemplated as static aprioris, but as functionally necessary fictions which enable the interaction of cognitively autonomous actors. Alternatively, as von Glasersfeld argues:

> The subjective element remains unavoidable because the semantic link which connects acoustic images with meanings must be actively constructed by each individual speaker.
>
> (von Glasersfeld, 1996: 219 – my translation)

Operative fictions depend fundamentally on the viability of cognitive experience in which viability should be seen as an accommodation to the world which offers a context for our uncertainties. Truth – and history, reality and objectivity – thus also becomes a relational concept and not just an objective law. Having re-established the intertwining relationship between communication and uncertainty, the task is now to ask how contingency (not rampant relativism) acts in a socially functional way.

Peter Hejl's concept of synreferentiality (Hejl, 1995) – a kind of 'functional community of perception' (Husserl, 1960: 122) – appears to offer a way out of the apparent aporias of pure autonomy and self-reference. It fulfils two functions: firstly, it acknowledges the self-referential operations of communication and, implicitly, the cognitive closure of the 'subject'. Secondly, it also accepts the existence of a realm above cognitively closed actors. This realm, which is not intermonadological or intersubjective, is populated by self-referential communications which can be accessed by actors as if they were a shared reality – in a non-ontological sense; this is where the media as *synreferential* generators play a key role as communicative constructions of reality:

> Understanding can be theoretically modelled in terms of what communication attributes to or requires of cognition on the occasion of the processing of media offers, or in terms of what consciousness presupposes as modus operandi of communicators during communication. Both communication and cognition cannot do without this imputation.
>
> (Schmidt, 1995: 322–3)

This complex communication realm seems to take a step back from the brink of any 'epistemological solipsism' in a manner reminiscent of Husserl's horizon of expectation.[4] The methodological gain is to be made in opening up inquiry to 'our' multiple fictions and their dramatizations in everyday life, in not painting the media, as specially mediatized forms of communication, as distortions of reality, but as differentiated fictions that become social codes for increasingly connected and fragmented subjects. This is one of the paradoxes of globalization.

Many basic factors can be held to account for communication uncertainties: communication takes place between social actors, that is, communicators, whose cognitive systems are closed. These communicators use languages whose reference functions do not map onto 'realities' outside communication, but realities which are communicatively constructed. In addition, our communications are always already dialogically, multiply constituted and emerge from multiply mediated contexts which are growing more dispersed and fluid over time with advances in new technologies. Against these insoluble uncertainties, the relationship between intentionality and understanding, truth claims or a putative intersubjective meshing of minds needs theoretical and epistemological revision. To access intentions, sift Goffman's 'ulterior motives', let alone achieve agreement or consensus or a reciprocal adopting of attitudes, implies reaching across cognitive closure and by means of languages which are freely enriched and radically interpreted (Recanati/Davidson) by these cognitively closed actors in the fluid contexts of communications which can no longer neatly be compartmentalized into mediated and face-to-face communications. The foregoing must now be related to theories of communication at a social level. Here, any attempt to assume that vagueness, cognitive autonomy and communicational uncertainty can be sublated and in this way a noise-free, originary dialogue or intersubjective world achieved, must involve a transcendental move. This particular move will not be effected here.

Even Luckmann and Linell's attempt to introduce greater empirical plausibility into their dialogue concept amounts to a reluctance to acknowledge the agentic, medial and contextual uncertainties of communication. Much more coherent and epistemologically daring is Luhmann's theory of asymmetry and related critique of the dialogical interaction paradigm, according to which inequality cannot be forced into a model of compatibility. For Luhmann, the survival of theories of dialogism and intersubjectivity is a reflection of a consciousness of imperfection/ perfectibility, based on the rationality paradigm, which is not prepared to accept the consequences of insights into cognitive self-reference, as Habermas has belatedly conceded. With the diffusion, if not actually the eclipse of the universalistic discourses (of liberation, emancipation or reason), any transcendental horizon of reference comes under pressure, the inherent uncertainties of communication emerge with greater clarity, demanding of theoretical reflection.[5]

Despite the empirical and theoretical need to explore the ruptures and instabilities in communications, Habermas continues to hold the view that rational lifeworld energies presuppose consensus, however improbable and infrequent he concedes this may actually be. Whereas the lifeworld depends on the (presumed) rationality of intersubjective communicative reciprocity, the system (understood as a self-referential organization in an environment) depends on performativity and self-referentiality. Systems logic does not completely colonize 'lifeworld' energies. Attempts made by the system to interfere in lifeworld spheres such as cultural tradition, social integration or education, inevitably conflict with the communicative rationality of these spheres – which have become differentiated from other spheres in the process of specialization. A further differentiation can be noted in the case of culture which, in achieving autonomy, has also become separated from the hermeneutics of everyday life. (This differentiation may also explain why Habermas neglects so consistently so-called parasitic forms of communication.)

As we have seen, in his *Theory of Communicative Action*, Habermas elaborated a complex theory of social action which links social cohesion to communicative consensus. Cohesion and consensus coalesce to generate a lifeworld which, although constantly under attack from the system, still offers an overarching horizon of references from which social actors derive their social bearings. Thus social actions and communicative practices coincide in rationality. On an epistemological level, therefore, the *Theory of Communicative Action* derives from a hermeneutic of rationalism.

Norms are also central to the concept of discourse introduced by Foucault in *L'Ordre du Discours* (1971), although Foucault did not seek an immaculate language in the form of a universal formal pragmatics: discourses are temporally and spatially legitimated languages linked to power and accordingly ruled by procedures of exclusion. In this model of internal and external exclusion procedures, Foucault must also assume stability: discourse is ruled by prohibitions, oppositions, manicheisms and disciplines, commentaries and author functions. Since he was not to conceive of volatile language until *The History of Sexuality* (originally 1976), Foucault must proceed from an ineluctable norm, defined by power. There is, in conclusion, little difference between Habermas and the earlier Foucault on the question of the norm. The difference lies in the conception of rationality: for Habermas rationality is an emancipatory force, for Foucault a disciplinary force. In Foucault's later analysis of the relations between sexuality and communication, he refers to the pluralization of modes of discourse – an 'incitation aux discours' (Foucault, 1984: 25). In this plural discourse universe, prohibition, control and censorship exist alongside regions of absolute silence which is part of a discoursal fermentation. These silences underpin and traverse discourses as part of the looser system of communicative management of sexuality and thus indirectly acquire an almost subversive potential. They are, to borrow the words of George Spencer Brown, unmarked communication spaces.

4. Social interaction

Both the early Foucault and Habermas proceed from the principle that rational communication is organized and thus restricts uncertainty. Habermas attributes to rational lifeworld communicative practices, the capacity for communicative renewal despite the threat of entropy, where entropy is the antonym of rational inclusive communication and acts as a source of noise or uncertainty which can be avoided. However, entropy is an inherent characteristic of any communication system, since the removal of uncertainty would result in pure statistical regularity or redundancy and no information. Given the cognitive uniqueness (and that means freedom) of each actor, this is, to say the least, improbable. Any control – disciplinary or epistemological – must therefore take place at the cost of a reduction of the very freedom that entropy guarantees. While intuition dictates that our perceptions maintain a noise-free contact with external reality, perception, as an act of cognition, is a self-referential process. Gerhard Roth defines it as a neurological process in a closed organ (the brain), in which direct contact with external reality is precluded. The environment of external 'reality' merely transmits electrical impulses which are incapable of penetrating the brain. Data processing (in neurological terms) is independent of outside reality to the extent that the language of the nervous system is independent of 'meaning'.

However, any notion of identical realities is implausible if the principle of cognitive autonomy is taken seriously. The contingency of our 'life reality' (von Glasersfeld) is not necessarily a synonym for alienation for there is arguably a paradoxical community of contingency in the sense that all actors are equally susceptible to risk at a system level and thus contingency at a cognitive level. It could be argued that contingency is a very important component of our shared experiences (Habermas, 1998). A specific case reveals the extent to which systems are contingent upon communications (in their interactions with their environments) and contingent *in* communications (they are the only media available for such interactions). Given this multiple contingency of communication, the legal system, for example, is as susceptible to noise (from the political, religious or scientific systems) as any other agency that is dependent on communication. In this way, the legal system can be viewed as being provisionally closed in its operations, but essentially porous. The only way in which social actors can gain purchase over the legal system, or indeed any other, is by participation in essentially porous communication. This conceptualization has two advantages: it neither relies on the counterfactual normativity developed by Habermas (i.e. universal communicative rationality), nor on an excessively ontological concept of systemic differentiation and temporary communicative stability as laid out by Luhmann. Instead, the concept of operative fictions seeks to remain sensitive to social and subjective construction and to heighten theoretical awareness of the precariousness/dynamic of social orders. This potentially heightened awareness of the fictionality of social construction has the potential to make us take subjective constructions more seriously, identify abuses of power, and wonder at the remarkably intricate interpersonal networks of social interaction. The more organized the communication, the lower the entropy. When entropy is lowered, so, too, is freedom of choice, and when freedom of choice is lowered, information becomes predictable. If entropy is a factor of uncertainty as opposed to redundancy, then it can be seen as the correlate of uncertainty in the domain of cognition.

By a process of formal analogy, it is argued here that communications provide a particularly relevant example of porous form since a communication is an acoustic or graphematic form amidst its non-form: silence or absence. And yet, this absence is a constitutive part of communication, which cannot be subtracted. While communications dwell in the interstices of silence, so, too, does silence dwell in the interstices of communication. Communications are latticeworks of morphological and semiotic properties; their free circulation is ensured by universal connections with all communicating agents, but their forms are constantly displaced by context, user, medium and receiver. No schematism can ever successfully fill the indeterminacies which are constitutive of communication. Social systems operate amidst such uncertainty for they are communication dependent. To preserve their stability as systems' institutions, they are endowed with codes or discourses as complex schematizations. These schematizations function as stabilizers of vague semiotics in which a vague residuum always persists (Peirce, 1955); potential destabilizing effects are fed back into the system recursively. Communicative stabilization requires communication, and with communicative interaction, risk commences. As Derrida put it: 'Every sign, linguistic or non-linguistic, spoken or written [...] can be cited, put between quotation marks; in so doing it can break with every given context, engendering an infinity of new contexts in a manner which is absolutely illimitable' (Derrida, 2000: 12).

As Schmidt (1994b, 2003a) and Baecker (2001, 2005) have also argued, a communication theory of uncertainty, with its emphasis on the instability of any referential operation, is essential to a theory of complex communication according to which cognitive and social contexts of use, reference and meaning remain inevitably porous. Contingencies are not so much doubled in the sense of Parsons, they are multiple in the radically dialogical constitution of the subject, the open appeal and contingent response of speakers and the mediated communication contexts in which we move. The concept of entropy in an information-theoretical sense means uncertainty or, in the classical Shannonian definition, the 'rate of generating information' (Shannon and Weaver, 1964: 58). When entropy is lowered, so, too, is freedom of choice, and when freedom of choice is lowered, information becomes predictable:

> In the limiting case where one probability is unity (certainty) and all the others zero (impossibility), then H [information] is zero (no uncertainty at all – no freedom of choice – no information).
>
> (Shannon and Weaver, 1964: 15)

Entropy and cognitive autonomy (Schmidt) go hand in hand, since one refers to uncertainty in communication, whereas the other asserts cognitive uniqueness. In Shannon's sense, meaning is certainty and thus closely related to redundancy in communication. Since his model deals essentially with discrete forms, the task here will be to enrich the entropy concept in pragmatic-semiotic terms and thus make it useful at the level of social communication theory.

In *Knowledge and the Flow of Information* (1976), Fred Dretske integrates Shannon's information theory with a semantic framework which comprises two additional commitments: truth and knowledge. The approach emphasizes the need to look beyond the formal properties of the communication medium to the *contents* of communication; thus a 'genuine theory of information would be about the content of our messages [...]' (Dretske, 1999: 40). While this work has clear innovatory potential, it stops short of a fuller consideration of pragmatic and semiotic dimensions which are crucial to the dynamics of communication.

As discussed above, it is well recognized that Shannon's classical work, *The Mathematical Theory of Communication*, suffered from 'semantic poverty' – a failure to deal with the semantic dimensions of information (although one should of course bear in mind that this was not his intention either). Dretske's semantic theory of information/communication (he uses the terms interchangeably) pursues the following aims:

1. The explanation of the 'cognitive importance of information'.
2. The uncovering of the connection between information and truth.
3. An understanding of the 'source (the intentionality of natural laws) of the *semantic* character of information'.

Two key normative attitudes emerge from this programme: knowledge and truth. Information is defined as 'something capable of yielding knowledge' (Dretske, 1999: 45). In consequence, since knowledge requires truth, so does information. Information points ineluctably to truth. It is the embeddedness of information in truth claims that 'relativizes' (Dretske's term) information, for how much information a signal contains 'depends on what the potential receiver knows about the various possibilities that exist at source' (Dretske, 1999: 79); knowledge of those possibilities is bound by truth. Moreover, the receiver's evaluation of that information is carried out against the background of 'communally shared knowledge' (1999: 80); 'common frame of knowledge is understood' (1999: 80). The intermonadological fallacy raises its head once more. Thus Dretske proposes a normative interpretation of information that distinguishes between information that is true and knowledge yielding and other forms of information, which, by implication, are neither true nor knowledge yielding. This normative dichotomy gives rise to the strong claim that false information is no information ('At least I had given you no information of the kind I purported to be giving' [1999: 44].) and that '*mis*-information' is no more information than 'decoy ducks and rubber ducks are kinds of ducks'. This truth–theoretical interpretation of information of course not only sustains epistemological bivalence (the distinction between true and false), but also makes assumptions about our ability to distinguish between sincerity and insincerity, dissimulation and transparency as if communications were diaphanous. If, as Dretske argues, reliable information is a tautology, then he marks a clear departure from Shannon's entropy theory and the embeddedness of uncertainty in information. Even leaving aside such relatively counter-intuitive arguments, intuitively we know that any information can yield knowledge, depending on what the receiver makes of it. This is precisely why the normatively constrained version of information stops the dynamic of communication in its tracks. Whether false or untruthful or truthful, information communicates. A broken promise is an act of communication. A further problem with Dretske's normative information theory is that it leaves little – if any – room for human agency, isolating the information source from its semiotic and pragmatic subsequent enrichment/distortion/misrepresentation/loosening etc. etc:

> [...] it makes no difference if one person knows that the signal he is receiving is reliable and the other does not. As long as the signal *is* reliable, whether or not it is *known* to be reliable, I_s (r), the information reaching the receiver about the source equals I (s), the amount of information generated at the source.
>
> (Dretske, 1999: 81)[6]

Dretske's truth–theoretic information theory excludes factors beyond the semantic. The signal is rendered inert, cut off from pragmatic and semiotic processes which generate uncertainty which in turn feeds communication forward. Dretske interestingly refers to the notion of a 'nesting relation' where 'nested information' conveys recognition that it is inappropriate to refer to a singular informational content – a recognition then of the contextualized nature of any signal. There are two types of nesting relations: analytical and nomic (truth-oriented). Nomic dependencies are lawful relations – they 'determine the amount of information [...] flows between two points [...]' (Dretske, 1999: 75):

> The ultimate source of the intentionality inherent in the transmission and receipt of information is, of course, the *nomic regularities* on which the transmission of information depends. The transmission of information requires, not simply a set of de facto correlations, but a network of nomic dependences between the condition at the source and the properties of the signal.
>
> (Dretske, 1999: 76–7)

Contentism (the need for a shift from the form of communication to the information content of communication Dretske proposes)[7] is a coherent part of this inert communication model.

While Dretske concedes that '[t]here is seldom, if ever, noiseless communication' (Dretske, 1999: 20), his truth–theoretical epistemicism leads him to an implausible account of what he describes frequently as the *transmission* process (the term in itself is indicative of a problematic view of communication as a dynamic). In this context, the key 'regulative principle' is the Xerox Principle, according to which 'If *A* carries the information that *B*, and *B* carries the information that *C*, then *A* carries the information that *C*' (Dretske, 1999: 57). Xerox is 'fundamental to the flow of information' (Dretske, 1999: 58) – not a narrow identity between source and reception but the assumption that 'enough information [is preserved] about the preceding link to keep the message intact according to the xerox principle'. And yet even this concession – this recognition of the unmarked residuum in communication – fails to resolve the core problem satisfactorily. As 'contents' are communicated and uncertainty increases through semiotic recontextualizations and pragmatic negotiation (as receivers process and therefore change the signals), the message becomes an unstable category. It is less the message that is kept intact than the communication. Dretske also argues that no correlation, no amount of dependency is necessary between source and receiver for the 'transmission of a message' (Dretske, 1999: 59). Thus for the communication of a message/content, one needs all the information associated with that content since 'Getting a message' is like being pregnant – there are no partial messages:

> [T]he information is either transmitted in toto or it is not transmitted at all: It does not make sense to speak of transmitting 99 percent of the information *that* it is raining.
>
> (Dretske, 1999: 60)

The receiver of the signal may be more *interested* in one piece of information than he is in any other, he may succeed in *extracting* one piece of information without another, but these differences are *irrelevant* to the information the signal contains.

(Dretske, 1999: 72 – emphasis added)[8]

Criticism of the semantic poverty of Shannon's model (see also Baecker, 1999a/b) which betrays its origins in information engineering, is of clear relevance to social communication theory. However, the deficiency of Shannon's model in terms of any use in the human and social sciences is not its syntactical bias, since Shannon deliberately set out to examine discrete sources. The problem is that if, as Luhmann argues, the signs we use to communicate are contingent, then semantics are not predetermined by structures, but also by the symbolic function of those structures in the constantly renegotiated contexts of subjects, institutions, systems or societies.

In a more complex communication model, which goes beyond the discrete characters Shannon had in mind, semantics cannot be ignored. Equally, communication as a social operation cannot be reduced to semantic or semanticist models and it must integrate the uncertainties of semiotic and pragmatic dimensions of communication agents. In Luhmann's terms, 'each participant knows for himself and of others that fixed forms of linguistic meaning are selected contingently' (Luhmann, 1997: 1.211). In telegraphy, noise is a disturbance in the channel, which the information engineer sets out to resolve. In social communication theory, noise is introduced by the dynamic uncertainties of communicative relations with the addressee(s), since cognitive autonomy means that signs can only ever operate as an appeal. Since this relation introduces uncertainty, communication can be said to be uncertain; 'messages' are always unstable.

Building, mutatis mutandis, on the information-theoretical distinction between meaning and information and constructivist insights, the concept of communicative porosity is introduced here in greater detail not only as a refinement of informational entropy and 'structural' accounts of the infinite iterability of language (see Derrida, 2000), but also as a critique of transcendentalist accounts based on intersubjectivity, consensus or dialogue. In order to illustrate the interdisciplinary utility of the concept of porosity and its connections with theories of vagueness, this section will briefly reconstruct its current usage in those fields in which it most frequently occurs. These fields appear remote at first sight. The concept of porosity is predominantly encountered in studies of porous media in geophysics and biology. In geophysical analysis:

> [A] porous medium is defined as a portion of space that is occupied partly by a persistent solid phase (= the solid matrix) and partly by a void space, the latter being occupied by one or more fluid phases.
> (Bear and Bachmat, 1984: 5)

Since the concept cannot be crudely imported from the geophysical modelling of porous media into reflections on social communication, it will be necessary to consider some of these physical properties before returning to communication processes. In other words, a simple operation in analogy[9] is not proposed here. Rather, the aim is to explore the use of the concept in terms of its formal and epistemological implications. It is important to observe that in a porous medium, solid and fluid properties interact. In terms of biological dynamics, the classic example of a porous structure is thus a membrane or open isothermal lattice system.

It would be wrong, however, to see the proposed focus on uncertainty as a denial in shape or form of social cohesion or communication. Rather, the intention is to work towards a theoretical model which is more sensitive to deep complexity and does not presume stability of interactions, relationships, conventions, rules, institutions or systems. There are thus similarities between the relationship between the solid matrix and fluid phase in geophysics and the biological dynamics of an open lattice system such as a membrane. In a theory of social systems, systems operate to preserve their stability despite the potential degeneration caused by uncertainty. To this end, institutions are endowed with codes or discourses and semantics. Semantics operate as stabilizers of vague signs: 'Languages enable us to codify the relation between the uncertainty and the meaning of a message (that can be expected to contain the information)'(Leydesdorff, 2001: 42).

In social communications systems uncertainty is recursively fed back into the system for the purposes of stabilization. Since they are actually defined by communications, social systems are environmentally open and thus remain sensitive to environmental instabilities, such as challenges from legislatures, coups d'état, public opinion or inadvertent leaks or even mendacious gossip. Instabilities are reduced by closed and self-referential semantics which orientate meanings for social actors (see Luhmann, 1997; Schmidt, 1994b). But these very self-referential semantics are also subject to uncertainty: nothing offers warranty for their survival other than their functionality as communications. This explains why social systems come and go in terms of the utility of their functioning (cf. also Baecker, 1999b: 52–9).

In terms of form then, the concept of porosity in communication-theoretical terms thus signifies an environmentally open hybrid state and dynamic process which in turn makes the operational closure of systems highly unstable. Examples of hybridity in communication terms can be seen as intertextuality, the confluence of private and public discourses, hacking, viral and virtual communication and so forth (cf. the varying accounts of Lacan, 1975; Luhmann, 1997; Baecker, 1999b; Derrida, 2000). Porous communication consists of a solid matrix which ranges from syntactical constraints to complex social codes, and a void space. In this void space, signs are vague, cognitive processes unique and contexts indeterminate. Thus, the concept of porosity implies the contingency of structure and the contingency of interactions with a fluid environment. In communication, the void space is not occupied by fluid phases, but by silence, and such silence is paradoxically part of communication. And yet porosity is more complex than Baecker's ambivalence concept and is also a much more contingent concept than the structurally defined notion of iterability as the capacity for written language to be continually repeated and modified. Derrida is more concerned with the structure of writing:

> My communication must be repeatable – iterable – in the absolute absence of the receiver or of any empirically determinable collectivity of receivers. Such iterability – (iter, again, probably comes from itara, other in Sanskrit, and everything that follows can be read as the working out of the logic that ties repetition to alterity) structures the mark of writing itself, no matter what particular type of writing is involved [...].
>
> (Derrida, 2000: 7)

For an analysis of porosity as a generally valid description of form, it is worth recalling Hegel's reflections on the same concept in the *Science of Logic* (1812). In Section Two on Appearance, Hegel provides a formal analysis of the Thing into which Matters 'circulate freely'. Furthermore, the determinateness of this Thing renders it, at the same time, dissoluble where dissolution is an external process of being determined (Hegel, 1976: 494). The Thing is an interrelation of its constituent matters – the one and the others, the self-related matters which are matters in relation to and by distinction to each other. There is, in the identity of the Thing, what Hegel calls interpenetration. Here, since the Thing is the 'also' of others, and the matters are determinate in themselves; they are 'indifferent' to each other and 'do not touch one another' (Hegel, 1976: 495). This is a description of the Thing as 'absolute porosity' – the interrelation of form and non-form:

> This thing has the two determinations of being first, this thing, and secondly, the 'also.' The 'also' is that which presents itself in external intuition as spatial extension; but the 'this', the negative unity, is the puncticity of the thing. [...] Therefore where one of these matters is, the other also is, in one and the same point; the thing does not have its colour in one place, its odorific matter in another, its heat matter in a third, and so on. Now because these matters are not outside one another but are one in 'this', they are assumed to be porous, so that one exists in the interstices of the other. But that which is present in the interstices of the other matter is itself porous; conversely, therefore, in its pores the other exists [...].
>
> (Hegel, 1976: 496)

The concept of porosity is directly related to the concept of entropy. Whereas the concept of entropy is a useful starting point in the study of uncertainty, it arose in information theory in engineering which was uncoupled from the agents of uncertainty. Porosity, by contrast, extends to the relations between speakers in the complexity of communication in an environment of noise. The role of the agents of communicative uncertainty is crucial. In terms of social communication theory, the use of the entropy concept – the uncertainty in communication as a source of information – implies that society builds on unstable or, in Derrida's terms, polycontextual structures (see also the definition of polycontexturality in Luhmann, 1997.1: 36f.).

5. From referential semantics to self-reference: implications for communication

The contingency of communication or its multiple risk factors one might say, also makes the notion of fixity of reference – or vagueness in a semiotic sense – problematic. While for Hilary Putnam, the 'reference is fixed by the fact that that individual is causally linked to other individuals' (Putnam, 1997: 203), there have been recent attempts from within the realist tradition to introduce greater instability without jettisoning referential semantics. For example, François Recanati's conception of 'semantic potential' argues that expressions can be applied to a 'real situations'. The problem remains that instability is destined to be underexplored if a realist epistemology is pursued. Thus, attempts to reconcile referential theories of reference to an external reality with polysemy achieve little in terms of a theory of complex social communication. Recanati (2004: 7) also refers to the 'gappiness' of pragmatic operations where the gaps are closed by the pragmatic engagement of the hearer. There are two such pragmatic processes: primary processes involved in the 'determination of what is said' and secondary processes as 'ordinary inferential processes which take us from what is said' to what is entailed by what is said (Recanati, 2004: 17). Another pragmatic process is free enrichment or specification of context as a pragmatic process which is not actually triggered linguistically. Other pragmatic processes not triggered linguistically include loosening (the application is contextually dropped) and semantic transfer (where the output is a different concept to that concept expressed by the input) (Recanati, 2004: 24–6).

Thus, Recanati challenges the semantic minimalist or invariantist view that semantic interpretation can deliver something determinate as a complete proposition, arguing instead that that interpretation can only deliver semantic schemata that require pragmatic contextualization.

> [...] Whenever there is semantic underdeterminacy, some form of pragmatic disambiguation must take place before the process of semantic interpretation can start.
>
> (Recanati, 2004: 57)

There is a clear connection between Recanati's concept of pragmatic gappiness (see chapter three) and underdeterminacy which is needed to take account of the fact that there is more to an utterance than discrete manifestation or 'ostensive stimuli' (Carston, 2002: 11). Her Underdeterminacy Thesis comprises three sub-theses, namely that: 'Linguistic meaning underdetermines what is meant', 'What is said underdetermines what is meant' and 'Linguistic meaning underdetermines what is said' (2002: 19). While the underdeterminacy thesis is a much more plausible contextualist account of pragmatic interaction, it also points to the mistaken view that contextualism is epistemologically radical. Indeed, for all the effort expended on a theory of underdeterminacy, the default epistemology is still the intermonadological fallacy. There is, as Carston argues, a 'mental interaction of speaker and hearer' (2002: 3). In other words, underdeterminacy does not equate to indeterminacy (no determination of the 'fact of the matter'); underdeterminacy means merely that the proposition 'cannot be determined by linguistic meaning alone' (Carston, 2002: 20–1) but will be determined by pragmatic extensions.

The argument put forward here is that even pragmatic extensions or enrichments cannot determine the proposition. One could argue that the semantically underdetermined utterance is a porous form of marked communication form and unmarked pragmatic processes of interpretation, disambiguation, selection, inferencing and so on.

A more radical paradigm shift was introduced by constructivist thinkers. It was the shift from reference to self-reference which encapsulates the implications of the fundamental shift in the theories of Luhmann and S.J. Schmidt. If, as von Foerster and the constructivists in general suggest, objectivity is a fiction, in the sense that it is the construction of an observer and not an ontological category, then the notion of reference (to what?, to whom?) becomes problematic. The observer does not make contact with the external world, but instead processes it internally. In simplified terms, it can be said that cognition (internal processing) is an operation in which the subject processes his environment by reference to his own prior knowledge and not by approximation to the 'reality'.

If cognition is in this sense a self-referential operation as opposed to one in which reference is made to an external reality, then this means communication with others occurs, as it were, despite the relative closure of cognitive processes. If cognition is indeed closed, in the sense that there can be no 'contact' between one mind and another, or indeed between one mind and 'reality' by means other than uncertain communications, then interaction should be reconceptualized to take account of such closure. For reasons of cognitive self-reference or 'closure', therefore, communicative interaction can be more adequately viewed as a precarious process. There are several dimensions to this precariousness.

As noted above, in terms of social theory, Luhmann provides a link between social communication theory and the implications of the shift from referential models to self-referential models of systems:

> Societies are a special case of self-referential systems. They presuppose a network of communications, previous communications and further communications and also communications that happen elsewhere. Communications are possible only within a system of communication and this system cannot escape the form of recursive circularity. Its basic events, the single units of communication, are units only by reference to other units within the same system. In consequence, only the structure of this system and not its environment can specify the meaning of communications.
>
> (Luhmann, 1990: 145–6)

According to this view, communications do not establish a connection with external reality, but recursively construct communications networks. Recursivity implies feedback, which implies redundancy and redundancy creates meaning (conventions are a classic case of the self-reference of communication codes where meaning is constructed from within, as it were). The recursivity of communication which Luhmann sees as being central to society requires closure upon itself. The cognitive autonomy it implies does not send us sliding down a slope into social atomism (see von Glasersfeld in Schmidt, 1994b) since social actors communicate by means of operative fictions of collective knowledge. The term fiction is used here since it is only ever collective knowledge as a social construction in which the cognitive autonomy of social actors is communalized. On the other hand:

> Meaning [...] is a completely open structure, excluding nothing, not even the negation of meanings. As systems of meaning-based communication societies are closed and open systems. They gain their openness by closure.
>
> (Luhmann, 1990: 146–7)

If entropy, as a correlate of the free enrichments of the autonomous homo communicans is inherent in communication, how can this entropy be reduced or stabilized as functional communication without denying freedom or pathologizing allegedly abnormal discourses as parasitic? If communication is indeed so precarious and fictions are all we have, how does society hold together? (cf. also Grant, 2001: 55). Even where communicative or discourse-theoretical approaches are adopted, the result of the amalgamation of Husserlian intersubjectivity, Mead's 'other-directedness' and Schütz and Luckmann's 'stock of common knowledge' is a modelling of communicative interaction in which the taking of another's perspective is reified and actors become 'entangled' in the perspective of the other. This entanglement is at variance with the modified constructivist approach set out above and induces positions which do not move far beyond intuitive transcendentalism – or the belief 'that in everyday life the environment I perceive and grasp is perceived and grasped similarly by fellow-beings endowed with a consciousness "essentially similar to my own"' (Graumann, 1995: 15).

As a consequence, mutuality is modelled as probabilistic despite a certain willingness to see interaction or mutuality as fraught with risk (Graumann, 1995: 17). However, this thesis is problematic since the features of instability and uncertainty outlined above – cognitive autonomy, vague semiotics and the unstable or polycontextual character of communication – render a dialogically modelled interaction model based on reciprocity impossible. A more plausible model in the communication and cognition terms developed above is provided by

Albrecht Wellmer's fallibilism[10] thesis, albeit in a discussion of truth and consensus. If communication is a fundamentally unstable process, then interactions take place in a world of communication contingencies with implications for social stability:

> We cannot ever rule out the emergence of new experiences, new arguments and new reasons which could require us to question or abandon truth claims held to be secure: a context-transcending concept of truth cannot therefore be founded in the terms of a theory of consensus, but instead only in fallibilistic terms.
>
> (Wellmer, 1992: 23–4 – my translation)

Jürgen Habermas argues that social actors are able to overcome the contingency or locality of their experiences by raising counterfactual validity claims (Habermas, 1999b: 26). Whereas it is certainly true that society reduces contingency in order to operate, a dualism is implied in the counterfactual concept (as an alternative to factuality). The frontier between the factual and what Habermas terms the counterfactual must be blurred since both are observer dependent; and if it is blurred, then we have no notion of the counterfactual and instead only different levels of construction (see also Wellmer, 1992: 30). This is the essential difference between realist concepts of counterfactual ideals and constructivist concepts of fictional constructions.

6. Conclusions

Some would argue that to see language and cognition as contingent and coupled only by fictions is to open a door beyond which descends a slippery slope of relativism and social atomism. And yet the concepts of cognitive autonomy, fictionality, vague reference and communicative uncertainty can be reconciled with social stability without recourse to dialogism, intersubjectivity and transcendental consensus. Any attempt to model communication as resolved or stable in pragmatic, cognitive or epistemological terms is destined: (1) to deny contingency and (2) neglect uncertainty and their precarious negotiation in communicative interaction. To recognize uncertainty in communication is not a recipe for relativism or anarchy. It is a conceptualization of a new form of subjectively negotiated normativity in which operative or functional fictions unmask the way in which norms actually undergo construction. Where normativity is seen as a rational predisposition or linguistically mediated transcendental lifeworld, its construction is already partially resolved. Where constructibility is emphasized, resolution is observed as a process. Existing interactionist paradigms, referential semantics, bivalent vagueness theories or universal pragmatics cannot adequately demonstrate the contingency of such constructions. Instead, if contingency is to be taken seriously in theoretical terms, there is a real need for a theory of uncertainty in communication rooted in a plausible account of vague reference, cognitive self-reference, the porous form of communication and the ongoing discursive renewal without which society cannot operate.

6
The Communicating Subject

L'unité avec autrui est donc, en fait, irréalisable.
—Jean-Paul Sartre, *L'Etre et le Néant*, 1986: 415

1. *Homo communicans?*

As we have seen, in *Social Structure and Semantics*, Niklas Luhmann argued that Enlightenment thinkers had extrapolated a general theory of society from idealized, face-to-face encounters in which reason would take shape and influence power. And yet, at the same time, the reciprocity implied in the powerful new paradigm of interaction was strangely at variance with a society increasingly driven by the functional needs of the economy in which reciprocity was disappearing. The semantic of interaction, thus, emerged in *deferred state* from the outset: given the conflict between social interactions and functional economic needs, an interactive model of society could only be proposed *counterfactually*. As a result, social theory retreated into what Luhmann (1993: 122) called *commonality*. Commonality is a concept based on nostalgia for an age of putative reciprocity and unity, and like the related concepts, common sense and its latter-day equivalent, intersubjectivity, is a paradox. Its thematization started as its prospects receded from view. Judith Butler brings this paradox neatly into view. For Butler, the Kantian rational subject and the concept of a 'transpersonal rationality' 'culminates in the claim that my reasoning presupposes the universalizability of my claim' (Butler, 2000: 15).

Let us take this powerful counterfactual further. The concept of rational interaction inherited from the semantic of interaction is accompanied by both weak and strong claims. According to the strong claim, interaction is synonymous with generalized modes of interaction, and often conceptualized as dialogue, exchange of meaning or even intersubjectivity. The broad aim of this chapter is to propose a theory of the communicating subject, which is at least designed to go beyond the semantic of interaction in Luhmann's critique and to consider the implications for the subject in this process. Here, I adopt the conventional separation of the self as a 'singular inner being' and a person as a 'socially defined, publicly visible embodied being' (Harré, 1983: 26); by contrast, the 'subject' is the epistemic confluence of both inner and social self and person with clear agentic properties. The central argument presented here is that, however defined, some prevailing conceptualizations of the communicating self remain within the semantic of interaction and need to deal more adequately with complex human communication. It is not sufficient to resolve the problem of solipsism which so exercised Husserl by invoking the intermonadological community or intersubjectivity as the solution of the problem.

2. Dialogue and dialogism

Where the 'semantic of interaction' concerns the counterfactually reciprocal code of social interaction and communication at the level of society. The modern-day understanding of the concept of dialogue, predicated on exchange and interaction, suggests duality and relationality and characterizes everyday expectations of the dialogical character of communication. In one of the most influential early accounts, George Herbert Mead put it thus:

> Meaning arises and lies within the field of the relation between the gesture of a given human organism and the subsequent behaviour of this organism as indicated to another human organism by that gesture.
>
> (Mead, 1967: 75–6)

The concept of dialogism which has evolved under Bakhtin's influence as an epistemology of discourse and society is not simply a description of communication dyads, but is a far more extensive programme – a 'general epistemology for cognition and communication' (Linell, 1998: xi). In simplified terms, dialogism claims to have resolved solipsism and can thus place monologism, and its emphasis on linear communicative transmission from speaker to hearer, with a model of interaction in which actors are 'mutually co-present' (Linell, 1998: 13). Where classical theories of dialogue viewed interactions through the prism of symmetry, reciprocity and freedom from coercion, dialogism is potentially more sensitive to such interactive features as hedges, vagueness and polyvocality:

> As an empirically grounded model of communication, such a view of dialogue based entirely on symmetry and equality would be unfruitful and counterfactual. In a modern empirical, yet dialogistic approach to discourse, another kind of definition of 'dialogue' seems more appropriate; 'any interaction through language (or other symbolic means) between two or several individuals who are mutually co-present' (cf. Luckmann, 1990).
>
> (Linell, 1998: 13)

However, dialogism assumes that shared realities are given which makes the notion of the autonomous mind a monological one; it also implies a 'thinking out loud together', 'cognition in practice', 'socially shared cognition' or 'distributed cognition' (Linell, 1998: 21). Two preliminary criticisms can be made at this point. On the one hand, dialogism, strongly influenced by the work of the Bakhtin circle, rightly acknowledges the multivoicedness of communication environments. However, while refuting the separation of cognition from communication, the uncertainties of that multivoicedness, in terms of cognition, communication and environments, are neutralized without justification under the horizon of an intermonadological community by means of the assertion of sharedness. The consequences of multivoicedness are at least threefold: (1) speakers and hearers are cognitively or *internally* 'dialogical'; (2) speakers and hearers are communicatively multivoiced; (3) speakers and hearers are ecologically distributed. In other words, the dialogical constitution of the self is an internal constitution rather than a mapping of an intersubjective orientation onto shared social positions. In addition, when engaged in communication, this internal dialogism is articulated or played out with other, internally dialogical actors. This makes shared meaning, let alone access to intentions or transparent, somehow noise-free communication, illusory. And were these factors of uncertainty insufficient in themselves, the fact that the cognitive or communicative context of our utterance is never fully the context of the hearer's utterance and the fact that these contexts of communication are multiply mediated (the rumour e-mailed to all staff on an office list), means that uncertainty interrupts any notion of sharedness. This account of uncertainty issues a number of challenges to the epistemology of intersubjectivity and dialogism.

The (rather Messianic[1]) affirmation that cognition is in some way socially shared short-circuits this multiplicity of voices. If communication and cognition are interrelated processes, then a multiplicity of voices must be accompanied by a multiplicity of minds. Thus, dialogism is not an ontology, and intersubjectivity cannot be 'achieved' as some kind of external aim, as if it were some kind of corrective to the solipsistic tendencies of the subject. This engineering approach to dialogue is frequently encountered in the literature. The communication of separate cognitive actors requires a conceptualization of uncertainty which dialogism, disappointingly, is not prepared to recognize:

> [...] dialogism would stress the interaction of the mind with the physical and social environment in all the activities of perception (intake), cognition and understanding (processing), remembering, and of course, a fortiori, overt interpersonal communication. These cannot be seen and understood in terms of information processing within autonomous minds.
>
> (Linell, 1998: 21)

Linell's dialogism rests on a realist social constructionism (with its emphasis on 'discourse as the vehicle through which self and world are articulated' [Gergen, 1999: 60]) and is distinguished from 'radical social constructionism' or 'radical interactionism'. The shortcoming of radical views (and here, Linell seems to conflate constructivism and constructionism) lies in its alleged lack of context: he maintains a belief in the existence of realities 'out there', stating that to see realities as the product of discursive construction is to remove context from communication and interaction (Linell, 1998: 52). In summary: 'constructivism conjures up individualistic ideas: the individual constructing his or her reality without a social context' (Linell, 1998: 59). And yet the key point is precisely that the social context is not some intersubjective construct and is entirely compatible with a view of the self as being cognitively closed. Communication is necessary as the means by which communication (i.e. social) contexts are created amongst autonomous actors and despite their irreducible self-reference. Moreover, while the critique of monologism and stability in theories of dialogism is pertinent, the definition of 'dialogue' as any interaction practice based on mutual co-presence is so wide as to suggest the risk of conceptual generalities. All too often in dialogistic approaches, interaction processes are conceptualized in such a way as to impose stability on communication.

3. Minds and communication

In social psychological and social therapeutic applications of dialogism, Hubert Hermans (2001) has set out to conceptualize the self as neither individualized nor self-contained. One key theoretical influence is the work of William James and in particular his distinction between the self as knower (the 'I') and the self as known (the 'Me') and the concept of the extended self, a self extending into an environment of relevant relationships. The extended self reaches beyond a self/other dualism, bringing the 'other' inside (Hermans, 2001; 245). The use of the other major influence, Bakhtin, is much less convincing (he is referred to as Bakhtin the literary theorist), since the theory of the dialogical self focuses on Bakhtin's literary concept of polyphony developed in *Problems of Dostoevsky's Poetics*. However, even without a fuller appreciation of Bakhtin's theory as a foundational epistemological one, the metaphor of multivoicedness remains relevant, if flawed. James's view that the various dimensions of the self vie with each other is coupled to polyphony understood as the novelistic multitude of characters. Despite creating this coupling between James and Bakhtin, Hermans highlights at least one salient difference in emphasis, namely James's conviction that the self was both discontinuous and continuous or unified through the force of the unifying 'volitional I', whereas Bakhtin's multivoicedness tends to challenge that very unity by 'decentralizing' it (Hermans, 2001: 248–9). The dialogical self is conceptualized as the 'dynamic multiplicity of relatively autonomous *I*-positions', combining a Jamesian continuity and a

Bakhtinian, contextually sensitive if not actually contextually constituted discontinuity or decentralization – 'they represent different
and perhaps opposed voices' (Hermans, (2001: 249). These relatively
autonomous positions can be internal (I as father), external (my
father) or outside the subjective horizon of the self:

> The dialogical self is 'social', not in the sense that a self-contained
> individual enters into social interactions with other *outside* peo-
> ple, but in the sense that other people occupy positions in a mul-
> tivoiced self.
>
> (Hermans, 2001: 250)

This view is distinguished from Mead's classical account of 'taking
the attitude of the other', resting instead on the assumption that the
other occupies a position into which the self can move. The theory
of the dialogical self assumes an intertwining of 'inter-psychological'
and 'intra-psychological' processes (Hermans, 2001: 255).[2] Dialogical
interaction is thus understood as communication in which the isolation of the subject is resolved; the idea that the mind is somehow
closed is simply 'solipsistic hell'. In place of this infernal solipsism is the
human who comes to awareness of himself 'in our dialogue with other
selves' (Friedman, 1992: 23; 5). Thus, 'individuality' is always contextualized by the 'ontology of the between' inspired by Martin Buber:

> [...] when two persons 'happen' to each other, the essential remain-
> der that is common to them reaches out beyond the special sphere
> of each. That remainder is the basic reality, the 'sphere of the
> between'.
>
> (Friedman, 1992: 3–4)

In this account, reality is disconnected from the subject and located in
a transcendental sphere of dialogue, a 'whole communal reality' or 'the
reality that is given to us' (Friedman, 1992: 42; 18). Thus, the fruitful
theoretical description of the multiply voiced self and the radical
potential of Bakhtin's and Hermans's work is undercut by two foundational assumptions about the social and the epistemological. On the
one hand, the dialogical self is a social self by virtue of its multiple constitution (where external selves occupy positions in our selves) while on
the other, an assumption is made about an interpsychological sharing

of knowledge. Consider the view that 'meaningful dialogue' assumes 'a certain degree of common understanding of the other and his or her world' with a 'misunderstanding as a possibility' caused by 'faulty assumptions' (Hermans, 2001: 256–7). Thus, the descriptive breakthrough is ultimately blocked by a theory of knowledge which assumes the possibility of intersubjective sharing – or the 'intersubjective intertwining of minds' and the 'amazing' regulatory capacity of the self amidst multivoicedness (Hermans, 2002: 147). The intermonadological fallacy remains unsolved.

Both social constructionists and radical constructivists provide useful critiques of such an account rooted in the intermonadological fallacy. For Gergen (1999: 60) meaning is an 'emergent property of co-ordinated action'. Radical constructivists also see social interaction in terms of a complex coupling of autonomous subjects by means of assumptions and imputations, meaning that cognitive closure and social communication, as an uncertain enterprise, go hand in hand. Understanding cannot be reduced to a world in which identities merge or fuse in mutuality or intersubjectivity and for both constructionists and radical constructivists the relation between mind and communication is complex. For Gergen (Gergen, 1999: 147), 'social understanding is not a matter of penetrating the privacy of the other's subjectivity', whereas for Schmidt (Schmidt, 1995: 322–3), as we have seen, understanding is the contingent, fictional construction across unique minds by communicative means. This theory of fiction is not to be confused with the concept of the 'fictional self' (see Elster, 1995) where the self is related to daydreaming or vicarious experience and therefore close to an understanding of fiction as a non-reality rather than fiction as 'reality' construction. Since for Gergen and Schmidt communication is seen in terms of the impenetrability of the mind of the other, transcendental claims raised with dialogism, the theory of the dialogical self, universal pragmatics and theories of intersubjectivity can be dropped in favour of detranscendentalized claims. Detranscendentalization means recognition that communication is contingent on contingencies – that minds, texts and environments can, as Luhmann said, always mean something different. The view adopted here does not attach private interpretations necessarily to collective interpretations, but argues instead for recognition of the vague residuum which persists between the private and the public or between the self and the person. Finally, the notion of shared knowledge can be seen in terms of the separateness of minds and as a functional or operative social fiction (see Schmidt, e.g. 1994b, 2001):

> Kant solved the problem of the connection between empirical (in the sense of subjectively experiential) and transcendent worlds by referring to the role played by heuristic fictions. Such fictions set up regulatory principles of the systematic use of reason used in the problematic conceptualization of objects considered possible. They operate here as the discourses in society that enable subjects or actors or individuals to communicate their constructions.
>
> (Grant, 2000: 12–13)

Even where there is recognition of the fact that the self must deal with complexity, it seems that the real complexities of multivoicedness are neutralized in the semantic of interaction and related dialogical theories. The commitment to stability and transcendence resolve from the outset contingencies of cognition and communication. And yet, it is possible to connect contingency to social stability as the societies in which we live demonstrate. Even if one were prepared to accept that the self really is intertwined, then it is not with other minds but with other voices in the sense proposed by Bakhtin. And this multivoicedness should not be seen in terms of a *normative stability* where conflicts, miscommunication and dissonance are *resolved*. If the self is enveloped in Bakhtin's 'mist of heteroglossia', then its communicative environment is multivoiced or hybrid. Contingency and complexity rather than intersubjectivity are the mark of communication of communicating subjects. Mead himself (1913: 377) offered a radical insight into the contingencies of the self in communication, where the self is 'a fusion of the remembered actor and this accompanying chorus' of others in society. This chorus is less harmonic than cacophonous, however and indeed Mead describes it (1913: 378) as 'different voices in conflict with each other'. In this connection, Mead's conceptualization of the self as growing 'out of a partial disintegration' (1913: 379–80) is a radical insight which is further pursued here with reference to communication and its impact on the self.

The insight that the subject acts amidst a chorus of conflicting voices and is therefore exposed to disintegrating or decentering forces is close to the theory put forward here, namely, (1) that the relationship between self and others is contingent upon communication (and this is admittedly a weak claim) and (2) that it is not transcendentally resolved by communication (and this is a stronger claim). In this sense, there is no room here for an acceptance of Mead's concept of communicability. It is worth recalling that for Mead (1967: 397), meanings require two characters: participation and communicability, where communicability derives from participation in that the individual can indicate to himself what he indicates to others. Meaning can only come about if participation is enabled and this means that 'some phrase of the act which the individual is arousing in the other can be aroused in himself'. Of greater significance in the current context is the connection Mead established between such participation and communicability. On the one hand, the participation character is not necessarily problematic since communication makes a difference. On the other, however, the communicability thesis is contentious: the individual may well be able to indicate to himself what he indicates to others, provided the individual is the perceiver of the indications. But in communications, perceivers or speakers can never know how the sign is being received, or what is being aroused. There is a communication gap – a pore – a *radical appeal to an interpretation that cannot be determined and flies in the face of intentions*. Where communication is a porous form of selected message and redundancy, there is a need to explore the unmarked spaces of communication, the interstices or gaps, the unspoken languages 'no-one has ever spoken or will ever speak'.

Baecker argues that communication is the 'determination of the indeterminate but determinable with the aim of understanding the determinate' (Baecker, 2005: 23). The indeterminacy of the range of communication options we have at our disposal in different cultures, different languages, different media and different social roles is not actually determinable at all. The porous form of communication actually means that even when we think we choose a clear, stable form, the penumbra of unselected communication remains. The relationship between the form of our communications and their non-forms is irreducibly dynamic. We communicate in order to accompany the dynamic of our interactions with the world. To be communicable is not to be determinable.

4. Opening intersubjectivity: Davidson on intersubjectivity and 'Interpretability'

The appeal to being capable of interpretation is all that remains. As Davidson argued in *Subjective – Intersubjective – Objective*, the key to communication – *being interpretable* – and the interpretations of self and other are irreducibly different. However, speakers are 'locked into a social nexus' which guarantees the 'objectivity of my beliefs' in a 'community of free selves' (2001: 91). While the self is irreducible and the individual the 'ultimate arbiter' of thought, that thought is inter-subjectively and thus also objectively embedded. Davidson argues further that the concept of the self can only come into being in relation to others and that means communication. There are three kinds of knowledge: knowledge of the objective world, knowledge of the contents of my mind and 'knowledge of the minds of others' (2001: 87). Davidson cannot do without a leap of faith across a divide that remains with subjects every time they take the risk to communicate. Interpretability means more than connected with self-reference, appeal and autonomy where there cannot be knowledge of other minds, motives or intentions:

> hearers have little access to what people have in mind apart from the interpretation of what they say. So interpretation would be a problem that hearers could not solve if they had to know what a speaker intended in order to identify the content of the context.
>
> (C. Gauker, MS, 2006: 7–8)

From within the philosophical tradition, Davidson plausibly notes that there is no satisfactory explanation of the 'asymmetry' between first and other person attributions of attitudes. The interpretation of an utterance 'cannot be the same for the utterer and his hearers' (2001: 12); there can admittedly be a move towards what appears to be a convergence, but this depends on 'clues to interpretation' (2001: 13); *interpretability* is the key to meaning. At first sight, interpretability seems to invite radical reflection, since to be interpretable is to be (interpretable) in the eyes and to the ears of *alter*. And yet Davidson's account is wedded to rationalism, for the interpretable self, so apparently open to the other, is locked into a social nexus 'that assures the objectivity if not the correctness of my beliefs' (Davidson, 2001: 91). This is a decidedly uneasy attempt at reconciliation between the self and the social which leads Davidson to adopt what appears to be a weak definition of intersubjectivity[3] (as interaction) and at the same time to assert that we exchange 'private notes' in our interactions: 'It is here that each person, each mind or self, reveals itself as part of a community of free selves' (Davidson, 2001: 91):

> Belief, intention, and the other propositional attitudes are all social in that they are states a creature cannot be in without having the concept of intersubjective truth and this is a concept one cannot have without sharing, and knowing that one shares, a world, and a way of thinking about the world, with someone else.
>
> (Davidson, 2001: 121)

Davidson's account, despite its intuitive appeal, is given a more radical translation here. Asymmetry, interpretability, the private character of our notes and the constitution of a community of free selves and a commitment to intentional interpretability as opposed to shared meaning suggest a radical reading of communications which could cast off the heavy weight of an intersubjective community. Davidson's criticism of Putnam on meaning is plausible here: two speakers must be understood by each other but 'don't [...] have to mean the same thing by the same words, but they must each be an interpreter of the other' (Davidson, 2001: 121). In potentiality at least, Davidson's interpretability thesis is compatible with a theory of uncertain communication. And yet, a theory of radical interpretability which recognizes uncertain semantics and semiotic appeal sits uneasily with his continued commitment to an 'intersubjective truth' (2001: 121). The notion that meanings can be shared and intentions inferred resolves the uncertainty of communication and the closure of speaking subjects, who, while sharing a world of communication, rely on communications to establish social relations with each other. As Christopher Gauker has argued, if interpretation were a question of accessing the intentions of alter, it would be an impossible task.

In the context of communicative relations between subjects in society, a *transcendental* understanding of dialogism guarantees the integration of speakers and allays suspicions of solipsism. Integration through dialogical relations (cf. Buber: 'In the beginning was the

Word and the Word was relation') presupposes reference to a common world that anchors speakers into a relation of reciprocal intersubjectivity. Linell's use of the concept of intersubjectivity as closely related to the dialogical model exposes the passionate belief in the new model which renders it blind to deeper implications of communication as an unstable process:

> The speaker is assigned the status of interpretive authority when it comes to the meaning of his/her own utterances. But this holds most unambiguously for reference, not necessarily for descriptive (or other aspects) of meaning. In other words, the speaker knows what the intended referents are, but s/he may be mistaken in her/his choice of words for describing them.
>
> (Linell, 1995: 180)

Despite references to asymmetries, the dialogism paradigm anticipates the resolution of communication in the form of shared meaning. It can be exemplified by Linell's three-step model based on Mead and Marková detailed below:

> Step 1: B understands *m* (where *m* is the meaning of the utterance)
> Step 2: A knows that B understands *m*
> Step 3: B 'knows that his understanding of *m* corresponds to what A wanted to make into shared knowledge'
>
> (Linell, 1998: 45)

The anticipation of a stable resolution implicit in Linell's dialogism means that premises are advanced without further critique. There are three concepts which can be made problematic: understanding, meaning and shared knowledge. If understanding is the grasp of external meaning, this model is plausible. However, understanding can be seen as an internal process of cognitive constructions made by the autonomous subject. Meaning is unstable – it is neither dependent on the form of the utterance nor on the intentions of the speaker. It is inferred, and thus always subject to a process of selection. On Brentano's understanding of the concept of 'intentionality', intending was held to be the act of 'pointing to', of 'direction toward an object', as opposed to the act of meaning or presupposing. Rom Harré has argued in *Personal Being* that intentions presuppose a cultural collective from which shared interpretations arise; intentionality is not only a property of public-collective action; it is also a property of the private and individual (Harré, 1983: 117). The key to this understanding is the conviction that intentions derive from the 'interpretative procedures of the collective' (Harré, 1983: 116). Without this collective context, intentions as semantic-semiotic directions, or 'pointings to', would be beyond the grammar of interpretation or what Harré describes as the 'social construction of the mind' ([w]ithout this sharing, nothing an actor does could count as displaying or declaring an intention' [Harré, 1983: 116]).

Bühler's language sign is 'a *signal* by virtue of its appeal to the hearer, whose inner and outer behaviour it directs as do other communicative signs' (Bühler, 1990: 35). If the sign is an uncertain appeal, then it goes without saying that meaning cannot be taken for granted. For the purposes of a simple comparison a three-step complex model could thus look like this:

Step 1: B selects from α (where α is the appeal of the utterance)
Step 2: A imputes the (appropriate) selection to B
Step 3: B may impute that his selection of α corresponds to A's intended selection, but this correspondence is a complex fiction which drives communication.
Alternatively, B may impute that his selection does not correspond to A's intended selection.

In this sense, communication cannot be separated from the complex construction of socially meaningful fictions. The term 'fiction' suggests a conceptualization of a contingency which is actually embedded in communication. The inherent fragility of the 'narrative of self-identity' does not simply derive from the 'backdrop of shifting experiences of day-to-day life and the fragmenting tendencies of modern institutions' (Giddens, 1991: 185–6), although these constitute undeniable factors of risk. Rather than seeing risk primarily or merely as an external object 'out there' (such as commodity capitalism or the pluralization of expertise [Giddens, 1991: 195]), it can be argued that communication without risk is inconceivable.

From within the dialogical paradigm, attempts have been made to introduce some complexity – notably with the concept of asymmetry as 'an intrinsic feature of dialogue' (Linell and Luckmann, 1991: 2–3) in communicative interaction. And yet asymmetry is not held to compromise intersubjectivity. In this sense, then, asymmetries can be resolved in and through communication: 'Asymmetries and inequalities are not only compatible with assumptions of mutuality and reciprocity, they are themselves essential properties of communication and dialogue' (Linell and Luckmann, 1991: 4). By contrast, Luhmann offers a more radical conception of asymmetry by unmasking the survival of theories of dialogism and related theories of intersubjectivity as a reflection of an enduring rationalist belief that understanding can be perfected (Luhmann).

Within a normative framework of understanding uncertainty is easily seen as a by-product. Under the assumption that intersubjectivity can be *achieved*, it can nonetheless occur that '[o]ther parts of individuals' understandings may remain private, and therefore communicatively irrelevant, until they somehow get expressed or "leak out"' (Linell, 1998: 79). In this way, leaks in communication are occasional dysfunctions or lapses. The alternative view proposed here is that such leaks are not occasional dysfunctions but are an integral part of the contingencies in and of communication. This dynamic of that uncertain appeal to interpretation lies in the fact that communications *are socially meaningful precisely because they do not confirm our expectations, but introduce the noise of other actors, compelling the forward development of forward communication.* As Butler, Laclau and Žižek argue, 'particular identities acknowledge that they share with other such identities the situation of a necessarily incomplete determination' (2000: 31).

5. Uncertain references

Luhmann's social theory sets out to provide a link between communication and the implications of the shift from a now problematic notion of reference to self-reference in a way that is directly relevant to the examination of contingency. In *Essays on Self-Reference*, one can read that:

> Societies are a special case of self-referential systems [which] presuppose a network of communications [...]. Communications are possible only within a system of communication and this system cannot escape the form of recursive circularity.
>
> (Luhmann, 1990: 145–6)

According to this view, communications do not establish a reference or connection with external reality (so there is no correspondence or even 'mapping'), but recursively construct communications networks. The concept of recursivity implies redundancy in communication, a reference in communication to further communication as opposed to an objective reality. Furthermore, redundancy creates meaning: for instance, conventions are a classic case of the self-reference of communication codes where meaning is constructed from the iteration of the convention. The concept of system closure can also be applied to neurological processes and perception.[4] Neurosemantic theorists stress the self-reference of the brain and the internal representation it constructs as if they were 'realities' (cf. Breidbach, 1996: 19). Just as in neurosemantic terms 'reality' is a self-referential construction built on previously existing schemata, so, too, in cognitive terms agents are self-referential in communication terms, in the sense that they do not intersubjectively engage, in that they are immersed in contingencies of contexts, other selves and voices. Schmidt's concept of cognitive autonomy thus stresses the autonomous constructibility of multiple realities but also relates this constructibility to communication and thus also to society.

6. The complex self

If we assume that (1) communication actors are capable of free pragmatic enrichment; (2) semiotic appeals are uncertain; (3) interpretability is radical (i.e. not an operation in understanding intentions or meanings) and (4) contexts are almost never saturated, then we might be tempted to conclude with Gergen (1991: 17) that the self is being overwhelmed by uncertainty and that 'the final stage in the transition to the postmodern is reached when the self vanishes fully into a stage of relatedness'. However, postmodernism – even if we accept that it means that the self is exposed (Gergen uses the term saturated) to a 'plurality of voices vying for the right to reality' (Gergen, 1991: 7) – does not obliterate the self, but merely exacts more of it. It is a symptom of the heightened awareness of the self in complex realities which have become pluralized (Schmidt). Elster's (1995: 3) notion of the multiple self offers more in opening up the contingencies of communication, selfhood and context; polyvocality or heteroglossia of reality does not efface the subject or the self. It is no coincidence that in social theory there is increased talk of risk or contingency or instability. This awareness of a 'community of contingency' (Habermas, 1998) also means a more acute sense of self-reflexivity. If, as argued here, there is no interpenetration[6] between minds, then how can a theory of social meaning incorporate complexity? The 'threat of meaninglessness' (Giddens, 1991: 201) is thus perhaps not so much a threat of meaninglessness because autonomous actors always construct meaning and communicate it, notwithstanding the invasive pressures of globalization. Rather than saturating the self, these pressures make the sense of self amidst complexity so acute that the effort to construct meaning becomes almost unbearable and therefore, paradoxically, unavoidable. Judicial processes and political systems recede further and further still into the distance. New forms of communication arise where old forms fade. The gulf between presuppositions of communicative rationality and the 'occasional commonality' (Habermas, 1992b: 1.125) of everyday language experiences becomes wider and wider. Uncertainties are an inherent part of the dynamics of social construction.

So, in an uncertain world, the demands placed on the self to manage complexities of environments, employment, identity, family and faith require higher levels of flexibility and performance. Bauman's 'liquid self' is the communicating self in multiply complex worlds and is perhaps embodied and disembodied simultaneously in reality TV shows, 'squeezing ever more lives into the timespan of mortal life' (Bauman, 2005: 8). It might even appear that that the multiple pressures of contemporary life make escape possible only in the form of solipsism or self-referential immersion:

> Diligently we prick our ears to the voices from 'inside', and yet hardly ever are we really, fully and beyond reasonable doubt, satisfied that the voices have not been misheard and that we've heard enough of them to make up our minds and pronounce a verdict.
>
> (Bauman, 2005: 17)

This is the communicating complexity of the radically multivoiced self and autonomous social agent whose internal multiplicity of voices, identities and selves is not resolved by some transcendental operation or miraculous intermonadological commununalization. That particular horizon has receded from view. Nevertheless, the eclipse of intersubjectivity does not cast the self into the darkest night of pure self-reference, for communication, however uncertain its form, its medium, its response, intention of interpretation, connects. Communication is necessary as the means by which social contexts are created amongst autonomous actors and despite their irreducible self-reference. And these connections serve up a particular paradox: of connection and separation – or, in other words, the paradox of contingency.

7
Radical Translation and Interpretation across Ideologies and Cultures

1. Quine, Davidson and uncertain understanding

This chapter takes a comprehensive view of translation beyond the confines of a linguistic view of cross-cultural communication, in order to underline the deep uncertainties of the processes of the translation and interpretation of reference or meaning in what might be termed *mono-cultural* or cross-cultural settings. In both such cases, a radical view of translation (adopting the work of Willard van Orman Quine) and a radical view of interpretation (adopting the work of Donald Davidson) will be taken.

In *Word and Object* (1960), Quine referred to the incompatibilities of translation as its fundamental indeterminacy, and this can be extended to both mono-cultural and cross-cultural translation activity. Part of the problem, as Quine described it, is that any linguistic act is an act in an environment at a point in time, but that same act extends back into multiple previous cognitive associations and responses to previous stimulations. Thus, the act of communication is a dynamic of the *form irrupting onto silence*, which can be heard or read, and a vast residuum – an unmarked communication history to which the hearer has no access. The recovery of a man's current language, Quine writes, is an act of radical translation – the 'translation of the language of a hitherto untouched people' (Quine, 1960: 28).

If so, then there can then be no identity of stimulus meaning from one speaker to the hearer or the next speaker, where stimulus meaning is the 'total battery of present dispositions to be prompted to assent to or to dissent from the sentence' (Quine, 1960: 39). Even if there is arguably some broad uniformity in use among speakers, in such cases where the sentence is almost a 'direct ostension', that uniformity lies at the surface of semiotic exchange, as Schmidt has argued (1994b). However, the multivoiced uncertainty of communication means that at any level of depth sentences are inevitably connected with other sentences and thus also past stimulations to which we are denied cognitive access. Amidst this internally and externally multivoiced network the 'randomness of personal history' makes reference uncertain whether in philosophical or linguistic accounts of translation:

> Now this random character has the effect not only that the stimulus meaning of the sentence for one speaker will differ from the stimulus meaning of that sentence for other speakers. It will differ from the stimulus meaning also of any other discoverable sentence for other speakers, in the same language or any other.
>
> (Quine, 1960: 45)

In *Subjective, Intersubjective, Objective*, Davidson similarly reminds us that the interpretation of an utterance 'cannot be the same for the utterer and his hearers' (2001: 12) and that while there can admittedly be convergence, this depends on 'clues to interpretation' (2001: 13); *interpretability*, rather than an immutable semantic essence, is the key to meaning. Nevertheless, while there are *prima facie* similarities with Quine's view of translation, Davidson is at pains to distinguish between translation and interpretation. Interpretation is not translation as an act of word substitution or similar, it is part of a theory of understanding (Davidson, 2005: 112–13). While interpretation is the key to pragmatic interactions, Davidson sees translation as a description a hearer might make of a speaker's utterances. Theoretically, there are two levels to his concept of interpretation – the prior and the passing theory. First, the hearer is said to be, in his prior theory, 'prepared in advance' to engage in interpretation; second, the hearer actually engages in the act of interpretation. For the speaker, there is a belief in what the interpreter's theory might be and also an intentional dimension, namely the theory he intends the hearer to use (Davidson, 2005: 101). Communication is about the second, pragmatic levels of interpretation, of use and intended use and not about prior beliefs or the foundational preparedness to engage in interpretative acts. Utterers are held to converge on these second, pragmatic dimensions as if suspending the preparedness for interpretation.

Davidson refers to the passing theories of actual interpretation and interpretation-intention as the imperfect, fortuitous use of 'private language' in interactions – the use of *wit, luck, wisdom and rules of thumb*. Thus we can at least suggest that communicators do not have access to each other's prior theories (of beliefs or preparedness to interpret) and nor do we have access to a shared language structure: 'We must give up the idea of a clearly defined shared structure which language-users acquire and then apply to cases' (Davidson, 2005: 107). And if it is true that we communicate private languages, then indeterminacy of reference, register or lexical use remain uncertain, *a fortiori* where more than one language is used for this means a further level of mediation to the associative frameworks of stimulus meanings. Despite this radical view of interpretation, Davidson still upholds the concept of 'mutual understanding' without actually saying how this mutuality might be reconciled across multiply private languages. While sharedness is evidently impossible, since private languages and precisely *private* languages are communicated, one might be tempted to say that language is not 'essential' and that speakers never need to speak as others speak. But Davidson pulls back from the brink of a solipsistic account of private languages by arguing that even if speakers do not hold to a social norm, they are 'responsible' to it; communication persists without shared practices. Crucially, however, the ontological principle of interpretability remains as the desire to be capable of interpretation and the desire to be interpreted. This opening between conformity to discourse convention and a linguistic practice which might be at variance with that convention is fruitful and clears the way for a more thorough examination of the negotiating moves and countermoves through uncertainties of speakers and hearers. Davidson offers a dynamic account of communication as the sustaining of ongoing communication, and this requires openness or the appeal (analogous to Bühler's use of the term) to interpretation:

> [...] what matters, the point of language or speech or whatever you want to call it, is communication, getting across to someone else what you have in mind by means of words that they interpret (understand) as you want them to.
>
> (Davidson, 2005: 120)

As noted above, Davidson cannot quite bring himself to concede that underlying this model of communication are all manner of contingencies: the selections we make, the assumptions, presuppositions and inferences which ultimately make the gap between speaker and hearer bridgeable only by the contingent, private communication appeals from speaker to hearer and from hearer to speaker. Still, the challenge to the intermonadological fallacy is well made:

> Interaction of the needed sort demands that each individual perceives others as reacting to the shared environment as much as he does; only then can teaching take place and appropriate questions be aroused. It follows that meaning something requires that by and large one follows a practice of one's own, a practice that can be understood by others. But there is no fundamental reason why practices must be shared.
>
> (Davidson, 2005: 125)

2. Myths of translational equivalence, subjects and ideologies

Linguistic theories of translation or intercultural communication typically make assumptions about the possibility of working towards an intersubjective understanding or a dynamic equivalence across language systems or the possibility of deriving the correct inference, assumption or belief and, in a process of transformation, translate across cultures removing distortion along the way. In this context, conceptualizing translation as uncertain intercultural communication (by virtue of impossible access to other meaning stimuli) aims to take the theoretical debate of the preceding chapters a step further and establish connections between intercultural communication and uncertainty as a social dynamic. The relatively recent 'cultural turn' in linguistic (as opposed to Quine's philosophical) translation theory has induced an interdisciplinary debate with literary, media and cultural theory which is welcome in that it sees textual practice – including translational activity – as social practice.

The popular conception of translation is that of a transmission process in which the translator seeks some kind of equivalence in the attempt to recreate the original (source) text. Where all else failed, this activity was held to involve capturing the 'essence' or even 'spirit' of the original so that new readers could be immersed in a new (target) text with a minimum of mediation. Translators were, as Venuti has argued, required to be 'invisible'. Since such unmediated equivalence is a chimera, then translation can be viewed as communication between two or more cultural or linguistic systems in terms of the *uncertainties* which any mediation induces. And such uncertainties extend equally to social and subjective value systems.

The diversification of approaches to translation as a socially embedded practice reflects attempts to increase the complexity of theoretical approaches to the field. As an ongoing self-reflective academic practice, translation theory continues to integrate new levels of complexity such as *Skopostheorie* (Reiss and Vermeer, 1984; Vermeer, 1996) or audience design, the role of institutions, power, gender or ideology, alterity and authority/authorship. It is to be expected, given the dynamics of communication processes generally, that theoretical complexity will itself become more complex as translation theory becomes increasingly exposed to its own theoretical premises.

As a counterpoint to assumptions we might make about ideologies as evaluative spheres of world communication society (cf. Japp, 2003), it is now opportune to explore the status of the subjective, private, untranslatable, language communicator in intercultural environments where there might be a marked desire to remove uncertainty and reach sharedness, but where in fact this must remain impossible. The prevailing orthodoxy in intercultural communication accounts is that there is a fundamentally possible universality of reference and understanding. In what follows, there will be discussion of both the subjective communication valuations of human agents as translators and also the ideological uncertainties of social communication systems across which translators operate. In other words, two levels of communication are conceptualized: social systems of evaluation as ideologies and subjective systems of evaluation as axiologies. As discussed above, axiology as a subjective value sphere is the irreducible subjectivity of evaluation in a social context. This subjectivity does not disappear in somehow stable, linguistically defined communities, systems or institutions and thus challenges the reifying view of ideology as a communication system or code outside the subject. It is empirically and theoretically plausible to view both subjectivity and rules or customs or conventions as constructions which require constant renewal if they are to maintain any validity or legitimacy. The tensions between source and target cultures can be more easily modelled and revealed by means of an analysis of two levels of construction: that of the subject and that of subsocial and social codifications. In the more immediate context, mediation at the subjective level is axiology, or subjective valuation, whereas mediation at the social level is ideology, or the discursive valuation of a social system. Bakhtin's views on axiological accentuation are also relevant here, particularly in view of the connections he establishes with heteroglossia:

> [...] in the process of literary creation, languages interanimate each other and objectify precisely that side of one's own (and of the other's) language *that pertains to its world view*, its inner form, the axiologically accentuated system inherent in it.
>
> (Bakhtin, 1998: 65)

This axiological, subjectively constructed accentuation of languages as social discourse practices is inevitable. In addition, this accentuation constitutes a belief system which is peculiar to the world view of a language and the communication agents who make use of it. This language is of course located amidst the tensions of centripetal and centrifugal forces of discourse. In dealing with translation as a complex communication operation, axiology needs to shift from an epistemological or ontological sphere to a pragmatic-interactional sphere which examines various levels of communication: agent communication, face-to-face interaction systems, subsystem communications, system communications and their imperfect frontiers. Equally, the morally embedded concept of axiology needs to be replaced by a more many-valued concept which focuses on all valuational moves in communication. A theory of axiological objectivism based on moral transcendentalism needs to yield to the socially subjective construction of axiology in order to offer a more plausible account of subjective agency. This subjective axiological construction can then be usefully contrasted with valuational spaces at a higher level, that is, thematic suborders and epistemic orders of discourses. At these levels, we encounter power or ideology. In bringing Bakhtin's radical dialogism together with constructivist (Schmidt) or systems-theoretical (Luhmann, Baecker) accounts of communication, ideology can be reconceptualized as a construct which is contingent and therefore constantly fighting against its own instability or ambiguity. If so, then it seems clear that there is a case for destabilizing the definition of ideology in texts.

The aim is thus to draw attention to the uncertain relationship between constraint and autonomy or ideology and axiology in textual manifestations at the interface of two communication systems. Such uncertainties are textually inescapable – however ideologically 'closed' a text may appear. And in the case of linguistic translation across two 'public' languages, mediation is rendered even more complex by the addition of an interpreter as an interlocutor in face-to-face exchange, as a translator in the written medium, or as the broadcast voices of disembodied conference interpreters. The point of departure for such a new exploration of translation is the potential of a theory of communicative uncertainty, not as confined to structures, but as an inescapable fact of any communicative activity on account of the openness of signs and the relative closure of the cognitive processes of communicators.

Existing attention in translation theory to such factors as context, text, subject, audience and ideology is informed by wider epistemological assumptions about reference, objectivity and truth, which still succumb to the intermonadological, universalist claim. Here, core concepts obey a dichotomy based on a distinction between subject and object and are mediated by referential operations between the two. Contexts and texts refer then to realities, subjects refer to each other in externally defined contexts, audiences are referred to in texts which are embedded in discourses and ideologies external to subjects and which refer to power relations. Realism operates with such dichotomies and stabilizes communication processes at variance with the porous or 'liquid realities' of today's information-rich worlds (Bauman, 2003).

If untranslatability and the contingency of interpretability are really taken seriously, then the response to the epistemological dilemma essayed above involves a paradigm shift from realism and referentialism towards constructivism and self-reference (Luhmann, 1995; Von Foerster, 2002; Schmidt, 2003b). The gain achieved by such a shift lies in the acknowledgement of far greater uncertainties in communication process, including translation, since such processes are no longer seen as stable references (to readers, institutions or worlds) but as constructs which are contingent on multiple levels (consider the impact of misreporting, misquoting and mistranslating in the contexts of mass media systems as exemplified by interactions with al Qaeda and other media-dependent groups). And yet, the multiple uncertainties of communication mean that contexts can be explored as multiple and shifting constraints which are temporarily stabilized by interests. Such interests – which can be codified as ideologies – are in turn generated as discourses and need to be continuously reactivated in order to sustain their validity (ideologically codified as 'legitimacy', for example). Ideologies are therefore codes which seek to establish contexts which reduce contingency in order to stabilize ambivalence (Baecker) or close porosity. However, such stabilization processes depend not purely on communication in the abstract, but on agents, including speakers, recipients and the agents of communication as translator-interpreters. In this sense, texts, as semiotic instantiations of communication, do not determine readings, but operate appellatively with a series of assumptions and expectations. These are in turn unstable, producing polycontextual interactions in which unstable ideologies interact with the unstable axiologies (subjective value systems) of subjects. These uncertainties are the uncertainties of globalization where interaction spaces are both truncated and extended by electronic media and where value systems are increasingly fluid.

3. Liquid ideology and text

The concept of ideology most commonly encountered in translation theory tends to be informed to a large degree by the writings of Michel Foucault and Roland Barthes. A constraint is thus directly imported into theories of linguistic translation, for while Foucault and Barthes stress the capillary or omnipresent nature of ideology, it is reified and denies the role of social agents in its construction. Thus, 'power' and 'exclusion' or the hegemony of the bourgeois semiotic point to an ideology somehow beyond human control. And yet, as discussed above, as complex communication codes, ideologies are schematizations and not objective fetters:

> Ideologies are, in other words, texts which contain something they do not contain, namely information about their authors and users. And in the conventional interpretation this means: information

about their interests. In other words, we are dealing with blindspots and the problem of latency.

(Luhmann, 1997: 2.1079–80)

It is therefore important to avoid seeking refuge in Foucault's concept of 'exclusion' in his theory of power where it acquires such stability that the notion of action or resistance is annulled. In *Les Mots et les Choses* (1966), Foucault used the term *discours* to signify the epistemes · of the classical age. The order of discourse is a relative, historically contingent order and can signify three things: (1) the general domain of all expressions; (2) an individualisable domain of expressions; (3) regulated practice. In all three cases discourses share one characteristic: they function as frameworks, structures and systems which restrict and exclude. Discourses are epistemic (communication) systems into which subjects are incorporated. These series are socially legitimated as discourses which are crystallized patterns of signification or semiotic codes, meaning that they are historically derived. Texts within discourses, e.g. a sermon or a catechism, are artificial constructs that seek to control dispersion. They are, as communications, potentially able to couple with other discourses (literary discourse, for example) and are thus intertextual, interdiscursive. Between the epistemic order of knowledge systems and texts as manifest instantiations of such knowledge systems lie suborders of discourse, where discourses are subdivided along thematic lines such as politics, religion and law. Discourses as epistemic orders are similar to cultural codes; they are communication systems differentiated functionally into suborders.

It is well known that Foucault had considered Bentham's *Panopticon* to be a prototype of the power/knowledge complex, since with the new organization of prisons introduced by Bentham, the prisoner was maintained in a state of permanent visibility. Not only did Foucault conflate power and knowledge in a nihilistic reaction to the colonization of the 1968 movement in France and elsewhere. Power was conceptualized as something so capillary and microbiotic that the very idea of the subject tended to be absorbed into its 'function of discourse', that is, a convention 'removed from its creative role' (Foucault, 1977: 130; 137); thus, the capacity for resistance is neutralized. At the same time, Foucault's conflation of power and knowledge and his anathematization of the Enlightenment flatten even this – socially fundamental – precariousness. Indeed, Habermas famously accused Foucault of retreating 'into the reflectionless objectivity of a non-participatory, ascetic description of kaleidoscopically changing practices of power' (Habermas, 1990b: 275–6).

Foucault's early 'discourse' concept, which has proved so influential in text and discourse linguistics, proceeds from the centrality of the discursive norm. Of course, Foucault did not seek an immaculate language. Discourses are temporally and spatially legitimated languages linked to power; accordingly, discourse is ruled by procedures of exclusion. In this model, Foucault must also presuppose stability: discourse excludes through the formation of dichotomies – prohibitions, oppositions, manicheisms and disciplines, commentaries and author functions. Since, until *The History of Sexuality*, Foucault did not explore volatile language use, he proceeded from an ineluctable norm of power/exclusion procedures. And yet, as social heteronomies, exclusion procedures are always relative: exclusions do not induce silence, but instabilities, as the paradoxical effects of censorship all too readily demonstrate. And yet exclusions leave a mark, an incision which can be inhabited. Thus, excluded communications do not disappear – they are part of a global communication system even where access to the Internet is not guaranteed. Consider how the 'silenced' voices of the East Timorese were 'heard' in John Pilger's TV documentaries in the 1980s.

Barthes's *Mythologies* (1957), of unquestionable influence in theories of translational communication, sought to examine what goes without saying (the silence of the sign, its legitimacy in itself), investigating second-order semiotic systems which build on other systems. Barthes takes us behind the scenes, strips away the surface of our cultural constructions, and shows how signifier and signified produce a new signifier for a new signified: second-order semiotic systems. His influential deconstructive inventory of mythologies is primarily driven by a critique which aims to unmask the false self-evidence or 'ideological abuse' of what 'goes without saying' (Barthes, 1957: 9). The false self-evidence is generated by an imposition of stability or clarity on the sign. In his analysis of a wrestling match, for instance, everything is described as being presented, evidenced to the point of exhaustion, 'leaving nothing in the shadows'. The euphoria performed releases spectators from the 'constitutive ambiguity of everyday life' where men are 'placed in the panoramic vision of a univocal

Nature' (1957: 23). The same applies to reified views of ideology as a fixed horizon manipulated by power interests when in fact it is a complex human construction. And yet, even here, such univocality is a communicative move, a self-referential code which can only perform its clarity or univocality as an appeal to subjects who can take it or leave it. Ideology fools no one – its frequent invocation the willing abandonment of subjective autonomy.

The result of Foucault's theory of microbiotic power and Barthes's critique of the bourgeois 'occupation' of semiotic space has all too often been to reify ideology and, in so doing, paradoxically stabilize it as an object of evil, as it were. The objectivistic approach to ideology can be crystallized into the primacy of dependency on a representation of objective worlds. And yet across a broad range of the human and social sciences, from constructionism to deconstruction, systems theory and conversation analysis, discourse ethics and constructivism, there is a recognition that ideology is much more fluid than is often assumed. As Brown asks, 'if there is no foundational reality exterior to those created in language, how are truth and power to be distinguished, much less separately judged?' (Brown, 1994: 31). Moreover, if ideologies are communicative constructs, then they are unstable. Texts are in Derrida's structural terms, infinitely iterable (re)writings (Derrida, 2000): 'My communication must be repeatable-iterable in the absolute absence of the receiver or of any empirically determinable collectivity of receivers (Derrida, 2000: 7).

Derrida's concept of iterability and Jacques Lacan's notion of the contingency of the signified are closely related to, but also distinct from the concept of porosity introduced above. The concept of porosity in communication-theoretical terms thus signifies an environmentally open hybrid *state and dynamic process* which in turn make the operational closure of systems highly unstable.

The reified view of ideology as an ultimate source of power and exclusion tends to present ideology as a stable horizon and curiously denies it of its lifeblood: the fact that it is communicable/interpretable into dichotomies which can be used to exclude. For if ideology is a complex communication code, it can only be communicatively regenerated time and time again in a territory of multiple contingencies. In other words, the danger is that the concept of ideology becomes a stable category: texts or discourses or (re)translations are, it is said, inevitably imbricated in ideological *discourse-operations* and the subject, the translational agent, is crushed. These operations are held to involve power relations with their asymmetries, exclusions, struggles and censorship. More often than not, ideology appears as the incarnation of manipulation or distortion of a reality which is assumed.

While there is an awareness that ideology is more than simply the crudely Marxist conception of a manipulation or distortion, ideology is still seen as one pole in a dichotomy – as an external force which forms society. Thus linguistic translation theories seem to conceptualize ideology as a theatre of power relations which means that 'inevitably, there is an ideological slant on the texts'. Calzada Pérez (2003) silently approximates ideology to public opinion and the formation of stereotypes; we are subject to ideological *pressure* and ideological *tensions*. Globalization is merely part of these dynamic of growing ideological tensions which can now simply be called the homogenizing 'globalized ideological tensions' (Calzada Pérez, 2003: 1). Both these views use a univocal (*sensu* Bakhtin) conception of ideology and indeed globalization, which reifies concepts by stabilizing them. Such views necessarily deny communication dynamics, Quine's multiple associations with meaning-stimuli, Davidson's open interpretability and Bühler's appeal to the hearer that make common ground permanently elusive.

However, just as globalization is a dialectic of resurgent nationalism *and* deterritorialization, globalization *and* glocalization, homogeneity *and* heterogeneity, the extended *and* truncated self, so, too, ideology is not a linear and stable text to which social actors (and therefore translators) automatically conform, but a precarious semantic manoeuvring between systems and their actors. In terms of a theoretical modelling of communication uncertainty, Baecker argues that a system is a precarious relationship between the system and its environment (Baecker, 2001). As noted, the introduction of such precariousness into the system concept as a self-referential communication realm is essential if reifications are to be avoided and the system concept de-ontologized (cf. Schmidt, 2003a: 27–33). According to Baecker, two causalities perform in this choreography: the external causal influence of the environment on the system and the 'self-determination of the system by the constraints under which it is placed and/or which it is ready to accept' (2001: 63); such 'split causality' is part of the openness of systems. Communication is inscribed into this double causality in the sense that it recursively generates the sets of possibilities (e.g. discourses, genres, conventions, types), for selection of communications require constant recursive generation. Thus, translation as intercultural communication can be conceptualized not as the transformation of one sign system into another, but of one unstable or, following Bakhtin, multivoiced semiotic into another multivoiced semiotic via a multivoiced subject. In this conceptual shift, new contingencies emerge: the source text is not a univocal phenomenon – and even in its most closed form where ideologies become marked – their porosity makes them susceptible to what Austin, Searle and Habermas have wistfully referred to as parasitism. The target text is also a 'dance' between pressures to impose univocality and remove contingency on the one hand and decentralizing tendencies in the form of the translator as a social agent and an interpreter-subject amidst constraints. The translator himself is also now conceptualized as a multivoiced agent (cf. Marková, 2001 and Hermans, 2002), whether we seek to recover the coherence of a 'source text' as a culturally embedded instantiation or alter's unknown language. To view ideology purely or predominantly in terms of external agency or constraint is to suppress subjectivity – and the subjective values which can never be subtracted from communication processes, including translation processes where such tensions become particularly acute. If we say that the authors are governed by ideologies, then we are saying that they are the objects of those ideologies.

Linguistic translation theory approaches to ideology typically operate with an internal/external dichotomy. Hatim and Mason (1997) refer to the ideology of translating and the translation of ideology, while Schäffner refers to 'extratextual and intratextual aspects of ideology' (Schäffner, 2003: 24). The recognition that ideology is not merely an external constraint, but also pervades communication (and therefore translation) is valid. However, two criticisms might be made. Firstly, ideology is communicatively generated, ie. an uncertain construct or semantic. Secondly, ideology is not an alien body to be incorporated or held at bay. The relationship between ideology and texts is richly imbricated and not one of external determination; an axiological subjective dimension must be part of it. As noted above, in epistemological terms the above approaches proceed from objectivistic positions according to which ideology is 'out there' and can be brought inside. Schäffner sees ideology 'as *reflected* in the text', texts as '*reflecting* different ideological traditions' and differences between texts 'explained as a *reflection* and/or awareness of ideological phenomena in the respective cultures' (2003: 29; 37; 41 – my emphases). If texts merely reflect ideology then ideology is reified; if ideology is reified, its communicative contingency is removed and it is objectified as an ultimate horizon beyond which no social actor can see. Ideology somehow has the power to tame subjects, reducing them to author-functions of discourse.

From within linguistic translation theory, Lawrence Venuti's work on foreignization and translator invisibility certainly moves within Foucault's shadow. Although Venuti rightly dismisses objectivity as an epistemological illusion, his theory of the subject – and that means of the translator as a social communicator whose communications occupy exposed positions between cognitive and social subsystems – remains locked within the subject–object dichotomy. Thus, the dialectic sketched in *The Translator's Invisibility* (1997) is weak: subjectivity is paradoxically the object of social determinations. While it would be subjectivistic to contend that subjects are not socially constituted, it is epistemologically limiting to argue, firstly, that subjectivity is determined when it is a co-determinant of communication and that, secondly, change is possible because of some quantitative heterogeneity of rules. Heterogeneity does not in itself guarantee the possibility of change, merely the possibility of predetermined variation.

This flattens the multitude of past associations and the multi-voicedness of communicating agents in complex environments. Harvey (2003) seeks to correct precisely this kind of reifying determinism by following Fairclough's distinction of ideology as structure and event, or, as Harvey puts it, text and system. He rightly points out that '[i]deological change in and through events is signalled typically by (often small) transgressions, contradictions and confusions' (2003: 45). Translation, as the '*interface* between competing ideological positions' (2003: 43), is an event within a system:

Conceived of as an 'event, a translation has the potential to reveal (and should be probed for) challenges, transgressions, contradictions and fissures, all of which are the outcomes of the interaction between, on the one hand, an underlying systemic configuration of values and assumptions and, on the other, the irruption of alterity within a domestic sphere.

(Harvey, 2003: 45)

While it is certainly true that some transgressions can irrupt more readily in translation than in what could be loosely described for the time being as other contexts, alterity is not the privileged domain of translation. Texts and complex configurations such as ideologies, discourses and the genres which sustain them, are not semantically stable units, but contingent communicative constructions. Thus even systems of values and beliefs are infinitely contestable by virtue of their very multivoicedness.

4. Intertextuality

As discussed above, the concept of contingency is a paradox, involving contact and thus dependency, but also risk, since this contact depends on a context which cannot be determined in advance. This contingency might – despite the constraints of university assessments, court or medical confidentiality, contractual obligations, conventions of genre and type – irrupt with greater force in translation in view of the semiotic incommensurability of different, private, language worlds now doubly mediated by translation as a form of intercultural communication. And yet communicative uncertainty means contingency is inscribed into source text and target text. The task for the translator – in multicultural or putatively monocultural settings – is one of transforming one heteroglot and yet temporarily stabilized text into another heteroglot and yet temporarily stabilized text.

Under the influence of the concept of intertextuality (Kristeva following Bakhtin), translation theorists have long accepted that texts are hybrids. This means that the organization of texts into types or genres is imperfect, and can be seen as a procedure of conventionalization designed to stabilize the contingency of communication for the purpose of epistemic and thus also social order. Despite the recognition that texts are hybrid, the implications of this recognition often do not seem to extend to the concept of ideology. For if texts are hybrid then it follows that discourses instantiated in texts are also hybrid. Ideology is only temporarily stable for it is a human construct and thus contingent as a temporary instantiation in communication. What appears stable is actually articulated by several layers of texts (e.g. edicts, manifestos, laws, speeches, regulations, agreements, constitutions) and remains dependent on communication in order to maintain its stability. All too often, the concept of ideology is reified as a source of irresistible power when actually it is textually constructed and texts can only ever appeal (following Bühler, mutatis mutandis) to ill-defined addressees. There is no historical evidence to suggest that even in the most bestial dictatorships of Nazism or fascism ideology completely infiltrates all discourse. The private spheres remain as private communication spheres, private codes are devised, demonstrations held and poems of resistance written. Ideology now needs to be conceptualized as a multi-layered code used for the stabilization of epistemic orders of discourse at the level of thematic systems – be they political, economic or religious. At the same time, the duration of this stability depends on social systems and their actors.

5. Private language, subjective evaluation and communication systems

If communications and their discoursal organization are unstable and if texts are hybrid for the reasons outlined above, then the valuational stance of each actor in communication is also constructed autonomously amidst a plurality of constraints. The mediations of translation cannot remove such an openness of interpretation and the multitude of associative possibilities with stimulus meanings (Quine, 1960). This also means that it is not possible to remove the autonomous valuational or axiological stance for in contrast to the ideology of the dominant semantic of a system (cf. Luhmann, 1993), axiologies are dependent on the actor or agent. The concept of axiology emphasizes the subjective residuum, that is, as cyberneticists would put it, the inescapable constructiveness of all reality levels (cf. Schmidt, 2003b). Ideologies, by contrast, are complex fictions used by systems and 'their' agents, to create the simulacrum of self-evidence that somehow ideologies deny resistance; as 'dominant discourses' they operate by attempting to reduce contingency (cf. Luhmann, 1979). And yet, as argued above, both axiologies and ideologies can be conceptualized as distinct communicative realms with their attendant codes, discourses and genres. Precisely as communicative realms, they are contingent upon contexts, receptions, iterations – in brief, the radical interpretability which gives communication its dynamic and its potential for social renewal and critique. In simplified terms, ideologies are the discursive organization of system values (van Dijk refers to ideology as 'the set of factual and evaluative beliefs – that is the knowledge and the opinions of a group' [2000: 48]).

Since both the communicating subject and the social system are dependent on communication, and since such communication is unstable in terms of context, reference and the appeal to interpretation, it is not possible to subtract uncertainty from the relations between subject and society or indeed between subjective value and system value. There is, in other words, a persistent centrifugal/centripetal tension between axiology and ideology (cf. Bakhtin, 1998: 276). Social communication systems are thus a complex tension between the colonizing self-reference of dominant social systems such as the economy or law and the dispersion of cognitive systems. And lest we forget: both depend on communications.

Rather like Hubert Hermans, van Dijk argues plausibly that both ideologies and values are 'the shared mental objects of social cognition', although he argues that values have a broader base on which ideologies are based, since values form the foundation of all evaluation processes. However, here again, his reading of values is tinged with positive connotations – truth, intelligence, beauty, enjoying a good life (2000: 74–5):

> Given the nature of ideologies as basic systems of group beliefs, we may assume that these typical societal values play a special role in them, as is indeed the case – virtually all major social and political ideologies will emphasize one or more of these societal values.
>
> (2000: 75)

While such intuitive views are foundational in theory building, some counter-intuitive thinking might indicate new directions. Values and ideologies are only values and ideologies inasmuch as they can be communicated – and if they can be communicated, they are contingent. Van Dijk's value concept explicitly deals with the need for the social organization of values in which actions and interactions require 'routines of evaluation'. Not only do values possess a routine character, they are historically embedded and handed down through ages where ideologies are 'terminal' and informed by short-term motivations or goals. The historicity, sharedness and routine character of values are taken to 'preclude their reduction to individuals' who 'may share, adopt or reject the values of their group', but whose ideals or goals are not values in themselves (van Dijk, 2000: 74). Thus, for van Dijk, values have a 'fundamental socio-cultural status'; they are, in other words social *aprioris*. In this way, subjective axiology is always seen as socialized and thus the inevitable tension between social values and cognitive values tends to be assumed to be resolved from the outset. In the question of socialized subjectivity, Anthony Giddens offers a not entirely dissimilar view of the irreducible social character of the subject:

> [S]ubjectivity is constituted by cultural and social determinations that are diverse and even conflicting, that mediate any language use, and that vary with every cultural formation and every histor-ical moment. Human action is intentional, but determinate, self-reflexively measured against social rules and resources, the heterogeneity of which allows for the possibility of change with every self-reflexive action.
>
> (Giddens, 1979 cited in: Venuti, 1997: 24)

There is more than a suggestion of objectivism in such a conception of values. Where values are seen as purely socio-cultural foundations, the question must be asked whether social agents are merely the objects (or, in Harré's words, *patients*) of such values. If so, then values are stable over time when we know them to be mutable (consider the fate of capital punishment, corporal punishment, ecological values, organized religions). And values are mutable because they depend on the discursive regeneration through agents who are indeed social, but still agents nonetheless. The axiological theory of evaluation essayed here seeks to avoid the subject-flattening objectivism of such approaches by acknowledging the autonomy of social agents without reducing such autonomy to solipsism or atomism. Autonomy and subjective valuation are constitutive social facts. They come together socially, not in collective knowledge or intermonadological commu-nalization, but in the communications and interpretations with their environments.

Translators are therefore engaged in multiple uncertainties – of systems and subsystems of source discourse and their manifold lan-guages. The multiplication of subjective heteroglossia and social het-eroglossia increases the number of communication variables considerably. A dominant, albeit precarious ideology, encounters an axiology which it must stabilize, codify or silence – but if it does, it jeopardizes its own communication success. The heterogeneity is subjectively guaranteed in the openness to interpretability and the impossibility of access to other multivoiced cognitive autonomous agents which make even universalist discourses contingent:

> [N]o assertion of universality takes place apart from a cultural norm, and, given the array of contesting norms that constitute the international field, no assertion can be made without at once requiring a cultural translation. Without translation, the very concept of universality cannot cross the linguistic borders it claims, in principle, to be able to cross. Or we might put it another way: without translation, the only way the assertion of universality can cross a border is through a colonial and expansionist logic.
>
> (Butler, Laclau, Žižek, 2000: 35)

8
New Communication Uncertainties and Mediapolitics

1. The semantic of interaction and mediapublics

The universalist semantic of interaction faces an acute dilemma. Not only are its theoretical premises questionable at least in the form in which that theory was framed; it is also seriously at variance with the liquid uncertainties of our realities today. The space of our interpersonal interactions has changed and many interactional transactions now take place electronically, giving rise to what Manuel Castells has termed the 'network society'. Diffuse, constantly changing networks 'constitute the new social morphology of our societies', while 'the diffusion of networking logic substantially modifies' our lives and challenges our conventional notions of the private and public, the 'lifeworld' of everyday culture and the 'system' of rationalization (Castells, 1997: 469). Ontological liquidity and technological diffusion coalesce with the fundamental uncertainty of the act of communicating.

The paradox of the intertwining of technological connectivity and communicative and existential contingency is nothing other than the process we call globalization – the shift from industrialism to 'informationalism' and Castells's network society bring about a shift from traditional conceptions of power to the power of financial and other flows which demand flexibility and the constant readaptation of social actors. The traditional forms of organization are yielding increasingly to new networks from virtual university research groups to terrorist groupings, anti-globalization resistance movements and citizens' discussion fora and global financial market operations.

Networks do not conform to the traditional hierarchical forms of business corporations or institutions but extend over *nodes*, or, as other theorists suggest, after Gilles Deleuze and Félix Guattari,[1] to rhizomatic forms of organization as integrated clusters. These open structures remain fluid and adaptable, capable of infinite new connections whilst maintaining the homeostasis (self-regulating stability), without which they would cease to exist as networks. These are the open structures of decentralized, diffuse organizations, and this is the fluid world where fetters have dissolved, where fluid form displaces traditional notions of direct intervention or action – where morphology gains pre-eminence over action (Castells). Work processes are increasingly individualized, a new, 'disaggregated', division of labour is in the process of emerging – one 'based on the attributers/ capacities of each worker rather than on the organization of the task' (Castells, 1997: 471). The nation state, too, is in flux (Grant, 2000): transnational civil society actors depend on intensive communication flows and the sharing of knowledge and in this way, some claim, they can 'sometimes outflank national government and international capital alike [...]' (Schiltz, Verschraegen, Magnolo, 2005: 347). The World Wide Web enables the emergence of 'loose coalitions, semi-spontaneous mobilizations, and ad hoc movements of neo-anarchists' displace permanent, structured, formal organizations (Castells in Schiltz, Verschraegen, Magnolo, 2005: 349). Vertical hierarchies built on states yield to horizontal heterarchies built on fluid networks.

Two preliminary points can be distilled here. Firstly, nodes are, as Castells himself observes, points at which curves intersect with themselves. There is thus the assumption of a necessary or adequate level of self-reference embedded in the metaphor of the node. Secondly, this self-reference of new organizational forms does not do away with the culturally and psychologically vital category of subjective agency since with the heterarchical form of distributed organizations across information nodes, far greater demands are exacted of the subject – to be agile, to engage in constant retraining, to absorb and adopt new practices, to interpret the interpretations of chatter, indeed, perhaps the hypercritical capacity for reinvention actually brings the autonomous subject back to his/her rightful place as an ethically responsible agent. Communication networks comprise not only informational codes in discrete channels, but also human communications in fundamentally uncertain channels, environments and minds. Risks are thematic, ontological and communicative – the 'objects of risk' thematized in communications about health, bioterror and environmental degradation, for example, the existential risk of life itself and the risks we take in interacting through the appeals to interpretation of our communicative acts. In suggesting that new connections presuppose the sharing of the 'same communication code' (Castells, 1997: 470), Castells leaves little room for the hybridization of those codes. Religious codes hybridize with political codes, commercial codes with legal codes, cultural codes with educational codes. And in this way, binary distinctions or schematizations become fluid.

2. Publics and relevance

Since political parties, NGOs, terrorist groups and commercial organizations rely so heavily on new forms of distributed, mass-mediated organization, it is appropriate to enquire after the status of the public sphere in the powerful, normative accounts of social communication which emerge more or less continuously from the Enlightenment through Husserl's work on intersubjectivity and finally Habermas's great works on the public and universal pragmatics. As we have seen, the intersubjective paradigm derives from the republican rhetorical tradition of the French Revolution, in the theory of Öffentlichkeit (publicness) and Enlightenment in Kant and in the literary enactment of dialogue as a means by which to overcome religious or courtly dogma. This paradigm still informs counterfactual theories of universal pragmatics, intersubjectivity, dialogism and, more often than not, our intuitive understanding of interactions to this day. Ostensibly an antidote to solipsism, having irrupted into Enlightenment thinking as an ideal at a contingent point in time, the intersubjective paradigm has exhausted itself in terms of its theoretical and empirical plausibility. Edmund Burke was already quick to decry the monstrous fictions of pro-revolutionary publics which claimed to speak for the majority and Hegel, equally determined to criticize the dissolution of publicness into 'mere public opinion'. However, the exhaustion of intersubjectivity has not simply come about because a once noble set of beliefs has been overtaken by rapacious technological advancement. Writing in the 1920s, Walter Lippmann offered a prescient account in *Public Opinion*, referring to the 'pseudo-environment' between men as 'populated by fictions' – the fictions, or social semiotic of public opinion detached from claims to reality:

> [...] the triangular relationship between the scene of action, the human picture of that scene, and the human response to that picture working itself out upon the scene of the action.
>
> (Lippmann, 1934: 16–17)

Lippmann saw propaganda as 'the effort to alter the picture to which men respond' (Lippmann, 1934: 26), but his innovativeness also lay in his awareness of the gap between ideals of the public and the limited resources of time, money and attention of the recipients of news or propaganda:

> We are concerned in public affairs, but immersed in our private ones. The time and attention are limited that we can spare for the labor of not taking opinions for granted, and we are subject to constant interruption.
>
> (Lippmann, 1934: 57)[2]

Clearly, in an information-rich global communication system, attention is limited and selection pressures unavoidable. Diffusion increases selection pressure and competition for relevance. Deselected information is no longer invisible, but a vast and exponentially growing residuum of information available at the click of a mouse. We are faced with a new 'logic of communication that contains a new form of publicness, information and "civil society"' (Castells, 1997: 348), for example, in the form of the Open Access and Creative Commons movements designed to enable local actors to gain access to public information goods especially in health and agriculture. The boundaries between State and civil society, private and public, become blurred. It is therefore difficult to see how public opinion can still be considered as 'the key ingredient of the type of bonding we call citizenship' (Hermes, 2006: 300). Does the fictional status of diffuse publics, despite the hope of Schiltz, Hermes et al., sound the death knell for active political participation?

Some have argued that although the classical civil society model is challenged by globalization, the Web now opens up new interactive opportunities for inclusion and symmetry. And yet to see this shift to networks, clusters and nodes as inherently more inclusive or interactive is probably a claim too far:

> These idealistic visions of open systems overlook the fact that networks are used to gain informational advantages, not erase them. They also ignore the fact that uncertainty and risk are the corollary to information abundance [...].
>
> (Mulgan, 1991: 4, cited in: Winseck, 2002: 93–122)

Against pessimistic or optimistic or simply quiescent theories of politics (and systems theory is open to this criticism), it is worth recalling that Habermas understood that the theory of publicness rested on counterfactual ideals of rationality and contestation (Habermas, 1996). Thus the question of any correspondence of a theory to 'the facts' is not really the issue here. Albeit implicitly, Kant himself had already drawn attention to the paradoxical unpublicness of publicness in terms of its male dominance and geographical limitations. If Kant was able to extrapolate an ideal social dialogue from a face-to-face communication context, this represented the advent of the interaction paradigm when in fact interaction was undergoing fundamental change from 'direct interaction' to 'mediated interaction'. The timing of the theory of dialogical interaction in a non-dialogical world, as Luhmann has pointed out, is no coincidence. Kant's public theory as a political interaction paradigm was already a wistful recollection of better communication days. If this incompatibility was already present in Kant's day, then it is even more acute with today's liquid interaction networks – rather too glibly disparaged as 'mediated quasi-interaction' (cf. Thompson, 1994: 35).

In view of these constraints (which only serve to highlight the risks of hypostatization in Habermas's model) the public sphere can be seen as a selection medium in which contributions from 'civil society' would be published in journals and newspapers according to the criterion of public relevance, rather than as a place for inclusion. This media system has been further differentiated functionally as social, political, cultural and other actors have differentiated. While these various communication subsystems jointly constitute what Klaus Japp (2003) has described as the world communication society, talk of a European or global public sphere rests rather too precariously and tenuously on a unifying metaphor of sharedness; even Castells has reproduced in his observation that networks work when the same communication codes are shared. And yet, I argue that human communications cut across and undermine those codes in dynamic, autonomous interactions.

Habermas's more recent reflections on the public sphere, some three decades after publication of *Structural Transformation of the Public Sphere*, criticize the new media, public relations and advertising for giving rise to media power – a new form of 'manipulation' which 'once and for all took care of the innocence of the principle of publicity' (Habermas, 1993: 437). Of course, a public sphere without an account of the medium – whether a literary pamphlet or an on-line discussion forum or blog – is inconceivable, or conceivable only if we adopt a truncated view of the public and communication. It needs to be said that not only can publicness – as communication – more adequately be construed as plural spaces in a fluid landscape in which information flows induce deterritorializations of nation states and public spheres with them (as outlined in the works of Lash and Bauman), but the associated concept of interaction itself should be reconceptualized if rational and normative claims are accepted as uncertainties (cf. Luhmann, 1993). For example, Lash, following Luke, sees the new global information society as consisting of a series of different zones: live zones of heavy information flows, wild zones of low information density, tame zones of high information density and dead zones of light information flows (Lash, 2002: 28; 37). These new information zones make the critical project of a public sphere highly problematic.

In a world of liquid life and liquid selves, where past structures are molten, and organizations and subjects in perpetual reinvention to keep pace with globalization, it is almost impossible to sustain belief in an immaculate communicative realm. 'Publics' – as self-thematizing clusters of relevance, are constituted by mediatizations which introduce uncertainties and transmit, challenge and renew reality levels with an almost simultaneous speed and intensity.[3] However, as pointed out at the beginning of this study, this impossibility is not merely a result of the revolution in media technologies, but more fundamentally a factor of a range of existential conditions: (1) the open dynamic of interpretation (as distinct from semantic mapping from one subject to another); (2) the impossibility of recovery of meaning stimuli from other speakers; (3) the multivoicedness of communicating subjects and

(4) our impossible access to other minds. As Christopher Gauker notes in his recent essay, 'Zero Tolerance fro Pragmatics', 'a hearer cannot reliably employ a method of interpretation that requires the hearer to have an independent insight into the speaker's intention' (Gauker, MS: 7). As Bauman himself has argued, the 'disengagement' between agents and systems has not been brought about by the colonization of the private sphere by the 'system', but by the 'radical melting of the fetters and manacles rightly or wrongly suspected of limiting the individual freedom to choose or to act'. Where it was a simple matter of assuming that ideology or systems lay somehow beyond the purchase of actors, with this melting process, we can, once more, turn to the vitality of human agency:

> Vision, indeed any system involving 'information', requires an interpreter, and that interpreter is the material human body grounded in the wetware of our sensorimotor systems.
>
> (Lenoir, 2004: xxiii)

The increasing use of computer-mediated communication (CMC) does not mean a seismic shift away from face-to-face interaction. CMC remains predominantly work-based (although the encroachments of work communications into private life are on the increase), still the preserve of professionals and younger, computer-literate generations; for the majority, the web remains a place of 'transient incursions' and CMC does not replace old networks – it reinforces them (Castells, 1997: 362–3). Indeed, in passing it is worth noting that there is a little-explored recursivity to this shift, namely the impact of computer-mediated interaction on face-to-face interaction for very often the solution to all-too frequent inflammatory electronic behaviour is to convene a face to face meeting in which matters are 'clarified'. Similarly, there must be a recursive loop social between, for example, reality TV shows, feeding forward into everyday face-to-face interactions, forming part of a communications environment in which public and private are blurred. For popular media environments are very much part of the everyday and offer points of cultural reference for millions worldwide.

There are many dimensions to the globalization process: connectivity and conflict, functional differentiation, detraditionalization (Zürn), but also retraditionalization, deterritorialization (the rise of transnational, postnational movements), contingency and risk. These are the twin processes of universaliztion and relativization where we have become acutely aware of the fluidity of our identities in cultural, cognitive or religious terms. Where Habermas refers to a paradoxical 'community of risk' others see identities as understandings of our incompleteness (Butler, 2000: 31). Thus the communicating subject is both *truncated* by the contingencies of dispersed media networks and also *extended* by the connections of the distributions these networks provide. We are both fragmented and almost permanently connected and reconnected.

In the age of uncertainty and the challenge to communicative understanding, normative accounts fail at this complexity gap and clash with the multiple contingencies of our communications: the selections of ego; the selections of alter; the mediatizations of our network extensions. Normative accounts of communication mask the intricacies of our assumptions, inferences and imputations and the need to rethink theories of meaning exchange, collective belief and referential semantics. Communication without uncertainty would be a statistically regular, almost ergodic exercise in redundancy and control. And yet we know that, *pace* intentionalistic models of communication, so much goes 'wrong' (misinterpretation, miscommunication, misfires, infelicities, misquotation) when we communicate. That uncertainty is a factor of human autonomy wrapped up in the freedom of interpretation and the incommensurability of radical translation and access to other minds. Why, then, does not uncertainty run riot? Have we resolved the intermonadological fallacy only at the cost of slipping back into the very solipsism we seek to evade?

3. Myths of the medium and limits of interactivity

Conventional models of democracy tend to be predicated on notions of a public domain in which citizens have their say. A conception of the public sphere, which remains blind to the impact of the media including electronic media, must therefore operate with extremely outdated concepts of social communication and interaction. For without doubt, the media have always played a crucial role in the formation of society (from the agora of ancient Greece to the Roman *Senatus* via the petition, from the printed press to the Internet).

The relationship between the uncertainties of communication and cognitive autonomy poses a problem for society, and ideal models of social interaction such as consensus, inclusion and democracy. If communication is irreducibly uncertain, and the social actor cognitively closed or self-referential, and society dependent on communications, then this might induce anarchy. And yet, society does come about and sustain itself – even if the fictional pseudo-environments are now merely media-constructions with competing reality constructions.

The classical ideal of democracy implies access to a public sphere, participation, exchange, freedom from constraint. *Prima facie*, e-networks appear to satisfy these democratic criteria and thus offer an ideal medium for democracy formation. However, the capacity of the public sphere (and therefore, accessible forms of political organization) to evolve with the emergence of each new medium can be viewed with scepticism in view of the porosity of communication and the hardware and software constraints of the medium. This means that the Internet is a paradox of transparency and selection in which the medium must be conceived as selective.

Even self-referential semantics (such as legal codes) remain, however residually, uncertain. Noise is not some parasitical deviation from the norm, but an embedded form of communication – not a manifestation of longer collateral communication damage, but an ontological or epistemic 'fact' demanded by the need to keep the space of communication open. No counterfactual schematism can ever successfully fill the indeterminacies which are constitutive of communication; systems theory and universal pragmatics have already demonstrated their limited reach and neglect of autonomy. Systems operate amidst such uncertainty for they are communication-dependent. To preserve their stability as systems or institutions they are endowed with codes or discourses as complex schematizations. These schematizations function as stabilizers of vague semiotics in which a vague residuum always persists (Peirce); potential destabilizing effects are fed back into the system recursively. In the case of strategic political communications designed by western agencies for intervention in winning 'hearts and minds' in the Arab world, this idea has also been embraced.

In liquid globalization, communication and connectivity, new forms of 'mediapolitics', might be said to be emergent. Blumler and

Gurevitch also invest considerable hope in the Internet's 'discursive role', as follows:

> [...] if Internet use tends to encourage and support a more active disposition to communications than mainstream media use, some of this should transfer over to people's reception through it of news, public affairs and politics.
>
> (Blumler and Gurevitch, 2001: 5)

New communication media have an undoubted impact on political life and their emergence has almost always accompanied by ambitious claims: Brecht's faith in the democratic potential of radio 1930s; and De Gaulle's televized presidential addresses in 1960s are two such examples. And yet, while television 'realigns' relations between public and politics, and e-democracy, e-governance, e-publics extolled as the latest new dawn, there are good reasons to exercise caution: the new media have a 'vulnerable potential to enhance public communications' (Blumler and Gurevitch, 2001: 2) with claims of the emergence of 'new politics' or a 'new political culture', popular culture and politics hybridize in a global mediaworlds; a danger emerges: the commodification of the 'public sphere':

> The product advertising campaign provides the underlying model for the political election campaign. Both instantiated the prominence of irrational appeal within a general legitimating discourse of rationality. Both are attempts to establish resonance with a massive number of people so that connections are drawn between the campaign's message and the interests of consumers/citizens.
>
> (Marshall, 1997: 205 cited in: Scott and Street, 2000: 224)

Forms of political organization remain contingent on a range of channels and audiences, which result in the increased dispersal of communications and juxtaposition of political, commercial and religious semantic codes. Given this dispersal, it seems to be over-simplified to claim that there is a tension between a 'cacophonic free-for-all' and 'forces for civility, integrity and coherence' (Blumler and Gurevitch), with the implied criticism of 'disorderly communication'.[4] Against the backdrop of an abundance of extreme communications (neo-Nazi groups, holocaust deniers, anti-semitic groups and fundamentalists of various hues and persuasions), and the impact of 'punk'-inspired spectacle politics the question will be to investigate the connections between dispersal and new forms of political communication.

On the interactivity potential of the web, Schulz claims that it is a more *active* medium, enabling greater citizen participation, greater capacity for community building and greater '*symmetry* of communicative power' (Schulz, 2000), where communication between citizens and politicians becomes more direct. And yet, these are also questionable claims since the medium itself remains a medium between cognitively closed agents who have no access to each others' inferences or intentions, *a fortiori* in multiple pseudo-environments populated by fictions. The Internet does not impose interactivity but does facilitate connections which extend systems and truncate them simultaneously. The communitarian ideals that accompany claims of enhanced interactivity or symmetry are at odds with a medium whose connections are simultaneously separations. The era of multiple contingency means that we are entitled to ask whether the medium creates a greater onus on politicians to be receptive or to provide good grounds for decisions by enhancing legitimation through feedback. In the deterritorialized world of globalization there is certainly an acute shock of discourses between a sense of risk, contingency and uncertainty, and a resurgence of 'semantics of unity' (Japp, 2003). Dispersal issues a challenge: as the world liquefies, the shock of civilizational or religious or political narratives becomes more acute – the communicating subject is cut loose from universal systems and counterfactual claims.

4. Mediaterror and world communication society

Theories of democracy or globalization require a theory of communication and the classical, normative understanding of a public sphere mediating between citizens and the state must now include an understanding of various communication media in social and political processes. The normative conception, derived from Habermas' counterfactual theory of discursive democracy, is based on contestation of validity claims, mediating sphere between lifeworld and system as a locus of rationale debate. When we think of globalization and ask whether globalization is actually global, we tend to ignore the core question, namely the uncertainties of mounting interconnectedness.

The answer to this question involves moving away from structures (access, regulation), representation (media), interaction (deliberative, discursive process) to an understanding of diffusion and reality construction and the contingency of grand narratives and the irreducible ethical imperative of each communicating subject. Globalization is profoundly paradoxical:

> There is a new dialectic of global and local questions which fall through the framework of national politics. These 'glocal' questions are part of the political agenda – in cities, countries, governments, publics, both nationally and internationally. This in turn requires a new political subject: the translocal social movements and national-cultural based parties of world citizens.
>
> (Beck, 1998b: 19)

Global mediaterror is a further example of the intertwining of connectivity and contingency – the fact that Al Qaeda's messages cannot be 'escaped' and that they fragment any notion of universal human rights. We are, as social subjects, faced with a new quality of multivoiced complexity, noise and uncertainty, which creates informational strain or an even greater need for complexity coping strategies for human agents.

In response to the new uncertainties of mediapolitics, the US government sponsored a strategic media intervention campaign and targeted the Middle East with children's TV series (Arabic Sesame Street), blogs, chatrooms, electronic journals, messages to 'delegitimize terrorism', NGO mobilization and language-qualified 'global messengers' (Report of the Defense Science Board Task Force on Strategic Communication: 68). This communications strategy formed part of a range of US international broadcasting services, including Voice of America, Radio Free Europe, Radio Free Asia, Radio Farda and Al Hurra. On the face of it, these outlets suggest an impressive panoply of strategic instruments, but there is a serious gap between strategic communication intention and impact. There is here a tacit acceptance of interconnectedness where control lies in the slender fact all unitary semantics of religious or political fundamentalism will fail as they seek to impose closure on the very uncertainties of human agents that keep communication going. The impact of the US-sponsored satellite broadcaster Al Hurra was reduced by a range of factors, including the saturation of satellite TV market, the perception that

Al Hurra was a US-government broadcaster, of poor reporting quality, little attention to in depth coverage of Middle East news, disappointed expectations of aggressive human rights reporting, names and accents of reporters assumed to be Lebanese Christians (Report Defense Board). In his testimony to the US Senate in 2004, William Rugh detailed the changed communication environment into which *Al Hurra* was pitched. Until Operation Desert Storm in 1991, the Arabic media had been largely government controlled. However, CNN offered 24/7 coverage of the war and provoked a satellite revolution in the Arabic-speaking world. The founding of *Al Jazeera* had marked a 'revolution' in Arabic media environment, with popular genres such as talk shows (fundamentalists versus feminists) and a range of local correspondents 'on the ground'.[5] The key fact is that both Al Qaeda and counterterrorism are media-dependent and actually form subsystems within a media system of which political system is increasingly one facet. It is possible to say that '[t]he history of terrorism is the history of communication' (Abrahms, 2005: 536) and that there is a curious communicational reciprocity to this relationship (cf. Grant, 2004; Crelinsten, 2002).

Goodall, Trethewey and McDonald argue that the rather specious top-down understanding of strategic political communication based on the transmission of intentions and the changing of minds is not possible and that dialogue, after decades of mistrust and conflict is not credible. A third way lies in the strategic ambiguity or the deliberate generation of noise and uncertainty. The origins of this model lie in research in organizations in turbulent environments and the pressure to share more information. In other words, message control is abandoned: 'The goal of strategically ambiguous communication should not be "shared meaning" but instead organized action' (Goodall, Trethewey, McDonald, 2006: 3–4). Today, the emergence of deterritorialized terrorism marks a new phase in the complexity of terrorist groups. And since such groups, with their reliance on the mass media, are communication organizations *sui generis*, this complexity generates new communicative uncertainty in the political and social systems in contexts of security and everyday life:

[...] meanings attributed to messages are – in a global mediated environment – interpreted locally and rebroadcast within those locally-interpreted frameworks to audiences who neither share our native language and culture, and who are fundamentally dubious about the truth value of our messages.

(Goodall, Trethewey, McDonald, 2006: 3–4)

While some political commentators view terrorism in terms of a good/ evil or rational/primitive manicheisms, Elliott and Kiel (2004), for example, examine terrorism as a series of 'complex adaptive systems' or, borrowing a metaphor from fluid mechanics, 'fluids'. It is not open to doubt that Al Qaeda is a particularly fluid organization for which communication is a core function. More than ever before terrorism relies on the mass media and without mass communication it would be denied its key function as a psychological weapon. Abrahms notes that Al Qaeda describes its terrorist acts as 'messages without words' (Abrahms, 2005: 530) when in fact the terrorist act itself is one of a range of instruments used by this *rhizomatic* group. In addition, there are audio and video recordings typically relayed to Al Jazeera. Here, it is striking how 'mainstream' Al Qaeda seeks to persuade 'public opinions' – or self-thematizing relevance systems – in western states by appealing to them to force their governments to withdraw troops from, for example, Iraq. There are also several subgenres at play: direct threats, blackmail, religious discourse, denials of responsibility and the claims of responsibility for attacks. The number of such communications has increased from 3 in 1996 to 2450 in 2005, with an increase in Internet for the broadcasting of such messages from 0 to 2439 over the same period (Torres *et al.*, 2006: 404; 405). This increase carries its own risk, namely one of attention overload for the audiences for which it is intended, and the result has been a diffusion of the propaganda effort (Torres *et al.*, 2005: 417). A ready contrast – and additional illustration of the competition for global media relevance – is offered by the videos of Zarqawi's Al Qaeda in Iraq group, whose communications were not so much additional instruments of terror, but embedded in the bestiality of live executions. Even if, as a dialogue, terrorism has failed (as a bargaining strategy it has failed), as a source of noise it is now firmly part of our global mediaworld. And that means pressure of interpretation selection:

The theory of functional differentiation also implies a world society communication system. Fundamentalism inevitably develops, even

if it does not wish to, in the context of functional differentiation
and not somehow as opposition from the outside.

(Japp, 2003: 56)

The choreography of relations between terrorist and counterterrorist
organizations is additionally complex since definitions of terrorism
and security have in themselves become, to borrow Bauman's
description, liquid. Crelinsten refers here to 'grey zones' or 'zones of
ambiguity' (Crelinsten, 2004: 79–80). These dyads are already a form
of schematization and support the view that if non-state based or
transnational groupings form systems, then state-based actors such
as governments or intergovernmental alliances are the environments
of such systems and *vice versa*. A certain communicational reciprocity
is thus built into these relations between terrorism and counterterrorism since a system can only exist by emphasizing its difference
vis-à-vis an environment. Al Qaeda seeks to promote instability in its
environment as a means to promote uncertainty, provoking attacks
and invasions by using misinformation strategically.[6] However, it is
not an anarchistic grouping and retains a strongly centralizing theo-
cratic core which rests on an interpretation of a canon by privileged
interpreters (first and foremost bin Laden). At the same time, an
analysis of communication complexity based merely on mutually
hostile systems has the potential to ignore the agents caught between
them. The subject is caught between the schematizations of two centralizing and yet also uncertain worlds of discourse in which he/she
is rarely if ever a direct participant. The management of such *multivoiced* complexity seems necessary and yet can place the agent under
severe informational strain where agents select relevance against a
background of deafening noise.

Caught between two dominant centripetal discourses (that is knowledge systems) built on manicheisms, we cope with flows of at least
new information and a system characterized by extremely high levels
of uncertainty generated by two unitary semantics. Counterterrorist
responses from governments or security agencies seek to reduce uncertainty with satellite broadcasts, intercultural exchanges and various
media reassurances and yet paradoxically create yet more uncertainty
since neither the sources of chatter nor the interpretation of that
chatter are divulged. Both communication worlds are hybrid: activist
rhetoric, the discourse of damnation and redemption, the discourses

of civil and universal human rights and free trade and the discourse of apostasy, spiritual superiority and the allegation of western decadence. The fluid forms of organization, complex interconnectedness of a mass mediated terrorism and counterterrorist operations leave communicative uncertainties unresolved for social agents, despite the use of manicheisms or binary codes on both sides.

5. 'Chatter' and the communicating subject as ethical interpreter

It is the core theme of this book that theories in the shadow of the 'semantic of interaction' such as intersubjectivity, understanding or consensus can be reconceptualized together with the epistemological foundations on which they are built. In pragmatic interactions, communicative uncertainties are bridged by contingent constructions such as assumptions, imputations and presuppositions between cognitively unique agents. Our knowledge of these uncertainties makes both transcendental theories of communication and understanding and overstabilized concepts of binary codes are problematic in equal measure. Thus it follows that systems which rely on communications such as western governments and media-hungry Al Qaeda itself, are porous in their communications – notwithstanding sophisticated encryption. In the case of the latter, the fluid organizational and porous communication structure could offer desirable additional operational capacity in making membership more decentralized and less hierarchical. At the same time, there is not a plurality of discourses in Al Qaeda communications since the organization seeks to operate with a far from complex apostasy/orthodoxy binary code.

As discussed above, Luhmann's theory of social systems suffers from a limited reach in tending both to overstate system stability and underestimate the inherent uncertainties of communication, arguing that 'there must be mechanisms that [...] produce adequate determinacy' (Luhmann, 1995: 83). Thus, despite the fact that disturbances or noise are constitutive of meaning processes, social systems operate with schematizations which facilitate connectivity. While communication systems do indeed use schematisms, binary codes or cultural semantics, it is still the case that all of these procedures depend on communications which are at the very least residually uncertain. Thus, it can also be said that binary codes (acceptance/rejection, legal/illegal, right/wrong) and schematisms are in themselves porous. After all, strategic information and strategic disinformation cannot be distinguished (Baecker, 1999a: 51).

Rather than simply presupposing schematism in every communication, as Luhmann suggests, it is proposed here to introduce greater uncertainty into open systems by conceptualizing stability, codification or schematization, not as 'momentary unamibiguity' [*sic*], but as tolerable uncertainty across a scale of interpretations. If communication is uncertain, this resolution is permanently polysemic; thus, the problematic sharpness of Luhmann's binary conceptualization of codes and schematisms is also revealed in the conception of social meaning systems which use 'linguistic coding' or 'the doubling of expressive possibilities by a yes/no difference' (Luhmann, 1995: 444). In such a system communication is coded as a proposal of meaning which can be accepted or rejected, understood or misunderstood. It is also the case that there is an increasing awareness in society of the uncertainty or contingency of rituals, binary codes or schematisms even if new schematisms and codes arise and take their place. The legal/illegal binary code is increasingly fuzzy in the case of international law (consider preventive military operations, humanitarian intervention and the shifting definitions of sovereignty).

In social terms, these connections and clashes form a new community of contingency (Habermas, 1998) with processes of sacralization, desacralization, detraditionalization and globalization/glocalization. These are instances and experiences when the reflexivity of our communicative practices and awareness of such paradoxes clashes against the self-referential closure of communications systems, and this clash in turn reveals the contingency of systems which observe themselves as being stable. And yet it would be wrong to underestimate the capacity of the autonomous agent to find a way through the noise, to evaluate and criticize. In other words, social agents are reflexively aware of the plurality of codes and rituals and their shifting diversification (consider also how the codes of politics and entertainment have become increasingly hybridized).

A further example of the complexity gap between systems theory or universal pragmatics and uncertain communication is provided by the belief that systems 'organize' systems in their environments by means of 'differentiation schemata'. It should be recalled that Luhmann sees the differentiation of systems as a source of indeterminacies which can be manipulated by a system. It could also be contended that the capacity for communication complexity means that communications constantly cross systems frontiers. In terms of cultural and social semantics, the processes of detraditionalization, denationalization and globalization/glocalization are examples of this system-crossing. In this way, communications actually challenge the internality of systems reference and induce a much stronger form of drift. If communications are uncertain by virtue of their dependency on producing and receiving agents, media and contexts and if systems have an operational dependency on communications then it follows that only uncertain distinctions can be constructed by a system. This inherent uncertainty also accounts for the dynamic process of systems evolution. Dynamic social systems can adapt to uncertainty without ever resolving it. Further, if systems depend on communications which are uncertain then it is more important for a system's capacity to adapt to be able to tolerate uncertainty within the system rather than seeing it as a source of exogenous contingency – as noise on the outside.[7] In their classic account of human pragmatics Watzlawick, Bavelas and Jackson (1967) made a similar point:

> The distinction between closed and open systems can be said to have freed the sciences concerned with life phenomena from the shackles of a theoretical model based essentially on classical physics and chemistry: a model of exclusively closed systems. Because living systems have crucial dealings with their environments, the theory and the methods of analysis appropriate to things which can be reasonably put in 'a sealed container' were significantly obstructive and misleading.
>
> (1967: 122)

The hybrid structural/spatial character of communication means that systems which rely on communications – social and human systems – have an in-built uncertainty. In such a conceptualization, there is a greater degree of tension between the capacity of systems to reduce or manage complexity and the uncertain communications on which they rely for their interactions with their environments.

As mentioned above, Baecker's distinction between well-defined and ill-defined systems shares some of the criticisms set out here. Whereas well-defined systems are like trivial machines in being stable in time, in ill-defined systems transitions between the stages in a system are not known, the probability of transitions is not known and the system itself is unstable in time. One such system is the human being. Agents interact better with poorly defined systems and do not wish to be confronted with over-determined systems in which their autonomy as agents is denied. In this way, it can be said that organizations are 'more or less manageable mixes of order and disorder, redundancy and variety, loose and firm coupling' (Baecker, 1999b: 25). While the correlation between uncertain communications and porous systems shares some common ground with Baecker's account, it places the systems-theoretical bias towards degrees of systems definitions (whether these be internal or external, well- or ill-defined) in a different context in which communications are the primary object of analysis. Descriptions by an observer of systems as having varying degrees of definition or sharpness tend to neglect factors which criss-cross all systems and to neglect these dynamic influences. There is therefore a need to reintroduce communications as universal and uncertain environments in which systems definitions and self referential process are always subject to risk and change. Crozier and Friedberg, too, in *The Actor and the System*, write that:

> [Structures and rules] create and circumscribe *zones of organizational uncertainty* which individuals or groups quite naturally seek to control for their own use in the pursuit of their own strategies [...].
> (Crozier and Friedberg, 2001: 78–9 – my translation)

Thus, while communications dwell in the interstices of uncertainty and schematization, so the obverse applies. The free circulation of communications is ensured by universal connections with all communicating agents but their forms are constantly displaced by context, user and receiver. No schematism or transcendental counterfactual can ever successfully fill the indeterminacies which are constitutive of communication. Social systems and universal paradigms operate amidst such uncertainty for they are communication-dependent. To preserve their stability as systems, institutions are endowed with codes or discourses as complex schematizations. These schematizations function as stabilizers of vague semiotics in which a vague residuum always persists (Peirce, 1955). Agents (the term is used here as a synonym for actor in the sense proposed by Crozier and

Friedberg) are also aware of the self-referential codes of such rituals and there is mounting evidence that agents are increasingly aware of the uncertainty of that self-reference in their ability to negotiate chatter, to interpret the interpretations of that chatter by security services, to 'read' mediasemiotics and deconstruct the ideological edifices of newspaper and TV editorial policies – consider also the rapid ironization of David Cameron's blog. This capacity of the subject to deconstruct multivoicedness, uncertainty in interaction and contingency in mediasociety is part of the ethical dimension of the autonomous subject as the interpreter of noise.

As Castells also notes in the field of finance, the logic of the market is not dictated by some pure economic laws of supply and demand, but informed by fuzzier factors such as psychology and society, gossip, rumour and noise (it is striking that Starbucks now have a 'Rumour Response' page on their corporate website). This new, global market 'responds to turbulences, and unpredictable movements, of noncalculable anticipations' (Castells, 1997: 474). Here, then, actors, who are not subsumed in communication systems, are dependent on the 'nonhuman capitalist logic of an electronically operated, random processing of information', where the randomness is generated by the recursive operations of financial systems turned in on themselves and bypassing individuals, a world of 'pure self-reference' or 'pure circulation'. This self-reference, precisely because it relies on information flows, is precarious: all information if porous, all subject to noise of various descriptions – the hacker, the electronic fraudster, the creative accountant, the collapse of a currency or regime, suspicions of misdeeds, or takeovers or mergers or interest-rate hikes. This uncertainty is the chance of the subject.

The theory of communication as a porous form of selected message and redundancy suggests the need to explore the unmarked spaces of communication, the interstices or gaps, the unspoken languages 'no-one has ever spoken or will ever speak'. Whereas Baecker argues that communication is the 'determination of the indeterminate but determinable with the aim of understanding the determinate' (Baecker, 2005: 23). I would suggest that the indeterminacy of the range of communication options we have at our disposal in different cultures, different languages, different media and different social roles is not actually determinable at all. The uncertainty of communication actually means that even when we think we choose a clear, stable form the *penumbra of unselected information* remains. The relationship between the form of our communications and their non-forms is irreducibly dynamic. We communicate in order to accompany the dynamic of our interactions with the world. To be communicable is not to be determinable but to remain interpretable despite the impossibility of intersubjectivity. The autonomous human communicator is the active interpreter of noise. That need to interpret is the chance of the subject freed from the weight of the paradigm of intersubjectivity.

Notes

Chapter 1

1. Donald Davidson, *Subjective, Intersubjective, Objective.* p. 108.
2. See, for example, Williamson (1998) and the exchange between Wright and Rosenkranz (2003).
3. Translations from this work are my own.

Chapter 2

1. The first published version of the *Meditations* appeared in the translation of Emmanuel Levinas and Gabrielle Pfeiffer in the Paris publishing house A. Colin in 1931. Publication of the first German edition was delayed by the arrival of the Nazis in 1933 and it was posthumously published in 1950.
2. Note the systematic use of the concept of relevance in contemporary theoretical pragmatics, exemplified by Sperber and Wilson's *Relevance* (1995). Schütz does not appear to have had a direct, acknowledged impact on their highly influential work.
3. But see Crossley, N. and Roberts, J.M. ed. (2004).
4. In a similar spirit I presented the papers 'Uncertainty and Dialogism' at the XIth International Bakhtin Conference at the Universidade Federal do Paraná in July 2003 and 'Bühler's Appeal for Complex Communication Theory: Towards a Theory of Constructivist Semiotics' at the Bakhtin Centre, University of Sheffield in November 2003.
5. Craig Brandist notes that '[...] Bakhtin does not argue for the final merging of all languages and perspectives when culture becomes self-conscious. The 'autonomous and independent value' of 'various cultural forms' are maintained rather than subsumed into a single and all-encompassing meta-form [...]' (Brandist, 2004: 147).
6. I rely on the reference made to Karcevskij in Holquist (1990: 47): By 1929, Karcevskij was arguing that relations between the sign and its eventual signification were asymmetrical in a manner reminiscent of Peirce's conclusion discussed in chapter one that the vague residuum in signs is irreducible.
7. Cf. Holquist's observations on the influence of relativity theories for Bakhtin (Holquist, 1990: 6ff.).
8. Van Dijk's approach to values explicitly deals with the need for the social organisation of values in which actions and interactions require 'routines of evaluation'. Not only do values possess a routine character, they are historically embedded and handed down through ages where ideologies are 'terminal' and informed by short-term motivations or goals. The historicity, sharedness and routine character of values are taken to 'preclude their reduction to individuals' who 'may share, adopt or reject the values of their

group' but are whose ideals or goals or not values in themselves (van Dijk, 2000: 74). Thus, for van Dijk, values have a 'fundamental socio-cultural status'; they are, in other words social *aprioris*. In this way, subjective axiology is always seen as socialized.

Chapter 3

1. See the extensive bibliographies of René Görtzen, *Jürgen Habermas: Eine Bibliographie seiner Schriften und der Sekundarliteratur 1952-1981* (Frankfurt: Suhrkamp, 1982).
2. In 'Further Reflections on the Public Sphere' in D. Calhoun, 1993, ed. *Habermas and the Public Sphere* (Cambridge MA, London: MIT Press, 421–61) and also *Die postnationale Konstellation*.
3. Uncertainty is a crucial component of communication if communication is to be associated with a society which can tolerate criticism. In authoritarian or totalitarian regimes attempts to control uncertainty – including the suppression of Milan Kundera's *The Joke* in 1967 – must fail. In this sense, uncertain communication theory refuses to abandon critical theory – it chooses to pursue the project by other means.
4. Cf. Whorf's classic *Language, Thought and Reality. Selected Writings of Benjamin Lee Whorf*, Carroll, J.B. ed. (Cambridge, MA: MIT Press, 1956).

Chapter 4

1. Translations from Luhmann's untranslated works are my own.
2. These titles are not currently available in English translation, and the translations here are my own. For translations of related works see: Schmidt, Siegfried J. (2003b). 'Histories and Discourses: An Integrated Approach to Communication Science' in Colin B. Grant ed. *Rethinking Communicative Interaction: New Interdisciplinary Horzions* (Amsterdam/ Philadelphia: Benjamins, 129–44) and Baecker, Dirk (2001) 'Why Systems?', *Theory, Culture & Society*, 1 18: 59–74.

Chapter 5

1. In psychological terms, Lacan refers to the 'vicissitudes of the subject' and the 'precarious life of the subject' (Lacan, 1973: 26; 85). Cf. also Cixous's work on the 'subject at risk' in H. Cixous and M. Calle-Gruber *Rootprints, Memory and Life Writing* (London: Routledge, 1997).
2. See Luckmann, Thomas (1977) *Lebensweltliche Zeitkategorien, Zeitstrukturen des Alltags und der Ort des historischen Bewußtseins*. Stuttgart: Reclam and Linell, Per and Thomas Luckmann (1991) 'Asymmetries in Dialogue: Some Conceptual Preliminaries' in I. Marková and K. Foppa eds., Asymmetries in Dialogue (Hemel Hempstead: Harvester Wheatsheaf, 1991).

3. See Vaihinger, H., 1924, The Philosophy of 'As if': A System of the Theoretical, Practical and Religious Fictions of Mankind (London: K. Paul, Trench, Trubner and Co.; New York: Harcourt, Brace and Co.). Some of the early interactionists also map out questions of potentially radical implications. W.I. Thomas refers to the 'as if' behaviour of social actors in an attempt to define the future reference of conduct. The potential virtuality of social behaviours thus comes to the fore. In other words, 'facts do not have a uniform existence apart from the persons who observe and interpret them' (Volkart cited in Meltzer et al, 1975: 27).

4. This is not the place to examine in detail Sartre's critique of Husserl, but one brief statement will suffice for the purposes of illustration: '[...] la seule réalité qui demeure est donc celle de mon intention: autrui, c'est le noème vide qui correspond à ma visée vers autrui [...]'. (J.-P. Sartre, *L'Etre et le Néant. Essai d'ontologie phénoménologique* (Paris: Gallimard: 280).

5. But Lyotard's conclusion that communication becomes 'agonistic' (Lyotard, 1988: 61; xxv) is too simplistic for these investigations.

6. Where I = information, s = source and r = receiver.

7. Dretske follows Sayre's "Philosophy and Cybernetics" in Kenneth Sayre and Frederick J. Crosson eds. *Philosophy and Cybernetics* (New York, 1967: 11).

8. '[...] what information is transmitted may depend on what the receiver already knows about the possibilities existing at the source.' (Dretske, 1999: 65) – I would argue that it *always* depends.

9. As pointed out by Krohn et al. (1994) in their discussion of the general applicability of concepts of self-organization in the social sciences.

10. Fallibilism: 'the doctrine relative to some significant class of beliefs or propositions, that they are inherently uncertain and possibly mistaken. The most extreme form of the doctrine attributes uncertainty to every belief; more restricted forms attribute it to all empirical beliefs, to beliefs concerning the past, the future, other minds, or the external world' – *The Cambridge Dictionary of Philosophy* (gen. Ed. Robert Audi) (Cambridge: Cambridge University Press, 261).

Chapter 6

1. It is not without interest that Linell himself admits that dialogism has a slightly 'Messianic ring' (Linell, 1998: 35).

2. Hermans refers to the 'complexity of the contemporary self' and even to the 'inevitability of dialogical misunderstanding' (Hermans, 2002: 157; 155). However, the assumption is always that the self is intersubjectively intertwined. Thus, complexity is reduced from the outset.

3. The term is misleadingly used by Luhmann and other constructivists.

4. Intentionalist theories continue to make mistaken claims about the relationship between the subject and communication. Gillett argues, for example, that the microprocessing shape of our brain is formed by the information our semantic environment presents to it. Thus, information is out there in an environment and not the product of active selection.

Chapter 8

1. Gilles Deleuze and Félix Guattari, *A Thousand Plateaus: Capitalism and Schizophrenia* (Minneapolis: University of Minnesota Press, 1987).
2. According to Robert K. Merton in *Mass Persuasion* (1946), people were becoming wary of 'commercial duplicity and pretended enthusiasms' and the 'feigning of personal concern with the other fellow in order to manipulate him the better' (cited in Simonson, 2006: 277).
3. *The Guardian* 17 November 2006.
4. 'Usenet groups reproduce chaos because discussion moderators or facilitators [...] are plainly absent' (Davis, 1999, in Blumler and Gurevitch, 2001: 4).
5. See Rugh, W.A., 'Comments on Radio Sawa and Al Hurra Television' retrieved from http:www.senate.gov/~foreign/testimony/2004/RughTestimony 040429.pdf
6. The founder of the World Wide Web, Tim Berners-Lee, has recently spoken of the risks of blogging and the potential for the dissolution of trust: 'The blogging world works by people reading blogs and linking to them. You're taking suggestions of what you read from people you trust. That, if you like, is a very simple system, but in fact the technology must help us express much more complicated feelings about who we'll trust with what.' Cited in Bobbie Johnson, 'Creator of Web warns of fraudsters and cheats' in *The Guardian*, 3 November 2006: 5.
7. In classical early communication theory it is interesting to note that where Watzlawick and others referred to the fact that open human systems are examples of complexity which can be considered analogous to Moiré patterns as 'optical manifestations of the superposition of two or more lattices' (Watzlawick, Beavin Bavelas and Jackson, 1967: 125). The fuzziness of systems which results from the twin processes of stabilisation and dissipation can be considered as lattice networks with a partial order (Negoita, 1981: 4).

General Bibliography

Abrahms, M., 'Al Qaeda's Miscommunication War: The Terrorism Paradox', *Terrorism and Political Violence*, 17 (2005) 529–49.

Adler, P.M. and Thovert, J.F., *Fractures and Fracture Networks* (Dordrecht, Boston, London: Kluwer, 1999).

Apel, K.-O., *Towards a Transformation of Philosophy*, tr. G. Adey and D. Frisby (London, Boston, Henley: Routledge and Kegan Paul, 1980).

Apel, K.-O., *Charles S. Peirce: From Pragmatism to Pragmaticism*, tr. John Michael Krois (New Jersey: Humanities Press, 1995).

Austin, J.L., *How to Do Things with Words* (Oxford: Clarendon Press, 1971).

Baecker, D., 'Kommunikation im Medium der Information' in Maresch, R. and Werber, N. eds., *Kommunikation, Medien, Macht* (Frankfurt: Suhrkamp, 1999a) 174–91.

Baecker, D., *Organisation als System* (Frankfurt: Suhrkamp, 1999b).

Baecker, D., 'Why Systems?', *Theory, Culture & Society*, 18 (1) (2001) 59–74.

Baecker, D., *Form und Formen der Kommunikation* (Frankfurt: Suhrkamp, 2005).

Bakhtin, M.M., *Problems of Dostoevsky's Poetics*, tr. R. Rotsel (Ann Arbor: Ardis, 1973).

Bakhtin, M.M., *The Dialogic Imagination: Four Essays*, Holquist, M. ed., tr. Caryl Emerson and M. Holquist (Austin: University of Texas Press, 1998).

Bakhtin, M.M., *Literatur und Karneval* (Frankfurt: Fischer, 1990).

Bakhtine, M.M. (Volochinov, V.N.), *Le Marxisme et la Philosophie du Langage* (Paris: Editions de Minuit, 1977).

Barthes, R., *Mythologies* (Paris: Seuil, 1957).

Bateson, G., *Steps Towards an Ecology of Mind: Collected Essays in Anthropology, Psychiatry, Evolution and Epistemology* (Chicago: University of Chicago Press, 1972).

Bauman, Z., *Liquid Modernity* (Cambridge: Polity, 2003).

Bauman, Z., *Liquid Life* (Cambridge: Polity, 2005).

Bear, J. and Bachmat, Y., 'Transport Phenomena in Porous Media – Basic Equations' in Bear, J. and Corapcioglu, M. Yavuz eds., *Fundamentals of Transport Phenomena in Porous Media* (Dordrecht, Boston, Lancaster: Martinus Nijhoff, 1984) 3–61.

Beck, U. ed., *Politik der Globalisierung* (Frankfurt: Suhrkamp, 1998a).

Beck, U., *Was ist Globalisierung? Irrtümer des Globalismus – Antworten auf Globalisierung* (Frankfurt: Suhrkamp, 1998b).

Bernard-Donals, Michael F., *Mikhail Bakhtin: Between Phenomenology and Marxism* (Cambridge, New York, Melbourne: Cambridge University Press, 1994).

Black, F., 'Noise', *The Journal of Finance*, 3 (XLI) (1986) 529–43.

Black, M., 'Vagueness: An Exercise in Logical Analysis' in Keefe, R. and Smith, P. eds., *Vagueness: A Reader* (Cambridge MA, London: MIT Press, 1997) 69–81.

Blumler, J.G. and Gurevitch, M., 'The New Media and Our Political Communication Discontents: Democratizing Cyberspace', *Information, Communication & Society*, 1 (4) (2001) 1–13.

Bostad, F., Brandist, C., Evensen, L. Sigfred and Faber, H. Charlotte eds., *Bakhtinian Perspectives on Language and Culture: Meaning in Language, Art and New Media* (Gordonsville VA, Basingstoke: Palgrave Macmillan, 2005).

Brandist, C., 'Mikhail Bakhtin and Early Soviet Sociolinguistics', *Proceedings of the XIth International Bakhtin Conference* (2004) 145–53.

Brandist, C., 'Law and the Genres of Discourse: The Bakhtin Circle's Theory of Language and the Phenomenology of Right' in Bostad, F., Brandist, C., Evensen, L.S. and Faber, H.C. eds., *Bakhtinian Perspectives on Language and Culture: Meaning in Language, Art and New Media* (Gordonsville VA, Basingstoke: Palgrave Macmillan, 2005) 21–45.

Brandom, R.B., *Making It Explicit: Reasoning, Representing & Discursive Commitment* (Cambridge MA: Harvard University Press, 1998).

Breidbach, O., 'Konturen einer Neurosemantik' in G. Rusch, and S.J. Schmidt eds., *Interne Repräsentationen. Neue Konzepte der Hirnforschung* (Frankfurt: Suhrkamp, 1996) 9–38.

Brown, R.H., 'Reconstructing Social Theory after the Postmodern Critique' in: Simons, H.W. and Billig, M. eds., *After Postmodernism: Reconstructing Ideology Critique* (London, Thousand Oaks, New Delhi: Sage, 1994) 12–37.

Bühler, K., *Theory of Language*, tr. D. Goodwin (Amsterdam and Philadelphia: Benjamins, 1990).

Butler, J., 'Restaging the Universal: Hegemony and the Limits of Formalism' in Butler, J., Laclau, E. and Žižek, S. eds., *Contingency, Hegemony, Universality. Contemporary Dialogues on the Left* (London, New York NY: Verso, 2000) 11–43.

Butler, J., Laclau, E. and Žižek, S. eds, *Contingency, Hegemony, Universality: Contemporary Dialogues on the Left* (London, New York NY: Verso, 2000).

Calzada Pérez, M. ed., *Apropos of Ideology: Translation Studies on Ideology – Ideologies in Translation Studies* (Manchester, Northampton MA: St Jerome, 2003).

Carston R., *Thoughts and Utterances: The Pragmatics of Explicit Communication* (Malden MA, Oxford, Victoria: Blackwell, 2002).

Cassirer, E., *The Philosophy of Symbolic Forms*, vol. 1, *Language*, tr. R. Mannheim (Yale University Press, 1955).

Castells, M., *The Rise of the Network Society – The Information Age: Economy, Society and Culture*, vol. 1 (Malden MA, Oxford: Blackwell, 1997).

Christis, J., 'Luhmann's Theory of Knowledge: Beyond Realism and Constructivism?', *Soziale Systeme* 2 (7) (2001) 328–49.

Cixous, H. and Calle-Gruber, M., *Rootprints, Memory and Life Writing* (London: Routledge, 1997).

Cooke, M., *Language and Reason: A Study of Habermas' Pragmatics* (Cambridge MA: MIT Press, 1994).

Crelinsten, R.D., 'Analysing Terrorism and Counter-terrorism: A Communication Model', *Terrorism and Political Violence* 2 (14) (2002) 77–122.

Crossley, N., *Intersubjectivity: The Fabric of Social Becoming* (London, Thousand Oaks, New Delhi: Sage, 1996).

Crossley, N. and Roberts, J.M. eds., *After Habermas: New Perspectives on the Public Sphere* (Malden MA, Oxford, Victoria: Blackwell, 2004).

Crozier, M. and Friedberg, E., *L'acteur et le système. Les contraintes de l'action collective* (Paris: Seuil, 2001).

Davidson, D., *Subjective, Intersubjective, Objective* (Oxford: Oxford University Press, 2001).

Davidson, D. *Truth, Language and History* (Oxford: Oxford University Press, 2005).

Davson, H. and Danielli, J.F., *The Permeability of Natural Membranes* (Cambridge: Cambridge University Press, 1952).

Derrida, J., *Limited Inc.* (Evanston IL: Northwestern University Press, 2000).

Dretske, F., *Knowledge and the Flow of Information* (CSLI Publications, 1999).

Dufva, H., 'Language, Thinking and Embodiment: Bakhtin, Whorf and Merleau-Ponty' in Bostad, F., Brandist, C., Evensen, L.S. and Faber, H.C. eds., *Bakhtinian Perspectives on Language and Culture: Meaning in Language, Art and New Media* (Gordonsville VA, Basingstoke: Palgrave Macmillan, 2005) 133–46.

Elliott, E. and Kiel, L.D., 'A Complex Systems Approach for Developing Public Policy toward Terrorism: An Agent-based Approach', *Chaos, Solitons and Fractals* 20 (2004) 63–8.

Elster, J. ed., *The Multiple Self* (Cambridge: Cambridge University Press, 1995).

Feather, H., *Intersubjectivity and Contemporary Social Theory: The Everyday as Critique* (Aldershot: Avebury, 1999).

Findlay J.N., *Axiological Ethics* (London, Basingstoke: Macmillan, 1970).

Fischer, H.R., 'Rationalität, Logik und Wirklichkeit. Zu einem konstruktivistischen Verständnis der Logik' in Rusch, G. ed., *Wissen und Wirklichkeit. Beiträge zum Konstruktivismus. Eine Hommage an Ernst von Glasersfeld* (Heidelberg: Carl Auer Systeme, 1999) 35–53.

Foucault, M., *L'ordre du discours* (Paris: Gallimard, 1971).

Foucault, M., *Language, Counter-memory, Practice: Selected Essays and Interviews*, Bouchard, D. ed., tr. D. Bouchard and S. Simon (Oxford: Basil Blackwell, 1977).

Foucault, M., *La volonté de savoir* (Paris: Gallimard, 1984).

Foucault, M., *The Order of Things: An Archaeology of the Human Sciences* (London: Routledge, 1991).

Frank, M. 'Subjektivität und Intersubjektivität', *Revue Internationale de Philosophie*, 4 (1995) 521–50.

Friedman, M., *Dialogue and the Human Image: Beyond Humanistic Psychology* (Newbury Park, London, New Delhi: Sage, 1992).

Garfinkel, H., *Studies in Ethnomethodology* (Cambridge: Polity Press, 1989).

Gauker, C., Zero Tolerance for Pragmatics (MS) 2006.

Gergen, K.J., *The Saturated Self: Dilemmas of Identity in Contemporary Life* (USA: BasicBooks, 1991).

Gergen, K.J., *An Invitation to Social Construction* (London, Thousand Oaks, New Delhi: Sage, 1999).

Giddens, A. *Central Problems in Social Theory: Action, Structure and Contradiction in Social Analysis* (Berkeley and Los Angeles: University of California Press, 1979).

Giddens, A., *Modernity and Self-Identity: Self and Society in the Late Modern Age* (Cambridge: Polity Press, 1991).

Gillett, G., 'Perception and Neuroscience', *British Journal for the Philosophy of Science* 40 (1989) 83–103.

Glansdorff, P. and Prigogine, I., *Thermodynamic Theory of Structure, Stability and Fluctuations* (London, New York, Sydney, Toronto: Wiley, 1971).

Goffman, E., *The Presentation of Self in Everyday Life* (New York: Doubleday Anchor, 1959).

Goffman, E., *Strategic Interaction* (Oxford: Basil Blackwell, 1970).

Goffman, E., *Interaction Ritual: Essays on Face-to-Face Behaviour* (Harmondsworth: Penguin, 1972).

Goffman, E., *Forms of Talk* (Oxford: Basil Blackwell, 1981).

Goodall, B., Trethewey, A. and McDonald, K., *Strategic Ambiguity, Communication, and Public Diplomacy in an Uncertain World: Principles and Practices 2006* June 21, 2006 (Report #0604 Consortium for Strategic Communication, Arizona State University)(http://www.asu. edu/clas/communication/about/csc/documents/StrategicAmbiguity-Communication.pdf).

Grant, C.B., *Functions and Fictions of Communication* (Oxford, Bern, Bruxelles, Frankfurt, New York, Vienna: Lang, 2000).

Grant, C.B., 'Vagueness, Porous Communication, Fictions of Society' in Grant, C.B. and McLaughlin, D. eds., *Language – Meaning – Social Construction: Interdisciplinary Studies* (Amsterdam, New York: Rodopi, 2001) 43–58.

Grant, C.B., 'Complexities of Self and Social Communication', Grant, C.B. ed., *Rethinking Communicative Interaction: New Interdisciplinary Horizons.* (Amsterdam, Philadelphia: Benjamins, 2003a) 101–25.

Grant, C.B., 'Destabilizing Social Communication Theory', *Theory, Culture and Society* 6 (20) (2003b) 95–119.

Grant, C.B. ed., *Rethinking Communicative Interaction. New Interdisciplinary Horizons* (Amsterdam, Philadelphia: Benjamins, 2003c).

Grant, C.B., 'Complex Communication and the Self at the Edge', *Theory and Psychology* 2 (14) (2004) 221–37.

Grant, C.B., 'Information Overload, Globalisation and Risks of the Dialogical Self', Hermans, H.J.M. and Oles, P.K. eds., *The Dialogical Self: Theory and Research* (Lublin: Wydawnictwo KUL, 2005) 27–41.

Graumann, C.F., 'Commonality, Mutuality, Reciprocity: A Conceptual Introduction' in Marková, I., Graumann, C.F. and Foppa, K. eds., *Mutualities in Dialogue* (Cambridge, New York, Melbourne: Cambridge University Press, 1995) 1–24.

Habermas, J., *Communication and the Evolution of Society* (London: Heinemann, 1979a).

Habermas, J., *Legitimation Crisis*, tr. T. McCarthy (London: Heinemann, 1979b).

Habermas, J., *Die Moderne – Ein unvollendetes Projekt* (Leipzig: Reclam, 1990a).

Habermas, J., *The Philosophical Discourse of Modernity. Twelve Lectures*, tr. F. Lawrence (Cambridge: Polity Press, 1990b).

Habermas, J., *Moral Consciousness and Communicative Action*, tr. C. Lenhardt and S.W. Nicholsen (Cambridge: Polity Press, 1992a).

Habermas, J., *The Theory of Communicative Action* 2 vols. (Cambridge: Polity Press, 1992b).

Habermas, J., 'Further Reflections on the Public Sphere' in Calhoun, D. ed., *Habermas and the Public Sphere* (Cambridge MA, London: MIT Press, 1993) 421–61.

Habermas, J., 'Replik', *Revue Internationale de Philosophie* 4 (1995a) 551–63.

Habermas, J., *Vorstudien und Ergänzungen zur Theorie des kommunikativen Handelns* (Frankfurt: Suhrkamp, 1995b).

Habermas, J., *Between Facts and Norms: Contributions to a Discourse Theory of Law and Democracy*, tr. W. Rehg (Cambridge MA: MIT Press, 1996).

Habermas, J., *Die Einbeziehung des Anderen* (Frankfurt: Suhrkamp, 1997).

Habermas, J., *Postmetaphysical Thinking* (Cambridge: Polity Press, 1998a).

Habermas, J., *Die postnationale Konstellation. Politische Essays* (Frankfurt: Suhrkamp, 1998b).

Habermas, J., *Erkenntnis und Interesse* (Frankfurt: Suhrkamp, 1999a).

Habermas, J., *Wahrheit und Rechtfertigung. Philosophische Aufsätze* (Frankfurt: Suhrkamp, 1999b).

Habermas, J. and Luhmann, N., *Theorie der Gesellschaft oder Sozialtechnologie – Was leistet die Systemforschung?* (Frankfurt: Surhkamp, 1972).

Hahn, T., Pethes, N. and Stäheli, U., 'Introduction: Popular Noise in Global Systems', *Soziale Systeme* 2 (9) (2003): 205–9.

Harré, R., *Personal Being: A Theory for Individual Psychology* (Oxford: Blackwell, 1983).

Hartmann, N., *Moral Values, Ethics*, vol. 2 (London: George Allen and Unwin, New York: Macmillan, 1932).

Harvey, K., ' "Events" and "Horizons": Reading Ideology in the Bindings of Translations' in Calzada Pérez, M. ed., *Apropos of Ideology. Translation Studies on Ideology – Ideologies in Translation Studies* (Manchester, Northampton MA: St Jerome, 2003) 43–69.

Hatim, B. and Mason, I., *The Translator as Communicator* (London: Longman, 1997).

Hegel, G.W.F., *Die Wissenschaft der Logik* (Frankfurt: Suhrkamp, 1976).

Hejl, P.M., 'Autopoiesis or Co-Evolution? Reconceptualizing the Relationship between Individuals and Societies', *Paragrana* 2 (4) (1995) 294–314.

Hermans, H.J.M., 'The Dialogical Self: Toward a Theory of Personal and Cultural Positioning', *Culture & Psychology* 3 (7) 2001: 243–81.

Hermans, H.J.M., 'The Dialogical Self as a Society of Mind', *Theory and Psychology* 2 (12) (2002) 147–60.

Hermans, H.J.M. and Kempen, H.J.G., *The Dialogical Self: Meaning as Movement* (San Diego: Academic Press1993).

Hermes, J., 'Citizenship in the Age of the Internet', *European Journal of Communication*, 3 (21) (2006) 295–309.

Herrnstein Smith, B., *Contingencies of Value: Alternative Perspectives for Critical Theory* (Cambridge MA: Harvard University Press, 1998).

Hirschkop, K., 'Bakhtin's Linguistic Turn', *Dialogism* 5/6 (2002) 21–34.

Holquist, M., *Dialogism. Bakhtin and His World* (London and New York: Routledge, 1990).

Husserl, E., *Cartesian Meditations. An Introduction to Phenomenology*, tr. D. Cairns (The Hague: Martinus Nijhoff, 1960).

Husserl, E., *Logisch Untersuchungen*, vol. 2, part 2, Geseammelte Schriften 3 (Hamburg: Felix Meiner, 1992).

Husserl, E., *The Crisis of the European Sciences and Transcendental Phenomenology*, tr. D. Carr, (Evanston IL: Northwestern University Press, 1997).

Iser, W., *Die Appellstruktur der Texte: Unbestimmtheit als Wirkungs-bedingung literarischer Prosa* (Konstanz: Universitätsverlag Konstanz, 1971).

Japp, K., 'Zur Soziologie des fundamentalistischen terrorismus', *Soziale Systeme* 1 (9) (2003) 54–87.

Jumarie, G., *Subjectivity, Information, Systems: Introduction to a Theory of Relativistic Cybernetics* (New York, London, Paris, Montreux, Tokyo: Gordon and Beach, 1986).

Jumarie, G., *Relative Information: Theories and Applications* (Berlin: Springer, 1990).

Kant, I., *Zum ewigen Frieden. Ein philosophischer Entwurf* in Kant, I., *Werke*, vol. 9, Schriften zur Anthropologie, Geschichtsphilosophie, Politik und Pädagogik (Darmstadt: Wissenschftliche Buchge-sellschaft, 1983a) 193–251.

Kant, I., *Kritik der reinen Vernunft Zweiter Teil* (Darmstadt: Wissen-schaftliche Buchgesellschaft, 1983b).

Kelly, M. ed., *Critique and Power. Recasting the Foucault/Habermas Debate* (Cambridge, MA/London: MIT Press, 1995).

Koczanowicz, L., 'Freedom and Communication: The Concept of Human Self in Mead and Bakhtin', *Dialogism* 4 (2000) 54–66.

Kristeva, J., *Le Texte du Roman. Approche sémiologique d'une structure dis-cursive transformationelle* (The Hague, Paris: Mouton, 1970).

Krohn, W., Küppers, G. and Paslack, R., 'Selbstorganisation – Zur Genese und Entwicklung einer wissenschaftlichen Revolution' in Schmidt, S.J. ed., *Der Diskurs des Radikalen Konstruktivismus* (Frankfurt: Suhrkamp, 1994) 441–65.

Lacan, J., *The Language of the Self: The Function of Language in Psychoanalysis* (Baltimore, London: Johns Hopkins Press, 1973).

Lacan, J., *Le Séminaire XX – Encore* (Paris: Seuil, 1975).

Lash, S., *Critique of Information* (London, Thousand Oaks, New Delhi: Sage, 2002).

Leask, I., 'Husserl, Givenness, and the Priority of the Self', *International Journal of Philosophical Studies* 2 (11) (2003): 141–56.

Leifer, E.M. and Rajah, V., 'Getting Observations: Strategic Ambiguities in Social Interaction', *Soziale Systeme* 2 (6) (2000): 251–67.

Lenoir, T., 'Foreword', Hansen, M.B.N., *New Philosophy for New Media* (Cambridge MA: MIT Press, 2004) xiii–xxviii.

Leydesdorff, L., *A Sociological Theory of Communication: The Self-Organization of the Knowledge-Based Society* (USA: Universal Publishers/ uPUBLISH. Com, 2001).

Leydesdorff, L., 'The Sociological and Communication-theoretical Foundations' in Leydesdorff, L., *The Knowledge-based Economy Modeled, Measured and Simulated: The Emergence of Anticipation in Networked Relations* (MS).

Linell, P., 'Troubles with Mutualities: Towards a Dialogical Theory of Misunderstanding and Miscommunication' in Marková, I., Graumann, C.F. and Foppa, K. eds., *Mutualities in Dialogue* (Cambridge, New York, Melbourne: Cambridge University Press, 1995) 176–213.

Linell, P., *Approaching Dialogue: Talk, Interaction and Contexts in Dialogical Perspectives* (Amsterdam/Philadelphia: Benjamins, 1998).

Linell, P. and Luckmann, T., 'Asymmetries in Dialogue. Some conceptual preliminaries' in Marková, I. and Foppa, K. eds., *Asymmetries in Dialogue* (Hemel Hempstead: Harvester Wheatsheaf, 1991) 1–20.

Lippmann, W., *Public Opinion* (New York: Harcourt, Brace and Company, 1934).

Locke, J., *An Essay on Human Understanding* (Harmondsworth: Penguin, 1997).

Luhmann, N., *Trust and Power: Two Works by Niklas Luhmann* (Chichester: Wiley, 1979).

Luhmann, N., *Observations on Modernity* (Stanford CA: Stanford University Press, 1988).

Luhmann, N., *Essays on Self-Reference* (New York, Oxford: Columbia University Press, 1990).

Luhmann, N., *Legitimation durch Verfahren* (Frankfurt: Suhrkamp, 1992).

Luhmann, N., *Gesellschaftsstruktur und Semantik*, vol. 1 (Frankfurt: Suhrkamp, 1993).

Luhmann, N., *Social Systems*, tr. J. Bednarz and D. Baecker (Stanford CA: Stanford University Press, 1995).

Luhmann, N., *Die Gesellschaft der Gesellschaft* 2 vols. (Frankfurt: Suhrkamp, 1997).

Lyotard, J.-F., *The Postmodern Condition: A Report on Knowledge*, tr. G. Bennington and B. Massumi (Manchester: Manchester University Press, 1986).

Marková, I., 'Dialogical perspectives of Democracy as Social Representation' in Grant, C.B. and McLaughlin, D. eds., *Language – Meaning – Social Construction: Interdisciplinary Studies* (Amsterdam, New York, NY: Rodopi, 2001) 125–39.

Marková, I., *Dialogicality and Social Representations: The Dynamics of Mind* (Cambridge: Cambridge University Press, 2003).

Mead, G.H., 'The Social Self', *Journal of Philosophy, Psychology and Scientific Methods* 10 (1913) 374–80.

Mead, G.H., *Mind, Self and Society from the Standpoint of a Social Behaviorist*, vol. 1, Works of George Herbert Mead (Chicago and London: University of Chicago Press, 1967).

Medvedev, P.N., Bakhtin, M.M., *The Formal Method in Literary Scholarship: A Critical Introduction to Sociological Poetics*, tr. J. Albert Wehrle (Baltimore and London: Johns Hopkins University Press, 1978).

Meltzer, B.N., Petras, J.W. and Reynolds, L.T., *Symbolic Interactionism: Genesis, Varieties and Criticism* (London and Boston: Routledge and Kegan Paul, 1975).

Mitterer, J., *Die Flucht aus der Beliebigjkeit* (Frankfurt: Fischer, 2001).

Morris, P., *The Bakhtin Reader: Selected Writings of Bakhtin, Medvedev, Voloshinov* (Oxford: Oxford University Press, 1997).

Nacos, B.L., *Mass-Mediated Terrorism: The Central Role of the Media in Terrorism and Counter-terrorism* (Lanham, Boulder: Rowman and Littlefield, 2002).

Negoita, C.V., *Fuzzy Systems* (Tunbridge Wells: Abacus, 1981).

Ongstad, S., 'Bakhtin's Triadic Epistemology and Ideologies of Dialogism' in Bostad, F., Brandist, C., Evensen, L.S. and Faber, S. eds., *Bakhtinian Perspectives on Language and Culture: Meaning in Language, Art and New Media* (Gordonsville VA, Basinstoke: Palgrave Macmillan, 2005).

Parsons, T., *The Social System* (London: Routledge and Kegan Paul, 1967).

Peirce, C.S., *Philosophical Writings of Peirce*, Buchler, J. ed. (New York: Dover, 1955).

Putnam, H., *Mind, Language and Reality*, vol. 2, *Philosophical Papers* (Cambridge: Cambridge University Press, 1997).

Quine, W.V., *Word and Object* (Cambridge: MIT Press, 1960).

Quine, W.V., *Methods of Logic* (London and Henley: Routledge and Kegan Paul, 1978).

Recanati, F., *Direct Reference: From Language to Thought* (Oxford: Blackwell, 1997).

Recanati, F., 'Déstabiliser le sens', *Revue Internationale de Philosophie*, 2 (2001) 197–208.

Recanati, F., *Literal Meaning* (Cambridge: Cambridge University Press, 2004).

Reiss, K. and Vermeer, H.J., *Grundlegung einer allgemeinen Translations-theorie* (Tübingen: Niemeyer, 1984).

Report of the Defense Science Board Task Force on Strategic Communication, September 2004 (www.acq.osd.mil/dsb/reports/2004-09-Strategic_Communication.pdf).

Ricoeur, P., *Husserl: An Analysis of His Phenomenology*, tr. E. Ballard and L. Embree (Evanston: Northwestern University Press, 1967).

Rorty, R., *Truth and Progress*, vol. 3, *Philosophical Papers* (Cambridge, New York, Melbourne: Cambridge University Press, 1998).

Rosenkranz, S., 'Wright on Vagueness and Agnosticism', *MIND* 112 (447) (2003) 449–63.

Roth, G., 'Erkenntnis und Realität: Das reale Gehirn und seine Wirklichkeit' in Schmidt, S.J. ed., *Der Diskurs des Radikalen Konstruktivismus* (Frankfurt: Suhrkamp, 1987) 229–55.

Sacks, H., *Lectures on Conversation*, vols. 1 & 2, G. Jefferson ed. (Oxford and Cambridge MA: Blackwell, 1995).

Sainsbury, R.M., 'Concepts without Boundaries' in Keefe, R. and Smith, P. eds., *Vagueness: A Reader* (Cambridge MA and London: MIT Press, 1997) 251–264.

Sartre, J.-P., *L'Etre et le Néant. Essai d'ontologie phénoménologique* (Paris: Gallimard, 1986).

Saussure, F. de, *Cours de linguistique générale* (Paris: Payot, 1968).

Schäffner, C., 'Third Ways and New Centres: Ideological Unity or Difference?' Calzada Pérez, M. ed., *Apropos of Ideology: Translation Studies on Ideology – Ideologies in Translation Studies* (Manchester, Northampton MA: St Jerome, 2003) 23–41.

Scheler, M., *Formalism and non-Formal Ethics of values: A New Attempt toward the Foundation of an Ethical Personalism* (Evanston: Northwestern University Press, 1973).

Schiltz, M., Verschraegen, G., Magnolo, S. 'Open Access to Knowledge in World Society?', *Soziale Systeme*, 11 (2005) 346–69.

Schmidt, S.J. ed., *Der Diskurs des Radikalen Konstruktivismus* (Frankfurt: Suhrkamp, 1994a).

Schmidt, S.J., *Kognitive Autonomie und soziale Orientierung* (Frankfurt: Suhrkamp, 1994b).

Schmidt, S.J.,'The Myth of Autopoiesis', *Paragrana* 4 (1995) 315–23.

Schmidt, S.J., 'Media Societies: Fiction Machines' in Grant, C.B. ed., *Language – Meaning – Social Construction: Interdisciplinary Studies* (New York, Amsterdam: Rodopi, 2001) 11–25.

Schmidt, S.J., *Geschichten und Diskurse. Abschied vom Konstruktivismus* (Reinbek: Rowohlt, 2003a).

Schmidt, S.J., 'Histories and Discourses: An Integrated Approach to Communication Science' in Grant, C.B. ed., *Rethinking Communicative Interaction: New Interdisciplinary Horzions* (Amsterdam, Philadelphia: Benjamins, 2003b) 129–44.

Schulz, W., 'Reconstructing Mediatization as an Analytical Concept', *European Journal of Communication*, 1 (19) (2004) 87–101.

Schütz, A., *The Phenomenology of the Social World*, tr. G. Walsh and F. Lehnert (London: Heinemann, 1972).

Schütz, A. and Luckmann, T., *The Structures of the Life-World*, tr. R. Zaner and H. Engelhardt Jr. (London: Heinemann, 1974).

Scott, A. and Street, J., 'From Media Politics to E-Protest', *Information, Communication & Society*, 2 (3) (2000) 215–40.

Searle, J.R., *Speech Acts: An Essay in the Philosophy of Language* (Cambridge: Cambridge University Press, 1969).

Searle, J.R., *The Construction of Social Reality* (Harmondsworth: Penguin, 1995).

Shannon, C.E. and Weaver, W., *Mathematical Theory of Communication* (Urbana: The University of Illinois Press, 1964).

Simons, H.W. and Billig, M. eds., *After Postmodernism: Reconstructing Ideology Critique* (London, Thousand Oaks, New Delhi: Sage, 1994).

Sperber, D. and Wilson, D., *Relevance: Communication and Cognition* (Oxford and Cambridge MA: Blackwell, 2001).

Thompson, J.B., *The Media and Modernity: A Social Theory of the Media* (Cambridge: Polity, 1994).

Todorov, T., *Mikhail Bakhtin: The Dialogical Principle*, tr. W. Godzich (Manchester: Manchester University Press, 1984).

Torres, M.R., Jordán, J., Horsburgh, N., 'Analysis and Evolution of the Global Jihadist Movement propaganda', *Terrorism and Political Violence*, 18 (2006) 399–421.

Vaihinger, H., *The Philosophy of 'As if': A System of the Theoretical, Practical and Religious Fictions of Mankind* (London: K. Paul, Trench, Trubner and Co., New York: Harcourt, Brace and Co., 1924).

Valsiner, J., 'Forms of Dialogical Relations and Semiotic Autoregulation within the Self', *Theory & Psychology* 12 (2002) 251–65.

Van Dijk, T., *Ideology: A Multipdisciplinary Approach* (London, Thousand Oaks, New Delhi: Sage, 2000).

Venuti, L., *The Translator's Invisibility: A History of Translation* (London, New York: Routledge, 1997).

Venuti, L., *The Scandals of Translation: Towards an Ethics of Difference* (London, New York: Routledge, 1998).

Vermeer, H.J., *A Skopos Theory of Translation (Some Arguments For and Against)* (Heidelberg: TEXTconTEXT Verlag, 1996).

Virilio, P., *La Machine de Vision* (Paris: Galilée, 1988).

Von Foerster, H., *Observing Systems* (Seaside: California, 1981).

Von Foerster, H., *Understanding Understanding* (New York: Springer, 2002).

Von Glasersfeld, E., *Radikaler Konstruktivismus. Ideen, Ergebnisse, Probleme* (Frankfurt: Suhrkamp, 1996).

Waismann, F., *Introduction to Mathematical Thinking: The Formation of Concepts in Modern Mathematics* (London: Hafner Publishing, 1951).

Waismann, F., 'Language Strata', in Flew, A. ed., *Logic and Language* (Aldershot: Gregg Revivals, 1993) 11–31.

Waldenfels, B., *Grundmotive einer Phänomenologie des Fremden* (Frankfurt: Suhrkamp, 2006).

Watzlawick, P., Bavelas, J. Beavin, and Jackson, D.D., *Pragmatics of Human Communication: A Study of Interactional Patterns, Pathologies, and Paradoxes* (New York, London: W.N. Norton, 1967).

Wellmer, A., 'Konsens als Telos der sprachlichen Kommunikation?' Giegel, H.-J. ed., *Kommunikation und Konsens in modernen Gesellschaften* (Frankfurt: Suhrkamp, 1992) 18–30.

Wellmer, A., *The Persistence of Modernity* (Cambridge MA: MIT Press, 1993).

Whorf, B.L., *Language, Thought and Reality: Selected Writings of Benjamin Lee Whorf* Carroll, J.B. ed. (Cambridge MA: MIT Press, 1956).

Williamson, T., 'Vagueness and Ignorance', in Keefe, R. and Smith, P. eds., *Vagueness: A Reader* (Cambridge MA, London: MIT Press, 1997) 265–80.

Williamson, T., *Vagueness* (London, New York: Routledge, 1998).

Williamson, T., 'On the Structure of Higher-Order Vagueness', *MIND* 429 (108) (1999) 127–43.

Winseck, D., 'Illusions of Perfect Information and Fantasies of Control in the Information Society', *New Media & Society* 1 (4) (2002) 93–122.

Wittgenstein, L., *Philosophical Investigations*, Anscombe, G.E.M. ed. (Oxford: Blackwell, 1968).

Wittgenstein, L., *Philosophische Grammatik*, vol. 4, *Werkausgabe*, Rhees, R. ed. (Frankfurt: Suhrkamp, 1991).

Wright, C., 'Rosenkranz on Quandary, Vagueness and Intuitionism', *MIND* 112 (447) (2003) 465–74.

Zürn, M. and Checkel, J.T., 'Getting Socialized to Build Bridges: Contructivism and Rationalism, Europe and the Nation State', *International Organization* 4 (59) (2005) 1065–76.

Index